DOING BUSINESS
WITH
Germany

Consultant Editors

Roderick Millar & Jonathan Reuvid

Deutsch-Britische
Industrie- und Handels-
kammer

German-British
Chamber
of Industry & Commerce

KOGAN
PAGE

First published 1997

Kogan Page Ltd
120 Pentonville Road
London N1 9JN
E-mail: kpinfo@kogan-page.co.uk

© Kogan Page 1997

British Library Cataloguing Data

A CIP record for this book is available from the British Library

ISBN 0 7494 2152 5

Typeset by JS Typesetting, Wellingborough, Northants
Printed and bound in Great Britain by Clays Ltd, St Ives plc

DOING BUSINESS
WITH
Germany

CUSTOMISED FINANCIAL SOLUTIONS FACILITATE ACCESS TO KEY MARKETS

If you are doing business with Germany, consider Landesbank Rheinland-Pfalz as a creative banking and finance partner. One of Germany's prominent public-sector financial institutions with total assets of more than DM 70 billion, Landesbank Rheinland-Pfalz offers a specialised range of commercial and investment banking services to international customers seeking to establish – or expand – solid links to the German market. Since every customer's objectives and requirements are different, we are committed to providing individually structured financial solutions – whatever the complexity of any given project. The cornerstones of our service potential are experience, flexibility, market know-how, and a continuous customer dialogue on a basis of close partnership.

To achieve smooth access to markets in Germany, take advantage of our proven financing concepts. Have a talk with the specialists at Landesbank Rheinland-Pfalz.

Landesbank Rheinland-Pfalz · D-55098 Mainz · Grosse Bleiche 54-56 · Phone (61 31) 13-01

LANDESBANK RHEINLAND-PFALZ

Contents

PART THREE: FINANCIAL AND ACCOUNTING FRAMEWORK

It's easy to get started here in the

Business Region Bruchsal

Overview

The Business Region of Bruchsal consists of 12 communities with its centre the metropolitan city of Bruchsal.
Population: 166,200
Employees: 50,700

Important companies

Du Pont, Siemens, John Deere, Vichy, SEW Eurodrive, Sulzer Weise, Goodyear, Huntsmann, SMG, Watlow, etc.

Leisure

Golf courses, thermal baths, castles, theatres and museums, annual Bruchsal „Baroque Days", recreational areas, cultural and sport clubs, wine & asparagus cultivation, etc.

Economy

More than 6,000 companies or entrepreneurs are located in the region. Examples of the broad range of regional industry represented here are electronics, information technology, automotive suppliers, machine manufacturing & construction, chemistry, pharmaceutical and food processing.

Wirtschafts-Region
BRUCHSAL

Infrastructure

Direct motorway accessibility: A5
Railway station with Intercity/ Interregio connection.
Nearest international airports: Frankfurt (60mls), Stuttgart (40mls)

NEW Our latest international location project:

Technology Village Bruchsal. It is the first development in Germany to integrate all phases of occupational and residential life into a single entity.

Contact us now ...

and enjoy our welcome-package:
Bruchsal Business Development Corp.
Wolfgang Kempermann
Dr.-Karl-Meister-Str. 12-13
D-76646 Bruchsal
phone (+49 7251) 8 10 28
fax   (+49 7251) 8 80 03

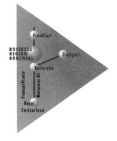

Is there
a Saxon in
you?

Last time you heard about the Saxons was when they settled
in Britain. Now find out what has been happening since then in
their German *heimat.* Nowadays they'd have no reason to emi-
grate. Quite the contrary: many Saxons are recalling their roots
and coming back to set up companies in Saxony. For a very good
reason: Saxony's economic growth rate is one of the highest
in Europe. Microchips and Meissen porcelain, environmental
engineering know-how and peak productivity in car manufacturing are all part of it. There's no need to wait for the next wave
of migration to profit from the situation. Wirtschaftsförderung
Sachsen GmbH, the Saxon Economic Development Corporation,
will be delighted to inform you free of charge about industrial
and commercial premises, subsidies, infrastructure, products,
trade relations and art and culture in Saxony. Wirtschaftsförderung Sachsen GmbH, phone +49/3 51/31 99-10 00,
fax +49/3 51/31 99-10 99, internet: http://www.saxony.com

SAXONY!

Foreword

Trade and investment are central elements of the British–German relationship. The Federal Republic of Germany is the UK's biggest trading partner, with total visible trade in both directions valued at £45.8 billion in 1995. Germany, the largest country in the European Union, offers a wide range of business opportunities to British companies.

New opportunities arise all the time. There are few things that Britain does not export to Germany. There is a strong market for electrical machinery, road vehicles and parts, office machinery, power generation equipment and chemicals. New opportunities are arising through the liberalisation of the German telecommunications market. At the consumer end, food and drink, giftware, clothing and footwear all sell well. Germany is also an important destination for UK invisibles. Transport, consultancy, financial and property services all feature prominently.

The UK was the No. 1 destination for German foreign investment in 1995. Over 1500 German companies now operate in the UK, some 300 with manufacturing facilities. The UK was also the leading investor in Germany in 1995 with investment valued at over £1 billion. Virtually all the leading companies have a presence in Germany either through subsidiaries or through joint ventures with local partners. Each year these ties are strengthened as our economies become ever more interdependent. We have a massive stake in each other's prosperity and my Government places great importance on the development of even closer business links between the countries.

This guide on *Doing Business with Germany* deals with many different aspects of trade, commerce and international finance. It is a valuable reference for newcomers to UK–German business and for those already active in this market.

Anthony Nelson, Minister for Trade

The German-British Chamber of Industry & Commerce

The German-British Chamber of Industry & Commerce is one of the German Chambers Abroad which form a worldwide network under the auspices of the Association German Chambers of Industry & Commerce in Bonn. It is both a membership organisation with nearly a thousand British and German companies and individuals as voluntary members and, at the same time, a consultancy business which provides members and non-members with a broad range of services.

Its core aim is identifying and securing export and import as well as direct investment opportunities in both countries and the provision of an extensive range of business services and information. These services include business and market information, market entry assistance, business consulting, business promotion, business partner search, VAT refund, trade fairs, legal and tax information and bad debt retrieval out of court. The Chamber also organises specialist seminars and other business events with prominent British and German speakers from industry, banking and politics. It works unbiased for British and German businesses alike.

The Chamber is in close contact with government departments and other organisations in both countries and lobbies both governments on behalf of its members. It provides a forum for its members and other interested parties where they can make face-to-face contact and share information on an informal basis. The German-British Chamber was founded in 1971.

List of Contributors

BDI (Federation of German Industries) is the umbrella organisation for 35 industrial sector associations and groups of associations in Germany. Its members represent about 80,000 private industrial enterprises employing over 10 million people. *Gabriele Hintzen* has been in charge of the BDI General Economic Policy Department since 1994.

British Chamber of Commerce in Germany provides a forum for British and German business people and represents its members' interests in both countries.
Bernard Wingenbach is General Manager at the BCCG General Office in Cologne.

Robert A Bischof, a merchant banker by trade, has spent most of his working life in Britain as Managing Director of Jungheinrich, a leading forklift truck supplier. In 1994, Jungnheinrich asked him to manage the restructuring of the new Boss Group Ltd.

Clifford Chance is a leading international law firm with over 1,500 lawyers and a total staff of approximately 3,000 in 23 business and financial centres around the world. The office in Frankfurt provides a full range of business and financial legal services including mergers and acquisitions, banking, media, telecommunications and tax law. Established in 1990, there are 40 lawyers in the Frankfurt practice: 29 German, 10 British and 1 Dutch.
Bernhard von Braunschweig, a Partner at the Clifford Chance Frankfurt office, oversaw the writing of the Clifford Chance articles. He specialises in corporate and tax law.

Commerzbank is Germany's third largest private commercial and investment bank. Its staff of almost 30,000 serves more than 3.5 million customers worldwide.
Klaus Holschuh is Head of Direct Marketing & Research Global Bonds and *Barbara Hain* is Trading Research Analyst at Commerzbank.

Coopers & Lybrand is one of the world's leading providers of professional services including accounting and audit, tax and consulting. Through its member firms, it deploys over 66,000 people on a globally integrated basis in more than 120 countries.

Wolfgang Suchanek heads up the German firm's UK desk from the Hamburg office. *Peter Combrink* is based in Frankfurt and specialises in serving international clients.
Christoph Schreiber is based in Hamburg and specialises in cross-border tax planning for both corporations and individuals. *Adrian Yeeles* is an international tax specialist based in London.
Wolfgang Wagner heads up the firm's Corporate Finance practice in Germany.
Günter Betz is a partner based in Düsseldorf who heads the firm's due diligence service for North Rhine-Westphalia. *Andreas Kopp* is an M&A specialist based in Frankfurt.

Laura Covill is an international financial journalist who has been based in Frankfurt since 1989. She also writes speeches for European business leaders.

Federal Institute for Vocational Training in Berlin and Bonn (BIBB) is the research and development body for vocational training.
Dr Hermann Schmidt is the President of BIBB and *Dr Lazslo Alex* is Director.

Kaevan Gazdar was for three years the director of the Management Information Service of the management consultancy, Dr Hofner & Partner. He joined the Publications Department of the Bayerische Vereinsbank in 1994.

German-British Chamber of Industry & Commerce is one of the German Chambers Abroad which form a worldwide network under the auspices of the Association of German Chambers of Industry & Commerce in Bonn. Its core aim is identifying and securing export and import as well as direct investment opportunities.
Klaus Balzar has been the Director General since his move to London in 1974.

Michael Harms is at the Bureau for East-West Co-operation.

Landesbank Hessen-Thuringen Girozentrale (Helaba) is a wholesale bank concentrating on financing, real estate business, asset management, liquidity and risk management, transactions and services as well as specialised business.
Stefan Mütze is an economist at the bank.

Dr Wolfgang Lecher studies in Sociology, Economics and Philosophy with the main subject of Industrial and Organisation Sociology in Tübingen and Frankfurt/Main.

Eric Lynn is Managing Director of LCT Consultants, Nuremberg, Germany. He has been living and working in Germany since 1984. He specialises in preparing German executives for specific assignments in English speaking and non-German executives for work in Germany.

Dr Peter Oberender has been Professor of Economics at the University of Beyreuth since 1980.

Brian Padgett is the Managing Director of The Technology Exchange Ltd, which he formed in 1985. It seeks technology for firms both in the UK and overseas and assists them with outward licensing through a network of over 4,000 partners.

Jonathan Reuvid was an economist at the French national oil company, Total, at the time of its UK market entry. He then moved into investment banking and financial consultancy. From 1984 Jonathan Reuvid has been engaged in the development of joint ventures in northern China and of technology transfers on his own behalf and for American and British corporate clients. Since 1989 he has been involved in business publishing.

Ute Sellhorst is the lawyer in charge of the International Department of CDH, the Central Organization of Commercial Agents and Brokers, in Cologne.

Walter Tacke is a management consultant and a former president of the Professional Association of the Marketing and Social Researcher in Germany.

Rolf Günther Thumann is Co-ordinator of the EMU Research Project. His article was written while he was at the Federal Ministry of Economics in Bonn.

John M Zindar is at the Foreign Investor Information Center, Federal Ministry of Economics, Berlin.

Part One

Economic and Business Conditions

1

Overview of Economic Performance

Jonathan Reuvid

UNIFIED GERMANY TODAY

In the second quarter of 1996 the German economy returned to growth and the recovery was maintained in the third quarter. GDP at market prices increased by 1.5 per cent in the second quarter, against the first quarter when GDP declined by 0.5 per cent against the 1.9 per cent annual growth registered for 1995. Effectively, the second quarter year-on-year growth was 1.2 per cent, compared to 0.3 per cent in the first quarter. As Table 1.1 shows, this welcome news confirms that the economy may be resuming its growth pattern after a period of reduced performance since 1991 and an actual decline in 1993.

However, optimism should be tempered with caution. The German economy has not yet digested the absorption of the five Eastern *Länder* and other indicators remain less encouraging. Although the OECD expects a year-on-year GDP growth of 0.5 per cent for 1996, rising to 2.4 per cent in 1997, employment is expected to fall by at least 1 per cent in 1996 and to do little more than stabilise in 1997. In August 1996 total unemployment fell marginally to 3.9 million, still about 8 per cent higher than in August 1995, before rising to a new peak of 4.04 million in October. The national unemployment rate now stands at 10.6 per cent, with the disparity maintained between western and eastern *Länder* rates of 9.4 per cent against 15.5 per cent respectively. High unemployment is attributable as much to rigidities in the FDR economic system as to integration of the former eastern Germany. The statistics in Table 1.1 confirm that German unemployment has increased continuously in

Table 1.1 *The German economy, background statistics*

	1986	1987	1988	1989	1990	1991	1992	1993	1994	1995
A. Percentage change from previous year at constant prices[1]										
Private consumption	3.5	3.4	2.7	2.8	5.4	5.6	2.8	0.5	0.9	1.7
Gross fixed investment	3.3	1.8	4.4	6.3	8.5	6.0	3.5	-5.6	4.3	1.5
Construction	3.1	0.0	3.1	4.4	4.9	2.7	9.7	0.9	7.8	1.2
Public	8.0	-1.2	0.4	3.1	-0.8	0.3	11.1	-3.3	1.8	-2.7
Residential	-0.6	-1.2	3.7	4.9	8.5	4.3	9.4	3.8	13.1	3.0
Business	6.0	2.5	3.6	4.4	2.8	1.6	9.4	-1.2	3.0	0.4
Machinery and equipment	3.7	4.5	6.3	8.8	13.2	10.0	-3.5	-14.1	-1.2	2.0
GDP at market prices	2.3	1.5	3.7	3.6	5.7	5.0	2.2	-1.2	2.9	1.9
GDP implicit price deflator	3.2	1.9	1.5	2.4	3.2	3.9	5.5	3.8	2.3	2.2
Industrial production	2.0	0.4	3.6	4.7	5.2	3.0	-2.6	-7.3	3.6	0.8
Employment	1.4	0.7	0.8	1.5	3.0	2.5	-1.8	-1.8	-0.7	-0.3
Compensation of employees (current prices)	5.2	4.2	4.0	4.5	7.8	8.0	8.0	2.0	2.2	3.2
Productivity (GDP/employment)	0.9	0.7	2.9	2.1	2.7	2.5	4.1	0.6	3.6	2.2
Unit labour costs (compensation of employees/GDP)	2.8	2.7	0.2	0.8	2.0	3.3	5.6	3.2	-0.6	1.3
Broad money supply (M3)[2]	7.3	7.3	6.4	5.7	4.5	5.6	8.2	7.9	9.0	NIL

Table 1.1 *The German economy, background statistics* (cont)

	1986	1987	1988	1989	1990	1991	1992	1993	1994	1995
B. Percentage ratios[2]										
Gross fixed investment										
As a per cent of GDP at constant prices	19.9	19.9	20.1	20.6	21.1	23.0	23.3	22.2	22.5	22.4
Stockbuilding										
As a per cent of GDP at constant prices	0.2	0.0	0.5	0.8	0.6	0.5	-0.1	-0.2	0.9	0.9
Foreign balance										
As a per cent of GDP at constant prices	5.1	4.2	4.4	5.1	5.5	-0.1	-0.7	-0.6	-0.5	-0.2
Compensation of employees										
As a per cent of GDP at current prices	56.1	56.5	55.8	54.9	54.3	56.5	56.6	56.3	54.7	54.2
Direct taxes										
As a per cent of household income	12.3	12.8	12.5	12.9	11.3	11.8	12.5	12.1	12.2	13.2
Household saving										
As a per cent of disposable income	12.3	12.6	12.8	12.4	13.8	12.7	12.8	12.2	11.6	11.5
Unemployment										
As a per cent of civilian labour force	7.7	7.6	7.6	6.9	6.2	6.7	7.7	8.9	9.6	9.4
C. Other indicator[2]										
Current balance (billion $)	40.5	46.1	49.5	57.2	48.9	-19.2	-21.5	-16.3	-21.4	-17.4

[1] From 1992 all Germany.
[2] From 1991 all Germany.
Source: Statistisches Bundesamt, *Volkswirtschaftliche Gesamtrechnungen, Reihe 1;* Deutsche Bundesbank, *Statistisches Beiheft zum Monatsbericht, Reihe 4.*

each year since 1990, supporting the conclusion that employment has consistently failed to regain former levels in periods of recovery from recession. There are high levels of elderly and long-term jobless, attributable, according to the OECD in its 1997 survey of the Germany economy, to 'distorted incentives built into the tax and benefit systems' and 'inflexible working practices, which reduce the demand for labour'. The slow reduction in the jobless totals prompted Chancellor Helmut Kohl, in his keynote speech to the annual Congress of the Chrisian Democratic Union in October 1996, to comment that he would be happy if unemployment fell to two-thirds of present levels against his previous target of halving unemployment by the year 2000.

Factors behind the recent return to growth of 1.2 per cent are not entirely reassuring. Between the first and second quarters of 1996 public sector consumption rose 3.6 per cent while construction activity jumped a record 11.5 per cent, more than offsetting the 9.5 per cent drop in the first quarter which was occasioned by severe winter weather. On the other hand, export demand increased by 2.5 per cent while industrial output increased on a year-on-year basis in the western *Länder* (0.9 per cent in August 1996) and for the whole of Germany (1.1 per cent in July and 0.7 per cent in August) against a 1.4 per cent fall in the east in August. German industrial output in August was revised downwards from 1 per cent growth to zero, and September output fell unexpectedly by 1.8 per cent, seasonally adjusted. As a result, industrial output in August and September was 0.8 per cent lower on a year-on-year basis. Although hopes of strong third-quarter growth have receded, the situation contrasts favourably with the recession of 1992–93 which followed the hectic dash of the post-reunification boom, when both industrial production and employment were in decline nationally (see Table 1.1).

The growth of private consumption has also remained at low ebb since 1992, although it started to recover in 1995. Retail sales levels have been erratic since the beginning of 1995 but achieved an increase of 2.5 per cent year-on-year in July 1996. The mail order sector is particularly strong. Household saving as a proportion of disposable income started to fall in 1993 from its 1992 peak of 12.8 per cent, but was still at 11.5 per cent in 1995. The scale of the task, and achievement, of integrating the two economic systems needs to be recognised. In population and employment terms, the total workforce increased by 22.7 per cent between 1990 and 1994, from 28.5 million to 34.9 million, while the gross population rose by 28.7 per cent, from 63.2 million to 81.4 million. The cost of integration, in terms of public financial transfers to eastern Germany to support the social security system and social services, investments in infrastructure and the refinancing of state-owned industry is summarised in Table 1.2.

Table 1.2 *Public financial transfers to eastern Germany (DM billion)*

	1991	1992	1993	1994	1995	1996 (forecast)
Gross transfers	139	152	168	168	185	181
Less:						
Federal tax and administration receipts from the east	33	37	39	43	45	50
Net transfers	106	115	129	125	140	131
As a percentage of:						
All-German GDP	3.7	3.7	4.1	3.8	4.0	3.7
West German GDP	4.0	4.1	4.5	4.2	4.5	–
East German GDP	52	44	42	36	37	–
Total public sector Debt	1182	1347	1592	1839	1974	1979
As a percentage of:						
All-German GDP	48.7	47.2	51.7	58.3	59.5	57.2

Source: OECD Economic Surveys 1996

The significance of the burden on the western *Länder* (and corresponding benefit to the eastern *Länder*) is measured in Table 1.2 by the proportion of GDP which these annual transfers represent. Plainly, the burden of supporting eastern Germany during a period of low economic growth continues to be heavy. West German support at similar levels is pledged for 1997 and 1998. In September 1996, the German cabinet confirmed that federal aid for businesses in eastern Germany should be kept 'at a high level' from 1999 onwards, but that level will not be judged until after the impact of tax changes in 1997 and further tax reforms planned for 1999 have been assessed.

In the meantime, the eastern *Länder* continue to be disadvantaged by too narrow an industrial base, with overly high labour costs and a shortage of capital for private companies, which currently generate only 2 per cent of Germany's total exports. The task of investing in eastern Germany's private industry has not been borne entirely by western Germany. In 1996 western support for eastern German companies is expected to amount to some DM25 billion, on top of the forecast DM131 billion in net transfers from western Germany. To some extent private investment in eastern Germany has been a substitute for German foreign direct investment (FDI) abroad, although FDI has remained healthy since reunification (see Chapter 2). However, the weak performance of the economy in 1995 and first part of 1996 has been attributed largely to the decline in business fixed investment in 1992–3 and the modest upswing since then.

Aside from the issue of EMU convergence, explored in Chapter 3, the main concerns surrounding the Germany economy for the medium term remain sluggish investment, the distortion of the tax and benefit systems and the rigidity of working practices, which in turn have contributed to a deterioration in investment returns and the general investment climate.

MONETARY CONDITIONS

Monetary policy remained cautious during 1995 as the economy began to recover, while interest rates, which had initially declined more slowly than in previous recoveries, continued to fall. In the first half of 1996, the market was surprised several times by the Bundesbank's continuing to cut interest rates, even at times when M3 growth exceeded targets. The real exchange rate, which remained unfavourable throughout 1995 and contributed to tighter overall monetary conditions, moved in Germany's favour from the beginning of 1996 and the deutschmark continued to weaken throughout the second and third quarters against the US dollar and sterling.

The German broad money supply (M3), whose progress is also recorded in Table 1.1, was static for 1995 but began to rise from the fourth quarter. The annualised growth rate of M3, which reached 9.6 per cent in June 1996, declined through 8.6 per cent in July and 8.7 per cent in August to 8.4 per cent in September, indicating that the cycle of interest rate cuts, which had culminated in a cut of the securities repurchase (repo) rate from 3.3 to 3.0 per cent in August, might be reaching its end. This was confirmed in October 1996 when the Bundesbank's chief economist warned that German interest rates would fall no further.

This policy statement coincided with the report from the IFO economic research institute in Munich of an upturn in its highly regarded business climate index, which revealed its highest level for a year in September. A positive factor in the present recovery is represented by current levels of inflation. For west Germany, consumer price inflation in 1996 remained below 2 per cent up to August when it stood at 1.4 per cent, while producer prices had fallen from February through to July.

RECENT POLICY ACTIONS

Since 1994 the government has focused on a broad programme of structural measures aimed at stimulating employment:

- A job creation scheme to support work in the areas of environmental improvement, social services and youth assistance, originally designed for the new *Länder*, was extended to western Germany.
- The programme to aid the long-term unemployed by providing wage subsidies up to a year for new hirings was extended up to 1999. The subsidy increases with the length of the previous unemployment, up to 80 per cent of the region's negotiated wage rates.
- A new law passed in October 1996 has cut the minimum statutory sick-pay benefit from 100 per cent to 80 per cent of wages.
- Enhanced government support has been announced in the areas of science and technology, particularly in high-technology fields such as biotechnology and IT, for research and to improve co-operation between the public and private sectors, with particular attention to small and medium-sized enterprises.

The 1996 tax reform led to a reduction in the tax burden for low-income groups, but did not eliminate unemployment traps for social assistance recipients over a broad income band. The new system of non-means-tested child benefits avoids the high effective marginal tax rates over some income ranges which were present in the previous system. However, non-wage labour costs increased with the introduction of the second stage of the long-term care insurance from July 1996.

A new 50-point action plan to promote investment, growth and employment and a further package of measures to revise the labour code, with the intention of promoting active job search and improved labour market performance, was submitted to Parliament in July 1996 and is working its way through the legislative process:

- In order to raise the retirement age and discourage early retirement, part-time employment of formerly full-time workers is to be encouraged by earnings supplements from the age of 55 up to retirement, provided that the employer compensates for reduced working hours by hiring unemployed or newly graduated apprentices. Benefits will be terminated for those who have worked and paid social security contributions for less than 150 days. In addition, it is intended that the entitlement level no longer be based on previous earnings but on the wages a participant would expect to receive under current conditions.

- Social assistance benefits are to be related more closely to employment opportunities. Benefit levels for recipients who refuse a 'suitable' job offer will be cut by 25 per cent.
- Shop opening hours were partially deregulated in July 1996. Shops may now remain open until 8 pm on weekdays and to 4 pm on Saturdays. Further liberalisation has been urged by the OECD.
- In July the telecommunications market was liberalised to facilitate the privatisation and public flotation of Deutsche Telekom, announced in October 1996.
- Proposals for simplifying planning approvals have been submitted for debate, allowing enterprises to proceed with projects which do not fundamentally change their environmental and other liabilities.

The changes in social assistance and employment benefits have not been accepted with equanimity by the trade unions. Gesamtmetall, the metal-working industry employers' federation, set out on its 1996 annual autumn round of wage negotiations with a determination to renegotiate 'the system', as well as to achieve a zero pay rise. The intention was to include as part of the package cuts in a string of costly fringe benefits such as sick pay, holiday pay and Christmas bonuses. The employers opened their campaign badly by seeking to change sickness benefits unilaterally, on the back of the statutory cut in minimum sick-pay benefit from 100 to 80 per cent of wages. They had to back down in the face of the threat of strike action by IG Metall members at many leading companies, including Daimler-Benz, Adam Opel and Ford's Cologne plant, and revert to the proper process of negotiation. By the end of October the talks were in disarray, with Gesamtmetall declaring that it was prepared to let the sick pay issue drop out of the regional industry-wide sector agreement. If this happened, it would undermine the regional wage-bargaining system, which has been viewed as the foundation of German labour relations. Companies and unions would then be forced to negotiate their own agreements in respect of any deviation from minimum statutory entitlements. On 26 October German industry was engulfed by one-day strikes by IG Metall members. The length and outcome of the dispute are unknown as this book goes to press.

THE MEDIUM-TERM OUTLOOK FOR BUSINESS FIXED INVESTMENT

The least satisfactory aspect of Germany economic performance has been the failure of business fixed investment to recover from the 1993 trough. It is true that the ratio of private non-residential investment was at its post-war peak in 1991 and that bankruptcies of eastern German enterprises have been on the increase, so it can be argued that there has been an element of adjustment from previous overinvestment. However, the effect of unification on recent weak investment can be overplayed. The phenomenon of bankruptcy a few years after the founding of an enterprise is normal. Of more concern, perhaps, is the inability of the eastern *Länder* to fund their own industrial development through private enterprise and the prospect of continuing dependence on federal transfers indefinitely which in turn will ensure that taxation remains high, thereby adversely affecting the overall levels of business investment.

The record of weak returns on investment in recent years is the main cause of depressed business investment. In spite of some recovery in 1993, the return on capital in 1994 was still below its average level over the previous 25 years. In view of the fact that the profitability of investment has not been restored to former levels, it is not surprising that investment intentions remain vulnerable in the climate of a faltering recovery. According to 1996 IFO studies on western German industry, net earnings before taxation of manufacturers employing more than 20 people will fall to 0.7 per cent of turnover for 1996, from 1.6 per cent in 1995.

The German Chamber of Commerce has also undertaken studies of investment intentions in 1995 and in the first half of 1996 among 25,000 mainly *Mittelstand* companies. According to the autumn 1995 survey, only 12 per cent of companies sampled in western Germany and 22 per cent of companies sampled in eastern Germany stated that the purpose of their investment was the widening of capacity. In western Germany, the main motive for investment is to reduce production costs, echoed by eastern Germany where the same motive of cost reduction ranks second only to replacement investment. In the pursuit of lower production cost and competitiveness, investment which reduces high-cost German labour content plainly makes sense. In some cases, the transfer of capacity, or, at least, the construction of additional capacity in lower-labour-cost eastern European countries, may be a more attractive option.

Inflation performance has improved considerably in 1996, as noted above. Before the October 'clash of the Titans' in the metal-working industry, the 1996 wage round had exhibited greater realism, with wage increases being held at below 2 per cent and more flexibility in working practices in the agreements signed. Between January and September 1996, the appreciation of the deutschmark in 1995 was offset by a weakening of the effective nominal exchange rate by some 4 per cent.

Allowing for a temporary adverse effect only on import prices and assuming that the remaining wage increases are held at less than 2 per cent, the prospect remains alive of containing inflation in 1997 to around 1.5 per cent, effectively a state of price stability.

If the government-sponsored tax changes to stimulate investment and encourage new business start-ups, approved by the Bundestag on 7 November, survive their second and third readings, the outlook for *Mittelstand* investment will be strengthened significantly. Perhaps these measures, coupled with the introduction of the Neuer Markt by the Frankfurt stock exchange early in 1997, will help to generate a more risk-friendly investment climate and the development of a robust venture capital sector.

2

European Competitiveness

Jonathan Reuvid

DEFINING COMPETITIVENESS

Economic competitiveness among member states of the EU, and those aspiring to join within the next few years, is an emotive subject. It is easy to arrive at facile judgments based on comparison of data relating to one or more narrow set of criteria, because 'competitiveness' can be defined in at least six different contexts:

- foreign trade;
- inward investment;
- financial stability;
- convergence to EMU criteria;
- living standards;
- overall economic performance.

Only by evaluating comparative performance in each of these contexts is a balanced judgment possible, either of current competitiveness or of the medium-term outlook for Germany and each of its trading partners in a global economic environment.

There is also a danger in attempting to evaluate Germany's competitiveness *vis-à-vis* its fellow EU members in isolation. The EU is not an economic island and the concept of 'fortress Europe' will become obsolete as the nascent World Trade Organisation continues to develop and the other geographically grouped economic alliances and their members interact with the EU and its members on a more level playing field.

Table 2.1 *Imports and exports of goods by regions (DM billion)*

	1986	1987	1988	1989	1990	1991	1992	1993	1994	1995
					Imports, fob					
OECD	325.3	325.9	351.7	404.7	442.4	509.5	505.8	436.5	470.6	477.3
EU	241.9	242.6	258.9	295.1	328.9	381.3	378.5	317.1	343.9	344.9
Austria	15.8	16.6	18.5	20.6	23.9	26.7	27.7	25.9	28.6	22.8
Belgium/Luxembourg	28.9	28.8	30.9	34.7	39.8	45.8	44.8	34.1	38.5	41.0
France	46.6	46.8	52.5	60.2	65.6	79.0	76.5	65.8	69.6	68.2
Italy	37.6	38.7	40.0	45.0	51.9	59.7	58.4	48.0	51.9	52.7
Netherlands	46.9	44.1	45.3	51.9	56.2	63.0	62.1	51.0	52.5	53.8
Sweden	9.5	9.4	10.2	12.2	12.6	13.8	13.4	11.9	13.3	12.2
United Kingdom	28.7	28.6	29.7	34.0	36.5	42.3	42.6	35.4	38.9	40.0
Other European	27.8	28.2	29.7	33.2	37.1	40.2	41.4	39.8	43.5	46.5
Switzerland	18.0	18.8	19.6	21.0	23.4	25.2	25.4	23.9	26.3	27.5
Other OECD	55.6	55.1	63.1	76.4	76.4	88.0	86.0	79.6	83.2	85.9
Japan	25.0	25.9	29.6	33.3	33.2	40.7	38.4	34.9	34.6	35.7
United States	26.1	24.6	28.4	37.1	36.9	40.9	41.5	39.3	42.9	43.5
Central and Eastern European countries[1]	16.2	13.8	13.9	17.1	23.7	29.9	31.8	32.6	40.1	47.0
Non-oil developing countries	41.2	39.7	45.3	51.5	55.0	63.0	58.5	58.1	62.9	66.5
OPEC	12.1	10.5	9.9	11.4	13.2	13.8	14.0	12.8	11.9	10.1
China	2.7	3.4	4.2	5.8	7.7	11.3	11.1	13.4	14.9	15.9
Dynamic Asian economies	15.7	18.2	20.9	23.2	25.6	31.9	30.0	31.2	33.8	36.4
Total imports	404.8	400.6	432.7	499.4	551.7	637.7	630.2	567.0	616.0	634.6

Table 2.1 Imports and exports of goods by regions (DM billion) (continued)

	1986	1987	1988	1989	1990	1991	1992	1993	1994	1995
					Exports, fob					
OECD	428.1	435.7	474.3	533.5	537.9	538.1	538.1	485.5	531.3	552.3
EU	312.9	324.9	362.4	414.3	413.8	421.2	424.7	368.1	401.3	414.6
Austria	28.1	28.3	32.3	35.9	37.5	40.2	40.4	37.7	40.1	39.6
Belgium/Luxembourg	36.3	38.1	41.3	45.5	47.5	48.2	49.0	42.5	46.5	46.6
France	61.2	62.5	70.6	83.8	84.2	87.5	86.9	77.4	83.2	84.3
Italy	42.5	45.5	51.4	59.6	60.0	61.2	62.3	46.9	52.4	54.4
Netherlands	44.6	45.3	48.8	54.2	54.7	56.3	56.1	48.8	52.6	54.0
Sweden	14.8	15.8	16.8	18.5	17.0	15.0	14.7	12.8	15.5	17.7
United Kingdom	44.3	46.3	52.7	59.1	54.7	50.5	50.9	50.0	55.4	58.2
Other European countries	43.1	43.6	45.4	49.6	52.1	51.4	49.1	48.6	50.5	56.3
Switzerland	31.0	32.1	34.8	38.8	38.9	38.0	35.7	34.1	37.2	39.7
Other OECD	72.2	67.2	66.5	69.5	72.1	65.4	64.3	68.8	79.6	81.4
Japan	8.5	10.3	12.9	15.0	17.2	16.3	14.5	15.2	17.3	18.4
United States	54.3	48.8	45.2	44.9	46.4	41.0	41.9	45.7	53.2	53.6
Central and Eastern European countries[1]	17.3	15.7	17.9	23.1	36.8	36.9	35.8	40.5	45.1	50.8
Non-oil developing countries	42.7	42.7	44.7	52.0	53.3	56.4	59.3	64.1	74.8	83.1
OPEC	17.6	14.0	15.3	16.3	18.3	21.4	23.0	18.4	17.7	17.0
China	6.1	4.9	4.9	4.6	4.0	4.0	5.7	9.5	10.2	10.6
Dynamic Asian economies	12.5	13.4	16.3	20.2	22.3	25.1	26.2	30.2	37.2	42.0
Total exports	522.4	522.2	566.8	640.5	663.8	667.6	671.6	632.7	696.0	732.6

[1] Poland, ex-USSR, former Czechoslovakia and Hungary.
Source: Deutsche Bundesbank, Statistisches Beiheft zum Monatsbericht, Reihe 4

For the purposes of the present assessment, therefore, competitiveness in each of the six contexts listed above is extended to the United States and Japan, the two largest OECD economies which affect the individual EU member economies most significantly.

FOREIGN TRADE

Germany's worldwide pattern of foreign trade is analysed by region in Table 2.1 over the 10-year period from 1986 to 1995. The balance of trade has remained positive throughout the period, with the annual surplus exceeding DM100 billion for each year up to 1991, when it fell to the DM40 billion level for two years before rising steadily in each of the three years to DM98 billion in 1995. The initial negative impact of reunification and the consequent recession has been reversed and, with the hardening of the US dollar against the deutschmark, the terms of trade have again moved in Germany's favour.

In spite of the deutschmark's strength relative to European currencies, Germany has maintained a favourable balance of trade with other EU countries in total and individually, except for the Netherlands in 1986 and from 1990 to 1994. Likewise, the balance has remained positive with other European countries, including those of Central and Eastern Europe.

Since 1988 imports from non-EU OECD countries have exceeded exports, although the balance of trade with the US has remained positive throughout the 10-year period. The reason is trade with Japan where there has been a continuous gap, although the deficit has narrowed from DM24.4 billion in 1991 to DM17.3 billion in 1995.

Exports to non-oil developing countries were in excess of imports, except for 1988, 1990 and 1991, and exceeded imports to OPEC countries in each year. Until 1994 imports from the dynamic Asian economies exceeded exports and since 1989 there has been a growing trade gap with China, with whom imports now exceed exports by 50 per cent at DM15.9 billion. The negative balance of trade with China is, of course, a world trade phenomenon.

There are two ratios by which the longer-term outlook for foreign trade is commonly judged: exports as a percentage of GDP, and the relative growth rates of exports and imports over the past five years. Comparative statistics for the OECD countries are currently available up to the end of 1994 only, but Table 2.2 is a summary of these ratios for Germany and its principal competitors having GDP in excess of US$1000 billion.

Table 2.2 *Ratios of foreign trade to end of 1994*

	Exports/ GDP %	Exports Growth %	Imports Growth %
Germany	23.0	4.4	3.5
France	17.7	5.6	3.5
Italy	18.6	6.2	1.9
UK	20.1	6.1	2.8
Japan	8.6	7.6	5.5
US	7.7	7.1	7.0

Source: OECD Economic Surveys

In relation to economic activity, Germany is the clear leader in export performance, followed by the UK and Italy. Working from a high baseline, export growth lags behind its competitors. However, the growth in imports is higher only than those of Italy and the UK, the two countries with the most positive trade balance on current account in percentage terms. On this evidence, there is no reason to doubt that Germany's long-term export competitiveness against its main OECD trading partners will remain strong.

INWARD INVESTMENT

Inward investment is the context in which Germany is currently labelled as uncompetitive by reason of its overall manpower costs, both in respect of wages and salaries, and their related employee social costs. In Chapter 3 various elements of cost which affect investment decisions are examined. In some cases, Germany compares quite favourably to its fellow EU members. However, it remains true that foreign investments in Europe, particularly from Japan - and now the Asian tigers – has been focused on the UK, whose current unit industrial labour cost is reported as 54 per cent below that of Germany.

However, growth in both producer prices and unit labour costs has been contained quite successfully in Germany over the period 1990 to 1995, compared to its five main OECD competitors, as Table 2.3 demonstrates. These statistics are expressed in index form against a common baseline index of 100 in 1985 for each country individually.

It is clear that Germany, followed by the US, has been the most success-ful in containing unit labour costs, while the clear leader on producer prices has been Japan which has actually engineered an overall price fall in the last five years. Since February 1996, Germany's producer

Table 2.3 *Comparative producer prices and unit labour costs*

| | Producer prices | | Unit labour costs | |
	1990	1995	1990	1995
Germany	101.0	107.5	110.3	110.8
France	107.1	109.7	109.6	118.1*
Italy	117.8	144.0	118.8	138.1
UK	121.0	146.0	122.7	134.2
Japan	95.7	92.0	108.2	138.3
US	113.9	122.2	104.0	105.4

Source: Financial Times
* 1993 statistic (last available)

prices also appear to have fallen by up to 1 per cent while unit labour costs have stabilised since March.

The outlook for foreign direct investment into Germany is therefore more positive than international public perception. Indeed, as the eastern Länder continue to prosper, following Germany's own massive direct investment, and the gap between their economic performance and those of other Central and Eastern European economies becomes more marked, Germany is likely to become a magnet for foreign investments directed towards that region.

FINANCIAL STABILITY

The Bundesbank's contribution to the performance of the German economy through its control of the country's monetary levers is much admired, although its rigid adherence to prudent policies has at times been a source of frustration to other EU members. Nevertheless, the financial statistics speak for themselves. The 1995 and second quarter 1996 growth rates for the narrow money (M1) and broad money (M2) supply, long-term interest rates and equity market yields are examined in Table 2.4 for the six leading OECD economies.

Looking back over the past 10 years, Germany's financial performance has been highly consistent. The M1 supply growth, which fell from 1990 to 1992 and dropped again to under 4 per cent in 1995, has revived to the 10 per cent level since February 1996 in line with economic recovery. Similarly, M2 supply growth, which fell away to nil in 1995, has recovered since the beginning of 1996, achieving 1993 levels from June.

While short-term interest rates have declined steadily from post-reunification levels, when they peaked at 9.52 per cent for 1992 and have

Table 2.4 *Comparative money and finance indicators*

	M1 Money		M2 Money		Long Interest		Equity Market yield	
	1995 %	'96Q2 %	1995 %	'96Q2 %	1995 %	'96Q2 %	1995 %	'96Q2 %
Germany	3.7	10.5	0.0	7.3	6.82	6.47	2.00	1.87
France	8.8	7.7	4.7	0.8	7.53	6.51	3.17	3.02
Italy	0.6	(0.9)	0.6	3.5	12.22	9.89	1.72	2.24
UK	6.0	6.5	7.2	9.9	8.16	8.09	4.15	4.08
Japan	8.2	15.7	3.2	3.8	3.39	3.24	0.86	0.72
US	(0.3)	(2.4)	2.0	5.2	6.57	6.70	2.61	2.18

Source: Financial Times

remained below 4 per cent since November 1995, long-term interest rates have remained within the range of 6.86 per cent to 6.07 per cent since 1993, except for January 1996 when they dipped briefly to 5.9 per cent. Likewise, equity market yields have ranged from 1.77 per cent (1994) to 2.04 per cent in the fourth quarter of 1995 and are currently stable at the 1.8 per cent level.

The financial system has proved itself sufficiently stable to accommodate the absorption of the eastern *Länder*. With inflation below 2 per cent since the second quarter of 1995 and the real value of the deutschmark only 10 points above its 1985 level, continuing stability in the medium term seems assured.

CONVERGENCE TO EMU CRITERIA

There are four criteria for admission to the EMU set down in the Maastricht treaty for potential participants. The two targets which are least likely to cause problems for Germany and its principal northern European partners are the requirements for inflation and long-term interest rates, where there is already clear evidence of convergence. The two remaining criteria which are more difficult for most EU members are:

- budget deficit as a percentage of GDP, where the maximum allowable is 3 per cent;
- government debt as a percentage of GDP, where the requirement is 60 per cent or less.

In September 1996, the International Monetary Fund (IMF) gave its predictions of the likely 1997 performance by each of the EU's 14 members towards achievement of the two latter goals. These predictions are summarised in Figure 2.1, suggesting that only Luxembourg, Finland, France and Germany are likely to qualify.

In terms of budget deficit as a percentage of GDP, Luxembourg, Denmark, Finland, Ireland and the Netherlands are expected to be comfortably within the targeted 3 per cent, with France and Germany, Austria, Sweden and Belgium hitting 3 per cent exactly. Of this latter grouping, France is widely expected to have the most difficulty in hitting the budget deficit goal, but that is achievable provided that the economy succeeds in expanding at an annual rate of about 2 per cent. The UK is predicted to fall short of target with a deficit of 3.3 per cent, but that is probably capable of correction, assuming that the present and next British governments do not talk themselves out of entering the race.

The government debt target is more problematic. Only Luxembourg and the UK are expected to have government debts equivalent to less than 60 per cent in 1997. Finland, Germany and France will be on the borderline, although all three have expressed their determination to satisfy the criterion. France already plans to employ creative accounting to meet the requirement – in the form of a one-off payment from France Telecom in compensation for assuming the state utility's pension liabilities. Germany's debt to GDP ratio is forecast to rise from 60.8 per cent to 61.9 per cent in 1997; however, it is certain that action will be taken to achieve conformity. In any case, it is inconceivable that the EMU could be launched without German participation. Operating the EMU without Germany would be akin to playing *Hamlet* without the Prince.

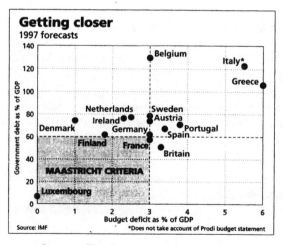

Source: The Economist, October 1996

Figure 2.1 *EMU Convergence*

If the other members of the early EMU clique, whose currencies are effectively regulated by the deutschmark, cannot manage to reach the required debt-to-GDP ratio, there will be a temptation to relax the admission criteria, but this will lower the odds against Spain and Italy who have both declared their intentions of gaining entry in the first wave. With their weaker economies, the early entry of Spain and Italy could have a destabilising effect on the EMU and would certainly cause concern to the stronger entrants. For Germany, whose EU competitiveness is solidly based, the substitution of a less stable currency for the deutschmark would be unattractive without safeguards, probably in the form of strict controls to be assigned to the new Central Bank.

LIVING STANDARDS

High living standards in Germany have been hard won over the years. The integration of the eastern *Länder* was accomplished at some cost to living standards in both West and East and, although standards of living continue to rise in the eastern states, the process is far from complete. The following comparison of statistics therefore refers to western Germany only in relation to its five principal OECD competitors and seven other EU members of the OECD. The statistics analysed in Table 2.5 are necessarily selective and include:

- private consumption per capita (1993) in US$, using current purchasing power parities (PPP);
- passenger cars per 1000 inhabitants (1990);
- television sets per 1000 inhabitants (1990);
- doctors per 1000 inhabitants (1992/3).

By these yardsticks, Germany is surpassed in each of the first three measurements by the US and in consumption per capita by all 11 countries listed except for the Netherlands, Austria, Denmark, Finland and Spain. In terms of car ownership, Germany ranks second behind the US, followed closely by Italy, Ireland and France. TV ownership is higher only in the US and Japan and there are more doctors per head only in Spain and Belgium. Except for Spain and Finland, living standards within the EU appear to be comparable.

OVERALL ECONOMIC PERFORMANCE

In Chapter 1 the current and medium-term outlook for the German economy was reviewed in some detail, albeit in isolation, although the impact of German reunification was discussed. In Table 2.6, key indicators of the German economy for 1994 are compared with those of the

Table 2.5 *Comparative living standards*

	Consumption per capita($)	passenger cars per 1000	TV sets per 1000	Doctors per 1000
Germany	10,733	480	556	3.2
Austria	10,546	382	478	2.3
Belgium	12,090	387	451	3.7
Denmark	10,402	311	536	2.8
Finland	8,814	386	501	2.6
France	11,395	413	407	2.8
Ireland	11,546	464	319	3.0
Italy	11,029	478	421	1.7
Japan	11,791	282	613	1.7
Netherlands	10,726	356	485	2.5
Spain	8,412	307	400	4.1
UK	10,942	361	434	1.5
US	16,444	568	814	2.3

Source: OECD Economic Surveys

Table 2.6 *Comparative economic indicators internationally*

	GDP per capita Billion US$	GDP growth over 5 yrs(%)	GFCF* % GDP	Savings % GDP	Consumer Prices(%) (Q2 1996)
Germany	27,826	0.8	18.5	21.0	2.9
Austria	24,670	2.5	24.8	25.3	3.4 (1994)
Belgium	22,515	1.6	17.4	22.2	2.8 (1994)
Denmark	20,546	1.9	14.8	17.0	2.1 (1994)
Finland	16,208	(1.6)	14.3	16.6	3.3 (1994)
France	19,201	1.1	18.1	19.0	2.4
Ireland	15,212	4.7	15.1	19.5	2.7 (1994)
Italy	18,681	1.0	16.4	18.8	4.2
Japan	20,756	2.1	28.6	31.2	0.2
Netherlands	18,589	2.3	19.3	24.4	2.8 (1994)
Spain	13,581	1.5	19.8	18.8	5.6 (1994)
UK	17,650	0.8	15.0	13.5	2.3
US	25,512	2.1	17.2	16.2	2.9

Source: OECD Economic Surveys, Financial Times
* Gross fixed capital formation (GFCF)

11 countries for which living standards were reviewed in the preceding section.

On the measurement of the GDP per capita, Germany takes first place, followed by the US, Austria and Belgium, but GDP growth shrank to less than 1 per cent over the five-year period to 1995 in line with the UK and France, the other two major, mature economies of the EU. However, the ratio of gross fixed capital formation to GDP has remained high in Germany, exceeded only by Austria, the Netherlands and Spain, but totally outperformed by Japan whose ratio of 28.6 per cent compares with 18.5 per cent for Germany and 17.2 per cent for the US.

Turning to savings as a percentage of GDP, the European countries and the US are again outperformed by Japan's 31.2 per cent, and at 21.0 per cent Germany's ratio is inferior to those of Austria, Belgium and the Netherlands within the EU. Finally, Germany's consumer price inflation is now below 3 per cent in common with Belgium, Denmark, France and the UK within Europe and with the US internationally. Japan's second-quarter inflation rate of 0.2 per cent is unlikely to remain at this unrealistically low level for long.

COMPETITIVENESS IN PERSPECTIVE

The overall competitiveness of Germany in relation to its EU partners is manifest within the six contexts reviewed in this analysis. Competitiveness in living standards and inward investment is less marked than in foreign trade, financial stability and overall economic performance. Of course, if the EU succeeds, competitiveness between members takes second place to the long-term competitiveness of the EU internationally. The continuing value of internal competitiveness within the market is as a mechanism for forcing up the economic performance of the weaker members, without which collective performance will be sluggish. Comparing the performances of France and Germany, who have striven to harmonise their economies, it is clear from Table 2.6 that the effort is succeeding, with one reservation. The GDP growth of both countries is now among the lowest in Europe and the OECD. It is true that Germany's GDP growth may have been slowed in the medium-term by the addition of the eastern *Länder* and their financial demands, but there may be a lesson from this experience. The long-term prosperity of the EU will depend on the interaction of its individual member state economies to achieve their highest common factors, rather than sinking to the level of lowest common multiples.

3

Inward and Outward Investment

Jonathan Reuvid

CAPITAL ACCOUNT TRANSACTIONS

In every year since 1985 direct German investment abroad has out-stripped foreign direct investment (FDI) into Germany, as Table 3.1 clearly shows. Over the ten-year period 1986 to 1995, cumulative FDI amounted to DM53 billion, against cumulative German outward invest-ment of DM300 billion. In contrast, German portfolio investment abroad has fallen short of foreign portfolio investment in Germany over the same period in every year except for 1988, 1989, 1990 and 1994. In the decade 1986 to 1995, foreign portfolio investment in Germany increased cumulatively by DM736 billion, against German foreign portfolio investment of DM484 billion.

The continuing net inflow of portfolio investment is a strong indicator of foreign investors' confidence in the German economy and in German industry and, in foreign exchange terms, has helped to ensure a favour-able balance on the capital account. As the final columns of Table 3.1 demonstrate, capital outflows over the ten-year period have been more than offset by foreign exchange inflows in each year since 1990, although there was a deficit on the capital account in the first five years from 1986 to 1990.

As noted in Chapter 2, the favourable balances on the capital account over the last five years are in contrast to negative balances on the current account over the same period, which have ranged between DM34.4 billion and DM24.9 billion annually. In contrast, current account

Table 3.1 *Inward and outward investment in Germany (DM billion)*

	1986	1987	1988	1989	1990	1991	1992	1993	1994	1995	Cumulative
Direct investment											
German FDI	21.9	17.4	21.2	28.5	38.7	39.3	30.5	25.3	27.0	50.0	299.8
FDI in Germany	2.5	3.3	2.0	13.3	4.0	6.8	4.2	2.9	1.1	12.9	53.0
Net outward investment	19.4	14.1	19.2	15.2	32.7	32.5	26.3	22.4	25.9	37.1	246.8
Portfolio investment											
German PI abroad	21.4	25.0	71.7	50.1	25.1	29.9	75.6	53.0	89.3	42.8	483.9
Foreign PI in Germany	72.5	32.3	7.4	45.7	19.4	71.2	122.5	235.3	45.4	84.6	736.3
Net PI inward	51.1	7.3	(64.3)	(4.4)	(5.7)	41.3	46.9	182.3	(43.9)	41.8	252.4
Total net investment inward/outward	31.7	(6.8)	(83.5)	(19.6)	(38.4)	8.8	20.6	159.9	(69.8)	(5.3)	5.6

balances were positive during each of the five years 1986 to 1990, when the net movement on the capital account was negative. Thus Germany's foreign exchange equilibrium has been maintained.

INWARD INVESTMENT

FDI in Germany rose from DM1.1 billion in 1994 (the lowest level in the last 10 years) to DM12.9 billion in 1995, the highest annual rate since 1989. Generally, FDI has remained relatively low over the period, compared with Germany's EU partners, reflecting the negative competitive factors discussed more fully in Chapter 2.

Relative overall FDI performance among the OECD countries is illustrated in Figure 3.1, which shows that cumulative FDI in Germany lags significantly behind France and the UK, although both are dwarfed by FDI in the US.

For inward investors, Germany's attractions as a business location, in particular its large and affluent domestic market, are outweighed by cost factors, notably employment costs – both wage rates and the associated social costs analysed in Chapter 1. In a recent study by the Federation of Germany Industry (BDI) thinktank, the Institute of the World Economy, it is reported that one hour's industrial labour in Germany costs DM45.52, compared with DM36.48 in Denmark, DM29.04 in France and DM 20.96 in the UK.

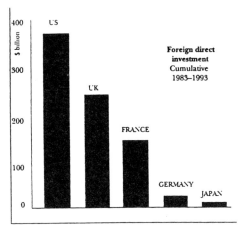

Source: OECD

Figure 3.1 *Relative FDI performance among OECD countries*

Only in certain high-technology industries, where wage costs account for no more than 8 per cent of total costs and the availability of a highly skilled and productive workforce is paramount, does the wage cost become a secondary consideration. In this context, the five Eastern *Länder* may become better placed, as in the case of Saxony which has recently attracted major investment in two semiconductor plants by Siemens and the US group AMD. Another favourable factor is the current oversupply of industrial and office property, resulting from a three-year recession, which is expected to affect property prices and rents. Similarly, for companies wishing to assemble products at cheaper facilities in the Czech Republic, Saxony is within easy reach of the border.

Against this, set-up costs in Germany are high. Expatriate, as well as local, salaries are higher in Germany than in other EU countries or the Czech Republic. Accommodation costs are similar to France, although lower than in the UK or Poland, while education costs are higher than other EU countries except the Netherlands and similar to the Czech Republic.

OUTWARD INVESTMENT

The integration of trade within the EU and of world trade more generally would be expected to stimulate rising outward direct investment, but German FDI is rather low by international standards, having remained below DM40 billion until 1995 when it rose some 85 per cent above the previous year's level to DM50 billion. Recent analysis suggests that, in Germany's case, the bulk of FDI is directed at opening up foreign markets to support German exports. However, in the decade from 1983 to 1992, transfers of production from Germany to abroad have been detected.

Evidence of this trend occurs in some industries, such as textiles, clothing and leather, where German FDI has coincided with a significant contraction of domestic employment. In other industries, such as chemicals, employment has stagnated domestically while expanding rapidly abroad. The primary motivation for FDI may now be shifting from the marketing and servicing of German exports to the pursuit of lower production costs, in particular to the nearby, developing central and eastern European countries beyond Germany. In eastern Europe, the most popular targets for investment were Hungary and the Czech Republic, accounting for 44.3 and 30.3 per cent respectively of the collective investment of 470 German companies included in a recent survey by the BDI in conjunction with the German East–West Trade

Committee. Russia, where companies were more concerned in ensuring a market foothold than in immediate benefit, accounted for a further 6 per cent.

Outward direct investment to the central and eastern European countries grew less rapidly in 1995 than in the period from 1990 to 1994, although the share of Germany's total FDI was 8.6 per cent, at US$2.8 billion, as compared with 3 per cent in 1991. In 1995 the principal beneficiaries of German FDI were other EU member countries and the US, in both of which investment more than doubled, accounting for 62 and 17 per cent respectively of the German total. China, where Germany is the biggest European trading partner with bilateral trade last year of DM27 billion, is also a major destination of German FDI. At the end of 1995, Germany ranked ninth among investors in the country, having invested $1.2 billion with a further $4.4 billion committed.

4

The Reunited Germany

R A Bischof, Chairman, Boss Group Ltd

German reunification happened at the end of a three-year growth phase in the business cycle in 1990–90; a cycle which was in fact just about to turn downwards. What followed was later described as the post-reunification boom, which lasted until about 1992–3 when, under a great deal of pressure from the Bundesbank, the overheating was halted and the inflationary pressures squeezed out of the system. The ensuing short recessionary phase was followed by another mini boom in 1994–5 and then a new, more severe, downturn in business activity from the third quarter of 1995 onwards and through to the present (second quarter 1996).

Bearing in mind the vast amounts of capital which had to be pumped into the former East Germany – DM150 billion per annum since 1990 – the Bundesbank did a remarkable job, keeping inflation under reasonable control and the economy just about on course.

The opportunities of re-engineering the former East Germany and selling consumer goods to its population, starved for 40 years of Western goods and services, were soon outstripped by three factors:

- High interest rates imposed by the Bundesbank had the nasty side effect of revaluing the DM or, to put it differently, led to devaluation of the currencies of Germany's main trading competitors – USA, UK, Sweden, Spain and Italy – during the period 1992–4.
- To pay for reunification, western German business had to carry still more taxes and social costs, although it already had the highest labour costs in Europe.
- The unions pushed through excessive wage claims which the employers agreed to, believing that they were at the beginning of

a new, sustained period of economic growth and thus could afford it.

These factors, together with the Bundesbank's tough monetary policy, have meant that Germany is being looked on as the sick man of Europe – social costs too high, wages too high, over-regulated, no flexibility in the workforce, no regard for shareholders, etc. The problems of *Metall-gesellschaft*, Mercedes-Benz and others have been cited with glee as telltale signs of economic decline. The poor unemployment record, with nearly 4 million unemployed in the united Germany, differs sharply from the falling unemployment in such countries as the UK and the USA, which both exhibit increasingly deregulated and highly flexible economic models, with a keen eye on shareholder value. The large inward invest-ment into the UK in the last two to three years is taken as proof of the preference of institutional capital and business for location in Britain rather than location in Germany. Conservative politicians and a large part of the UK's press could make one believe that the country has indeed become the enterprise centre of Europe, if not the world.

However, for business people who have to make logical, long-term decisions with far-reaching consequences, it is important to take a more balanced view, away from political posturing or ideologically motivated wishful thinking.

If the UK is so successful compared to Germany, why is it not doing better? In spite of all the inward investment, manufacturing output is flat and manufacturing investment negative (second quarter 1996). Germany, despite a near 20 per cent revaluation since 1992 (from DM2.95 to 2.30) still had a DM12 billion trade surplus with Britain (1995). Over 50 per cent of all exports to Eastern Europe from EU countries come from Germany, against a mere 5 per cent from Britain, and Germany is the most important trading partner for virtually all SoutheastAsian economies among its EU competitors, including the UK.

These few facts should act as a small reminder of the true position in the economic world. Germany not only had to create new jobs – real ones by western standards – for 16.5 million East Germans, but also for around 3.5 million, mainly Eastern European, immigrants since 1990. West Germany's population stood at 60 million in 1989 and at over 80 million in 1995.

In 1989, before the Berlin wall fell, East Germany proudly boasted full male and female employment. This amounted to about 8 million people in work. By West German standards of productivity and investment, at least 50 per cent were mere 'passengers'. Additionally, the country's economy was lopsided by Western standards: virtually no service industries such as banking, insurance, distribution etc, hardly any construction industry, almost no consumer goods industry, but a huge, oversized and COMECON-oriented heavy industry, large surface mining and chemical industry, the latter two with State-endorsed licences to pollute.

An example may highlight former East Germany's plight (for more details see Bischof *et al.*, 1993).

The Baukema Kombinat, a heavy construction equipment manufacturing conglomerate, with 12 subsidiary companies in 12 locations dotted around East Germany, was typical. Its 20,000 employees were engaged in building large excavators, graders, road surface-laying machines, concrete and asphalt-mixing towers; there were six foundries in the group and a plant making machines to produce pre-cast concrete panels for industrial buildings and private dwellings, etc.

In 1989–90 the group's turnover of about DM1 billion (converted 1:1 from East to West) consisted of 70 per cent exports to the Soviet Union, 15 per cent home sales and 15 per cent exports to other mainly Communist countries. By 1991–2 exports to the Comecon countries had all but gone. The necessary reduction in manpower was accelerated by a productivity drive aided by state-financed investment in modern machinery. The biggest problem was trying to sell products which were hopelessly out of date and only useful for unsophisticated markets. Against Western competitors such as Caterpillar, Liebherr and Komatsu, to name but a few, they had no chance. Additionally, managers were not used to taking decisions on their own; nor did they know much about the concept of selling or marketing. The Eastern economies were driven by constant shortages compared to the Western economies, which are characterised by over-supply and excess capacities. No balance sheets or profit and loss accounts existed in 1990 in any of Baukema's companies.

The time between 1991 and 1993 was spent in restructuring the conglomerate from top to bottom: balance sheets were created, an organisation chart, two-tier boards of management, product development, management and workforce retraining, downsizing to about 20 per cent of the original workforce and ridding these companies of unrelated business and involvements.

By 1993, all but 1 of the 12 subsidiaries of the Baukema Kombinat had been restructured and successfully privatised through a total of 20 different deals. Only 2500 employees out of the 20,000 remained in their original industry/jobs. Most others were either sent into early retirement or retrained for jobs outside heavy engineering.

The new states' economic performance went into free fall in 1992–3, bottomed out in 93–4 and started growing at a reasonable pace in 1994–5. The speed of advancement would have been faster, if wages in East Germany had been in line with productivity – unfortunately, it was agreed in the early stage of reunification, before the extent of the problem was recognised by politicians, trade unions and employers, that wages in East and West would be set to equalise over a four-year period. They started at about 50 per cent of West German wages, when productivity was one-third of West Germany's and, on average, wages had always been ahead of productivity. This has caused many firms to struggle and not a few to go under. The start-up rate in the East is proportionally very much higher than in the West; however, so is the failure rate.

Nevertheless, a number of companies are now performing ahead of western German companies and can, therefore, take advantage of the remaining wage differential, approximately 25 per cent.

The new states (*Neue Länder*) now have the most advanced telephone communication system, and soon will have one of the best road and railway infrastructures in Europe. The gigantic task of trying to bring East German standards of living, productivity, skills investment and quality of life up to West German standards will probably take another 10 years. However, the major part of it has been done. One dreads to think how long it will take the other Eastern European countries to get to Western standards, without a big brother helping them. Their only advantage is the fact that their wages are a fraction of those that East German industry has to cope with.

One often underestimated part of the change that had to take place in the East was to change people's minds and attitudes, to give them confidence in themselves, their decisions and their abilities. This has been more difficult with the older generation and, in many cases, downright impossible, as the vote of about 20 per cent for the PDS, the ex-Communist party, still shows. However, the young and the young at heart have taken to the new-won freedom with both hands. They have often turned out to be more entrepreneurial than their rich, over-fed and over-regulated cousins in the West.

The old East Germany also brings another great asset to the economic battle for the future: long-established ties to all East European countries, knowledge of language (Russian was the first foreign language in all of Eastern Europe) and inter-cultural skills. Its industries supplied the Soviet Union and the Republic of China for decades before the fall of the Iron Curtain. These connections are there to be used and are taken advantage of by the new owners of the old businesses, predominantly, of course, West German firms.

I believe that Europe should concentrate largely on the development of its own backyard, the old Eastern bloc economies, where there is a market of 300 million people who, in contrast to their rich Western neighbours, have nothing and want everything. The 'Tiger' economies of Southeast Asia are certainly impressive, but Hong Kong, Taiwan, Singapore or Malaysia are comparatively small markets. China will develop and eventually dominate, with Japan, that part of the world, and one should not neglect those markets, but on Europe's own doorstep lies the biggest opportunity.

If Europe is not afraid of exporting jobs to those countries, in other words giving them work and buying simple goods from them, then their economies will start to grow. Their people will have disposable income to buy more and more sophisticated goods from the West, and Europe could see 30–50 years of growth from these markets, always provided that a managed equilibrium is maintained.

Germany, in particular the old East Germany, the *Neue Länder*, is geographically, culturally and industrially in the best position to take advantage of this development.

It is true that some of Germany's companies have taken their eye off the ball and neglected shareholders and short-term profits in the pursuit of long-term strategic positions in various markets. And it is equally true that Germany is over-regulated in areas where it should no longer be, such as financial services. It is also true that Germany's employees and unions have, in the last few years, begun to misuse the system, which has given them high wages and living standards, security in and out of work and in retirement.

The German government has realised this and has started to take measures to roll some of the excesses back, reduce employee power and social costs and encourage companies to look after their shareholders' needs. German business has already responded and has started to refocus on profits and shareholder value.

Neither, however, wants to go anywhere near the Anglo-Saxon, purely shareholder-value-driven model, with its exploitation and disregard of the employees and a short-term profit-dominated culture, which does not allow strategic development of markets, neglects training and skill advancement, as well as research and development and investment in capital equipment.

In any event, it would not be possible to go overboard, as the German constitution clearly states that the Federal Republic is a democratic and social state, and also because the three main German political parties support wholeheartedly the principles of the social market economy, with its emphasis on competition and social fairness. The business community also believes that this model is ultimately superior to the Anglo-Saxon model and that it is more in line with modern aspirations and the twentieth century's requirement for democratic processes, not only in public life but also at the workplace.

That does not mean, however, that even the best models or economic systems do not, from time to time, need a thorough overhaul and cleansing of excesses. This is clearly underway in Germany.

Germany's trading position, as well as her attractiveness as a manu-facturing location, has improved since there has been a correction in the exchange rates of those countries whose currencies had been devalued the most during 1994–5. The US dollar hardened, not only against the Japanese yen, reversing some of Japan's problems, but also against the deutschmark. One must not forget that when the US dollar falls or rises, it concerns all the countries in the dollar bloc, not just the United States; currencies which are tied to the dollar include a number of Southeast Asia's Tiger economies.

In a reversal of its previously held beliefs, the German Employers Federation, the BDI, confirmed recent economic research which proved that two-thirds of Germany's problems with competitiveness had been the result of exchange rate movements, and only one-third was home-made – in other words, due to increases in wages and social costs and the inflexibility and 'red tape' which goes with highly regulated countries.

In any event, the latest pay round in Germany has been very modest indeed and, as was said earlier, the social state will be rolled back and, in the coming years, the burden of financing the new states will also be reduced.

Germany's traditionally highly trained, highly skilled workforce will also continue to play a decisive role in the country's success. Every year approximately 600,000 young people enter full apprenticeships, still the best vocational training model in the world. Half of them go into craft-related jobs such as engineering, computing, carpentry, plumbing, hairdressing; the other 300,000 go into commercial or banking apprenticeships, which gives Germany its commercial backbone. Some 67 per cent of young people enter working life like that, many after A-

Levels (*Abitur*) and before they go to University. The apprenticeship system is a living thing: recently it was found that large companies, such as Siemens, saw a need for a new apprenticeship called chemical bioengineering and, within a year, a new career possibility was created.

The old East Germany had the same vocational training system and, in spite of upheavals and restructuring, over 90 per cent of apprenticeships were finished, although some youngsters had to change from one industry into another.

It is very advisable to take Germany, the largest market in Europe, as a place in which to do business seriously. All rumours of terminal decline are premature.

REFERENCE

Bischof, R., von Bismarck, G. and Colin, W. (1993) From Kombinat to Private Enterprise: Two Case Studies in East German Privatisation.

5

Development of the European Union

Klaus Balzer, Director General, German-British Chamber of Industry & Commerce

GERMANY'S ROLE IN THE FURTHER DEVELOPMENT OF THE EU

Germany plays a key role politically, economically and financially in Europe. The German federal government, led by Chancellor Helmut Kohl, is a strong proponent of the further development of the European Union, including European Monetary Union and the widening of the EU to include a number of countries in Central Europe which have opted for democracy and the principle of a market economy following the collapse of communism. The guiding thought in this is that Europe will never again have to experience the wars that were commonplace until the second half of the twentieth century. Democracy and economic prosperity for all European countries are seen as the best safeguard for such a development. At the same time Germany is trying not to create a 'fortress Europe', but to keep Europe open for free world trade and for a close alliance and co-operation with the United States of America. These aims are supported by the vast majority of Germans. There is, however, an apprehension among Germans with regard to the stability of the currency once the European Monetary Union (EMU) is a reality. Germans do not want to see the 'Euro' weakened against the deutschmark if and when other EU-countries with weaker currencies join EMU. For many Germans the deutschmark is the symbol of stability and trustworthiness and reflects the country's success over the past 50 years.

While the majority of German business supports EMU, surveys show most ordinary Germans to be sceptical of it.

After the Second World War the German population demonstrated that it knows how to overcome difficult times. Universally admired, the Germans rebuilt their country after 1945 with enormous energy; not least with the support of its Western neighbours, particularly with the assistance of the US and the Marshall Plan, West Germany created an economic miracle. Between 1950 and 1960 GNP tripled and full employment was secured for the following two decades. In the space of 20 years, Germany created Europe's strongest economy. West Germany's success was so striking that the communist leaders of East Germany built the Berlin Wall in 1961 in order to prevent people from this part of Germany moving into the western part of the country. Following Germany's reunification on 3 October 1990, the former West Germany invested enormous sums in a country which had been driven to economic ruin by the communist planned economy. A fundamental restructuring of the economy in eastern Germany began, which will continue over a number of years. Huge transfers of funds contributed to the economic downswing in Germany from mid-1995 to end 1996. Germany now faces two great problems: meeting the criteria for EMU set by Maastricht and the reconstruction of the eastern German economy. There is, however, no doubt that Germany will achieve these tasks. It continues to be the largest trading nation in the world and the deutschmark is among the world's strongest currencies. With 80 million people, Germany is Western Europe's most populated state.

However, Germany would never have been in a position to create such a politically and economically stable nation without the co-operation and good will of its European partners. When the Treaty of Rome was signed in 1957, Germany was one of the six founder states along with France, Belgium, Luxembourg, the Netherlands and Italy. The Treaty of Rome, whose founders included Jean Monet (France), Konrad Adenauer (Germany), Alcide de Gasperi (Italy) and Paul Henri Spaak (Belgium), signalled the start of European Union. In 1967 the European Community was created, consisting of the European Community for Coal and Steel (1952), the European Atomic Energy Community (1957) and the European Economic Community (1957). This was a decisive step in the development of the EU. In 1979, the European Monetary System was created with the function of stabilising movements in exchange rates. In 1992 the Treaty of Maastricht was concluded, stipulating the introduction of a single European currency on 1 January 1999. Membership of the EU has increased to 15 countries and the completion of the Single European Market came about at the end of 1992.

Germany's importance in the future development of Europe is plainly evident from the role of Berlin. Before the Second World War Berlin, was, like the other great European cities, a leader in the fields of economy, finance, science and the arts. Following Germany's reunification, Berlin is about to resume this role. It is again the capital of Germany and from 1999 onwards it will also be the seat of the German federal government. The fact that Germany is the geographical centre of Europe provides the country with a prominent role. This also concerns trade with Eastern European countries, whose further integration into the European Union has to be taken into consideration. For them Berlin is the 'gateway' to the world. With Berlin as its capital in the heart of Europe and with its important historic background, Germany will play an essential role within the European Union.

THE BUSINESS BENEFITS OF THE EU FOR COMPANIES IN EUROPE

After the borders between the EU member states were opened, the idea of the Single European Market could be put into practice, although there were initial difficulties. Customs formalities have been abolished, the barriers to free competition between all companies in Europe have been removed and each national of an EU member country is allowed to take up residence in any other EU member state and work there. This has provided a tremendous boost to the further internationalisation of the European economy. However, further steps must be taken in order to realise all the benefits of the EU. EMU, for instance, promises to provide companies with more accurate business calculations, an improvement in their competitiveness and a more transparent market. Additionally, further employment could be created and investments made easier.

Membership in EMU is dependent on strict adherence to the convergence criteria which were agreed in the Treaty of Maastricht in 1992. This treaty stipulates for member countries low inflation rates, a public indebtedness which does not exceed 60 per cent of GNP and a public sector borrowing requirement no higher than 3 per cent of GDP. The monetary authority of each member state participating in EMU will be transferred to a politically independent European Central Bank, whose core task will be to secure price stability in all countries which adopt the 'Euro'. The 'Euro' will become a world currency, thus boosting competition. The single European currency will therefore improve the effectiveness of the European economies and will contribute to the creation of new and the safeguarding of existing workplaces. There is broad-ranging agreement among politicians and economic experts in all countries of the EU that European Monetary Union will not be feasible without the participation of France and Germany. The participation of the other member states is equally important.

The introduction of European Monetary Union is now firmly on the cards for 1999, but doubts remain that a number of European states wishing to join EMU may not fulfil the requirements of the Maastricht Treaty by that time. However, the notion that this may delay the start of EMU has been dispelled by the EU summit held in Dublin in December 1996. In order to fulfil the Maastricht criteria for Germany's participation in EMU, the German Cabinet in early November 1996 decided on serious cuts in many areas of government expenditure. Chancellor Kohl will use all means available in order to achieve EMU and develop the European Union further. The Chancellor is profoundly convinced that only the creation of a unified Europe, where forces are combined in the fight against crime and drugs and joint decisions are taken on foreign policy, defence, the economy and the environment, will prevent further disasters from happening to Europe as a whole. He also stresses that the creation of such a union cannot be compared with the United States of America, since Europe has a much older history with very diverse cultures, languages and peoples.

There is no consensus on the time scale for the beginning of EMU. According to the President of the Association of Germany Chambers of Industry and Commerce, Hans Peter Stihl, Europe should not put itself under pressure in fulfilling the convergence criteria for the creation of EMU. Should it be apparent that there are not enough member states in 1999 which fulfil the conditions for entry into EMU, a delay in the creation of the single currency should be considered. What is most important is that EMU will be created; it does not matter when.

The German economy requires an agreement on stability so that previous endeavours towards stability are not weakened whenever another state enters European Monetary Union. Germany's Finance Minister, Theo Waigel, has proposed sanctions if and when participating member states surpass a deficit of 3 per cent of GNP in planning their budgets or in the actual pursuit of their financial policy. Between the decision in 1998 on the qualification of member states for EMU and the beginning of EMU in 1999, there will be nine months during which the participants will have been selected but the exchange rates of the participating currencies will not have been fixed. Companies should be informed as soon as possible how the exchange rates are to be fixed. Monetary Union itself is not a single step, but a process. Some countries either cannot or do not want to enter EMU right from the start. These countries will closely co-operate in exchange rate policies with the European Central Bank. In Germany, industry and commerce, in particular the retail trade, broadly favour the switch from national currencies to the 'Euro' on a given date. Too quick a change from national currencies to the 'Euro' will lead to high costs. To continue to use national currencies for a period alongside the 'Euro' would increase the costs even more.

A GERMAN VIEW OF THE EU'S FUTURE DEVELOPMENT AND ITS BENEFITS TO EUROPEAN BUSINESS

Given the political will to make the European Union successful and to use its full potential, the European Union will provide tremendous benefits to the peoples of all member states in political, economic and cultural matters. European business stands to benefit equally.

In most member states deregulation has a high priority in order to increase the potential for European competition. This applies not least to Germany, where taxes, salaries, wages and supplementary wage costs are too high. Bureaucracy has to be reduced and more flexibility in the labour market is needed. All member states have to observe strict budgetary control.

Countries must give up protectionism and distortion of competition and there must be even stricter control of subsidies on a national level. Increased competition in the economy has great benefits, not only for the consumer. Without competition, many investments and developments in new technologies which actually provide long-term benefits for companies would not otherwise be undertaken. A single European currency eliminates the risks of exchange rates and makes business transactions easier to calculate. A harmonised legal system also contributes to security and justice. The European Parliament must obtain real legislative power in order to secure democracy in Europe, even though national parliaments should retain their legislative power in certain areas. Germany has ample experience with her Länder system, all of which retain legislative powers in areas special to them and excluded from the federal or national Parliament. However, the European Parliament should be answerable to all people in the European Union. The legislative power of the European Parliament must be checked by the jurisdiction of a European Supreme Court. The principle of subsidiarity must be accorded a high priority. This means that problems which can be solved on a national level should be solved there without committing other EU member states.

German companies expect from the European Union a number of positive effects such as:

- no barriers to market entry in other EU countries through which companies hope to increase their competitiveness both as suppliers and purchasers;
- speedier transactions through the elimination of non-tariff trade barriers and an increased use of distribution networks in the EU;
- an improvement in competition through the harmonisation of technical standards in Europe which will create further synergies;
- easier access to public tendering in other EU countries as a result of the harmonisation of tender procedures and the liberalisation of markets.

Nevertheless, there are also some negative aspects facing companies in EU countries:

- the competitiveness of individual companies can be weakened as a result of the entry of more European competitors on the national market;
- increased pressure on price levels and other conditions owing to the competition in other EU countries being able to produce at a lower price. These pressures will be particularly evident if companies are only able to adjust their cost structures in a limited way;
- many companies fear an increase in takeovers and concentration of business activities into large companies at the expense of small and medium-sized businesses;
- in Germany, many more companies transfer investments into low-wage countries and pursue more economic rationalisation measures which has severe effects on the home labour market.

Germany must lower taxation, wage and supplementary wage costs in order to make it a more attractive location for foreign investors, but also to keep domestic companies within the country. However, never will Germany, or for that matter, any other highly industrialised EU Member country be able to compete on labour costs prevailing in some Eastern European and Far East countries. Non-wage elements such as superior quality innovation and excellent service have to make up for this. It will be necessary to limit salary increases; both companies and employees should be amenable to flexible working hours in order to make the most of the latest high-value technology.

Harmonisation is required in many areas such as taxation, environmental protection laws, rules governing foreign trade and ultimately, taxation. In order to simplify trade between different EU countries, standardised contracts have to be divised which must be as simple to use as possible. But business must also be clear on the continuing validity of long-term contracts. German industry and business are firmly behind the idea that subsidiarity should be the guiding principle within the EU. The EU consists of pluralist societies which believe in freedom and a market-oriented economy. Subsidiarity is a principle which safeguards the pluralist order. German business and industry welcome the intention of the federal government to back the introduction of subsidiarity in the EU. According to the spirit of subsidiarity, the areas of jurisdiction of the EU and the member states must be clearly defined. Working to the principle of subsidiarity will also decrease bureaucracy and the lengthy procedures of European administration.

All countries in the EU should be open to its expansion towards the East and Central European states. On no account should a 'fortress Europe' be built after the frontiers between EU member states have been removed. Protectionist measures can only worsen competition on the internal market. The EU should therefore adopt a positive and open policy towards the further integration of Eastern and Central European countries, which until recently were guided by a centralist approach and a planned economy. Problems with integration will certainly arise, but the fears of existing member states that the EU will somehow be weakened by the extension into Central and Eastern Europe are largely unfounded. Obviously, the EU will have to guard against additional financial burdens, particularly concerning the Common Agricultural Policy, which is already in urgent need of reform. But in many other respects, the countries of Central and Eastern Europe have already successfully carried out decisive reforms and stabilisation measures and they are beginning to show results. In particular, Germany is very much interested in integrating these countries into the EU, in order to secure peace in Europe, but also to increase trade. Like Germany, all EU countries must have an interest in the political and economic well-being of these states whose background and culture are European.

In future, Germany will play a full part in European defence policy. Until recently, German soldiers could not be used for fighting purposes outside the NATO area and could only fulfil a non-military, peace-keeping role such as in Bosnia, for instance, providing medicines and hospital equipment or delivering food to Asia and Africa. In future, however, German soldiers will also be part of multinational fighting units for securing peace. This makes Germany a fully integrated member of the EU in every sense.

Despite certain risks, which are inevitable with a venture as huge as building a united Europe, the positive aspects and opportunities within the EU are predominant. The EU must be turned into a success for the good of all people in Europe and for the European economy to be competitive in a global world.

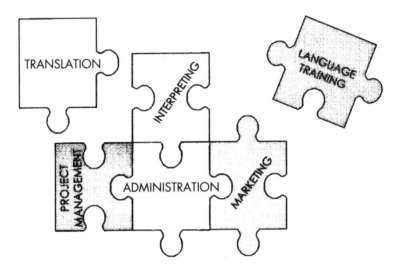

6

The Role and Influence of European Monetary Union

Rolf Günther Thumann, Co-ordinator of the EMU Research Project

A HISTORICAL PERSPECTIVE

The Treaty of Maastricht says that European Monetary Union (EMU) will start on 1 January, 1999. This means that there is not much time left for preparation. In fact, critics have argued that EMU is being introduced with too much haste. However, economic and monetary union is not being created overnight. EMU will be the result of a learning process which started with monetary cooperation within the European Community in the 1960s and developed into the conceptual thoughts of the Delors Report of 1989. This report in turn was the basis for formulating the Maastricht Treaty, which became effective in late 1993 and which envisages the creation of an economic and monetary union in three stages over a number of years.

In the 1960s monetary cooperation among the six founding members of the European Economic Community (EEC) was not greatly developed. In the late 1960s/early 1970s difficulties with this infant system of cooperation led to an ambitious project, the Werner Plan. This envisaged the introduction of an economic and monetary union in three stages based on a gradual strengthening of economic and monetary policy coordination and a narrowing of intra-EC exchange rate fluctuations. Based on this plan, in April 1972, the Central Bank Presidents laid down the details of a system of exchange rate coordination (the so-called 'snake') which aimed at limiting exchange rate fluctuations to +/–2.25 per cent. Mainly reflecting the final breakdown of the Bretton Woods system in 1973, the turmoil in the aftermath of the first OPEC oil price explosion and problems in the coordination of member states' policies, the snake system encountered major difficulties. The more ambitious elements of the Werner Plan – economic and monetary union – had to be shelved completely.

The idea of an economic and monetary union in Europe received renewed impetus with a further plan – initiated by Giscard d'Estaing of France and Helmut Schmidt of Germany – to replace the unsuccessful 'snake' with a workable exchange rate system, the European Monetary System (EMS). At the core of the EMS has been the use of a basket currency – the ECU – as an anchor and a unit of account, combined with the rules of the Exchange Rate Mechanism (ERM) and the provision of certain financing mechanisms. However, over the years the deutsch-mark has attained the role of de facto *Leitwährung* of the system. The Bundesbank has set the rules of monetary policy in the system, putting Europe on a downward inflation path and thus adding to the credibility of the EMS. However, realignments which are subject to multilateral agreement were at times delayed and this led to disruptive developments, e.g. the exit of Italy and the UK from the exchange rate mechanism in September 1992 and the widening of fluctuation margins from +/–2.25 per cent to +/–15 per cent in August 1993.

The demand by the French Finance Minister Balladur in late 1987, supported by the German Foreign Minister Genscher, to create a European Central Bank led to the establishment of the Delors Group by the European Council in Hanover in June 1988. The mandate of this group was to check and suggest concrete steps to realise an economic and monetary union in Europe. The Delors Report, published in April 1989, proposed to establish this union in three stages: stage I, which was to start on 1 July, 1990, included closer coordination of economic and budgetary policies, strengthened Community competition policy, the completion of the Single Market and a comprehensive liberalisation of the capital markets; stage II would prepare the necessary institutional structures, and in particular establish the European Monetary Institute (EMI) as the forerunner of the future European Central Bank; stage III would mark full-fledged economic and monetary union.

From December 1990 to December 1991 two Intergovernmental Conferences, one on economic and monetary union and the second on political union, worked out the text of the European Union Treaty which was endorsed by the Heads of State or Government in Maastricht on 9 and 10 December, 1991. This so-called Maastricht Treaty defines in legal terms the blueprint of EMU. It was signed in Maastricht on 7 February, 1992 and became effective on 1 November, 1993. Stage I of EMU began in July 1990, stage II in January 1994. Stage III is envisaged by the Treaty to start on 1 January, 1999 (at the latest).

THE EMU TIMETABLE

The timetable for EMU was outlined in the conclusions of the Madrid summit of the Heads of State or Government in December 1995. This timetable marks four key dates.

First, the decision of who will participate in EMU initially will be made as early as possible in 1998 on the basis of actual 1997 economic data. The procedure under which a member state qualifies is spelled out in Article 109j of the Maastricht Treaty. Based on a report and a recommendation by the EU Commission and a report by the European Monetary Institute, the ECOFIN Council assesses which member states fulfil the necessary conditions for the introduction of the Euro (formerly the ECU) and makes a recommendation to the European Council (Heads of State or Government). The European Council decides with a qualified majority which member states are fit to participate, based on the recommendation of the ECOFIN Council and taking into account the above mentioned reports and the opinion of the European Parliament. The requirement of qualified majority voting implies that at least 62 out of 87 votes and at least 10 out of 15 member states are necessary for a positive decision. Following the decision on the participants, the European Central Bank (ECB) will be established.

Second, on 1 January 1999, EMU begins. The exchange rates of the EU member states participating in the Euro area are irrevocably fixed among each other and with respect to the Euro. These conversion rates are to be set in a unanimous vote by the ECOFIN Council in the composition of the states adopting the Euro, based on a proposal by the EU Commission and after hearing the ECB (Maastricht Treaty, article 109 l (4)). The Euro becomes the common currency of the participating member states and the ECB conducts the common monetary policy in this currency. Because Euro notes and coins will not be available in sufficient quantities in the early stage of EMU (reflecting production bottlenecks at the printing presses and the mints), national currencies will remain legal tender for a transition period lasting up to three years. During this period, according to the principle of 'no compulsion and no prohibition', the Euro can be used on a voluntary basis. The governments of the Euro zone are expected to issue marketable debt in Euro from 1999 and the banks will probably be quick to offer Euro customer accounts. Big companies are also expected to switch to the Euro early on.

Third, three years after the start of EMU at the latest, Euro notes and coins will finally be available and the Euro will become legal tender. Within a period of at most six months the Euro must replace completely national notes and coins. During this period, which is known in EMI terminology as phase 3b, there will be a parallel currency regime, with the Euro having legal tender status while the national currencies retain much or all of their legal tender status. Final decisions on the details of this parallel currency regime have not been taken.

Fourth, by mid-2002 at the latest, national notes and coins will have lost their legal tender status and the Euro will be the only lawful and legal tender currency. However, it will still be possible to exchange national notes and coins into Euro after that date.

For this timetable to work in practice two essential conditions must be fulfilled. First, a politically acceptable number of member states must qualify for EMU by early 1998. As of summer 1996 the financial markets appear to assume that a group of countries, including Germany, France, the Netherlands, Belgium, Luxembourg and Austria, will qualify. However, there remains a risk that even some of these countries could miss the budgetary criteria of the Maastricht Treaty. Second, the participants must be 'technically ready' for the introduction of the Euro. The EU institutions, the EMI, the Central Banks and the national governments face an immense workload and bottlenecks might emerge. Moreover, firms and households have to prepare themselves for the changeover period – the former both on a technical as well as a strategic level, the latter mainly psychologically. It is important to understand that the Euro can be introduced successfully only if it is accepted by the public at large.

EUROPE IN TIERS?

In contrast to hopes existing at the time of the Maastricht Treaty negotiations, it has become quite clear meanwhile that only a limited number of countries will be in sufficiently good economic shape to launch EMU in 1999. Other countries will not qualify in time and two countries which could qualify may use their option not to participate (UK and Denmark). Hence, at least in the early phase of EMU, there will be 'ins' and 'outs'. EMU critics fear that this situation will damage the internal market and cause political friction, possibly putting the Union at risk.

However, the probability that a multi-speed EMU will end in a 'Europe in tiers' appears rather limited. First, most of the 'outs' have a strong political preference for joining EMU as soon as possible. Hence, they will most probably persevere, at least for a while, with their current anti-inflation and budget deficit reduction policies and be able to join EMU with only a limited delay. Second, the 'outs' have the option to join the EMS II, the successor to the present exchange rate mechanism. This will help them to stabilise their exchange rates and reduce the risk of 'competitive devaluations'. Third, although the 'outs' will not have a seat on the ECB Council, they will share responsibility for monetary cooperation within the European System of Central Banks (ESCB). More generally, they will continue to work together ever more closely with the 'ins' in the ECOFIN Council, the Economic and Finance Committee (the successor to the Monetary Committee) and other EU institutions. Fourth, the 'ins' have economic interests of their own to bring as many of the 'outs' on board as quickly as possible in order to reap the full benefits of EMU.

There is, however, one important caveat. An 'out' country that is perceived not to be interested in joining EMU but to be merely trying to benefit without sharing the burdens may face disadvantages. One major cost could be higher domestic interest rates in that country compared with EMU rates reflecting economic policy and exchange rate risks. There is also a danger that the financial markets of the outsider could lose importance or even become marginalised. Another type of cost could be related to isolation in decision-making processes at EU level.

Specific negative effects on businesses of an 'out' country are limited by the rules of the Single Market which aim at securing a 'level playing field'. Nevertheless, as the ongoing discussion about the access of banks to the TARGET system demonstrates, there may be cases in which the role of an outsider entails disadvantages. On the other hand, businesses of an 'out' country do not have to bear the transition costs related to the introduction of the Euro. Moreover, they do not have to face the direct additional competition that comes with greater price and cost transparency in EMU. However, in the longer run this lack of competition may slow down adjustment and increase inefficiencies which would translate into a loss of business opportunities.

Other specific practical effects on businesses of an 'out' country will probably be limited because the Single Market rules out discriminatory behaviour.

THE MACROECONOMIC POLICY REGIME UNDER EMU AND ITS EFFECTS ON BUSINESSES

EMU will have a decisive impact on the conduct of macroeconomic policies in Europe. The stance of monetary/fiscal policies will probably be tighter compared to a regime without EMU, provided that the participating member states stick to the rules laid down in the Maastricht Treaty. Hence interest rates should be lower and exchange rates *vis-à-vis* third countries more stable than otherwise. The Maastrich rules on budget deficits and public debt should also, over time, allow governments to lower the tax burden and reduce the share of the public sector in the economy. These developments should on balance create an economic climate which is favourable to more vigorous growth. However, if member countries violate the Maastricht rules with regard to monetary and fiscal policy, the impact on businesses could turn out to be quite unfavourable.

The Maastricht Treaty is rather specific about monetary and fiscal policy but says very little about wage and labour market policies. The absence of clear rules in these areas could lead to inconsistencies and tensions in macroeconomic policies. Due to the common monetary policy, the constraints on fiscal policy and the lack of exchange rate adjustment within EMU, a participating member state loses some degree of freedom in conducting economic policy. Therefore, to avoid inconsistencies and tensions, a member state's wage and labour market policies must become more flexible.

The institutional structures of wage determination and labour market regulations differ markedly between EU countries. Moreover, labour market reforms are particularly difficult to achieve in light of the vested interests involved. In order to safeguard a proper functioning of EMU, policy makers as well as employers and unions in the participating member states will have to tackle this highly complex problem in time, hopefully before the start of EMU.

THE COMMERCIAL BENEFITS OF EMU

In an assessment of EMU the Federation of German Industry (BDI) comes to the general conclusion that, on balance, monetary union will benefit German businesses. Other studies, e.g. those of the German Banking Association, support this view of the BDI. As many details – e.g. participants, conversion rates, monetary instruments, legal specifications for the transition period – still have to be decided, it is quite obvious that no reliable detailed quantifications of the positive and negative effects of EMU on business profitability can yet be provided.

Nevertheless, a number of commercial benefits of EMU can be identified even now. Essentially, there are five factors that will have a positive impact on German companies' cost competitiveness:

- the elimination or reduction of outlays for exchange transactions or currency hedging;
- the absence or the lowering of exchange rate risk in investment decisions and in selecting markets for outputs and inputs;
- the improvement in price competitiveness for those companies which have suffered from distorted medium-term currency appreciation;
- companies' transaction costs are reduced due to the introduction of large-scale money-transfer systems;
- substantially more liquid and broader financial markets in Europe will reduce companies' user costs of capital.

The magnitude of these cost savings will vary considerably between sectors and increase with the number of participating countries. Clearly, the lion's share of the above-mentioned benefits will be reaped by the export sectors, i.e. chemicals, steel, mechanical engineering and motor vehicles. However, the non-tradeables sectors will benefit from lower user cost of capital directly and from the other factors indirectly, through linkage and multiplier effects. To the extent that EMU leads to lower interest rates, interest-sensitive sectors such as housing construction should also gain.

EMU – reflecting better price transparency and reduced risk – will enhance business opportunities for European companies. In particular, lower financing costs and the removal of exchange risk for intra-EU business will probably induce higher volumes of cross-border trade and investment and lead to a more efficient allocation of resources in the Union. The financial institutions will benefit from a broader and more liquid European market for their services, although banks are set to lose part of their forex (foreign exchange) business. Small and medium-sized companies in the tradeables sectors with lower value-added production will find improved chances for cross-border activities which thus far, in the face of high transaction costs, have not been profitable enough. Moreover, the transition from national currencies to the Euro will directly create a massive, though temporary, increase in orders for the computer, software, paper, printing, automated machine and consulting industries – risking the emergence of severe bottlenecks in some cases. As with cost savings, it is not possible at this stage to quantify the additional business opportunities.

Clearly, the transition to EMU will also entail costs to businesses. Accounting systems must be adjusted, long-term contracts must be checked, employees must be trained – all key business activities must be re-evaluated. EMU start-up costs across sectors and businesses will be distributed unevenly. For instance, the financial institutions will have to make major efforts, at a very early stage, to be able to implement all necessary conversion obligations, create as well as satisfy demands for new financial products and provide information and advice to customers. The retail trade is faced with problems related to pricing in national currency and Euro, cashier systems and – perhaps – confused customers.

Those adjustment costs may be significant. The European Banking Association estimated the total conversion costs over three to four years to banks in all EU countries at between DM15 and 18 billion, equivalent to up to 2 per cent of current annual operating costs. The German Association of Retailers (HDE) calculated adjustment costs of German retailers at DM10 billion. It is important, however, to understand that these costs will be temporary, while the benefits of EMU will be permanent. Moreover, to keep costs down it is of crucial importance that the EU governments:

- create a clear legal framework for the use of the Euro, securing as far as legally possible the continuity of contracts (intra-EU and *vis-à-vis* third countries);
- find appropriate rules for 'rounding';
- minimise (subject to sector needs) the length of the parallel currency period;
- avoid (subject to legitimate consumer interests) complicated double-pricing legislation.

The legal framework for the use of the Euro will be specified in a Council regulation which will become effective on 1 January, 1999. Currently the EU Commission is preparing the technical details. *Inter alia*, this Council regulation will probably address the issue of continuity of contracts in a general fashion, stating that the introduction of the Euro shall not in itself give the right to change a contract *unilaterally* unless the parties to the contract have agreed otherwise. Under existing German jurisdiction, the introduction of the Euro in itself would not as a rule be sufficient cause to plea for *Wegfall der Geschäftsgrundlage* (the basis on which the contract has been concluded no longer exists). Nevertheless, there may be exceptional cases in which adjustments to a contract could be appropriate. But those cases cannot be subjected *ex ante* to EU-wide or national legal rules, but will have to be investigated by the civil courts, if the need arises.

Matters become more complicated if a contract is subject to the laws of a non-EU country. Whether an understanding between the EU and third-party countries regarding the continuity of contracts issue can be found needs to be investigated further.

All told, EMU will bring with it an unusual density of changes and innovations. For businesses this will create a window of opportunity though accompanied by additional risks. Those companies quick to adjust are likely to gain; the laggards, however, may lose. Moreover, the EMU's effects on businesses will be spread unevenly across sectors and over time. The best advice that can be given to companies at this stage is probably: start getting ready now.

7

German Business Culture

Eric Lynn, Managing Director, LCT Consultants, Nuremberg

It takes time to do a thing well. (German proverb)

Recently, Bill, a new recruit to the Manchester subsidiary of a German corporation, was sent on a five-day seminar to Hamburg. It was his first visit to Germany. On arrival at the seminar hotel, he met his German colleagues and was taken aback at the formality of the atmosphere and the seriousness of his new colleagues. Although he found the work interesting and despite the fact that they seemed to loosen up at the bar in the evening, he began to wonder whether he had made the right decision in joining the company.

It is 15 March and Tony received an angry call from his Munich head-quarters asking for a set of quality reports which they claim they requested in November. On checking his files, Tony discovered the fax. It seems he had simply forgotten the deadline. 'No problem,' he said, 'I'll get them to you in the next couple of weeks.' He sensed that this made his German colleague even angrier.

These are two examples of misunderstanding due to differences in the way people work in Anglo-Saxon countries and Germany. Differences are not a problem: not understanding why they exist and how they affect business relationships is.

Culture is simply the way things are done in any one particular place. The place may be Britain, the United States, western Germany, eastern Germany, or anywhere else. It may also be a subgroup within a society such as a corporation. It is important because it is the driving force behind the way people deal with others, challenges, problems, work –

life. Understanding the influence of culture on international business is vital because, whatever the technology and whatever the benefits of a particular product, all business deals are made by people.

People behave differently for a variety of historical, political, sociological and psychological reasons. If we ignore these differences, we cannot hope to understand what motivates and drives our business counterparts from abroad and we risk making very expensive mistakes as well as not achieving optimal results from those deals that we do pull off.

This chapter will look at the way Germans do business and consider how Germans tend to manage their dealings with business partners domestically and abroad. The most significant factors affecting German behaviour patterns and the driving forces behind these behaviours – values, society norms, historical factors – will be covered. You will gain an understanding of the reasons for German behaviour to enable you to interpret specific situations appropriately as well as to modify your behaviour when dealing with German counterparts.

The business culture of Germany in the late 1990s is influenced by historical factors (eg the effects of the hyperinflation of the 1920s), political factors (eg the reunification of the country in 1990), sociological factors (eg the emphasis laid on specialisation in the education system) and psychological factors, which include not only these aspects but also the pressure from society to conform to accepted norms. Furthermore, it is guided by the people active throughout all levels of business life whose actions are motivated (whether positively or negatively) by the values that underlie society.

STEREOTYPES

Stereotypes exist about almost every ethnic or national group. Both Bill and Tony may have attributed some of these stereotypical behaviours to Germans: they are humourless, aggressive, distant, stubborn, unfriendly, sticklers for detail.

People who have been fortunate enough to get to know their German business partners well, and who have been able to consider why they behave as they do, will have realised that these stereotypes are anything but true.

Stereotypes and generalisations develop when one's own view of reality is imposed on a *foreign* (in this case German) situation. To a Briton or American used to a working atmosphere where fun is combined with hard work, the German, for whom work is 'serious business' may appear to be humourless, if judged by *foreign* standards (in this case British or American).

Did the aggressiveness, personal distance or unfriendliness that Bill and Tony *perceived* really exist or did they misinterpret the signals? In his book *How Real is Real?*, Paul Watzlawick says: 'The most dangerous delusion of all is that there is only one reality.' He also says: 'our everyday, traditional ideas of reality are delusions which we spend substantial parts of our daily lives shoring up, even at the considerable risk of trying to force facts to fit our definition of reality instead of vice versa.' How many readers can honestly claim never to have been guilty of this kind of attitude?

Germans do tend to take longer to reach decisions. However, just because they favour analysing situations thoroughly rather than the pragmatic short-term solution-oriented approach preferred in Britain, for example, can we really claim that they take *too long* to reach their decisions?

The best thing to do with stereotypes when doing business abroad is to forget them! Meet the challenge with an open mind and open eyes.

GERMAN VALUES AND BEHAVIOUR PATTERNS IN BUSINESS

Germany has one of the most successful and envied economies of the second half of the twentieth century. Companies have achieved success by *hard work* and *efficiency*, both highly valued character traits. The *quality* of products is recognised throughout the world. Organisation is tight and *precise* (well *ordered*); everybody knows his or her function. Decisions are made after careful, *thorough* and *precise* analysis. Risks are minimised; *security* is a lifeline. Time schedules are strictly adhered to: *punctual* delivery means on the day precisely! *Formality* is a necessary sign of respect. Business is *serious* business. These are the values that pervade society and are the foundation on which German managers build.

Forming successful business relationships with German companies does not entail taking all of these values on board, but recognising their importance to your business partner. It may also mean modifying your behaviour in the interests of achieving your business goals.

German business is male dominated. Although women account for about 40 per cent of the workforce, they are underrepresented in management ranks. Specific sectors such as fashion and advertising are an exception. A woman in a position of responsibility may invoke surprise in her German (male) counterpart, which could lead to embarrassing situations whereby he assumes that she is a secretary or accompanying person! I even know of one business deal that broke down when a Canadian businesswoman felt so insulted that she got on the next plane home. You may ask yourself whose fault this was. The only realistic answer is that both parties were guilty of ethnocentricity and attribution (assigning their own norms to the behaviour of someone from another culture).

As most German managers you will meet will probably be male, they are referred to in the male form in this chapter. Please rest assured that this does not indicate any bias on the part of the author!

Managing people

Important qualities expected of a manager in Germany include the ability to assert oneself, willingness to work hard, ability to lead, analytical ability and knowledge of the business area. A manager will usually have attained his position by rising through the ranks, having displayed these qualities. He will probably have at least one degree (65 per cent of German managers have) in which he specialised in engineering or business studies. He will initially have entered working life as a specialist and have proved his ability by producing quality solutions to specific problems, very often displaying the persuasive powers necessary to get himself noticed.

British (but not American) managers may be surprised to read that the ability to assert oneself is considered a quality. Both Britons and Americans may be surprised that analytical ability and knowledge of the business area are considered so important, having probably had a broader education which has prepared them for the world at large and endowed them with more general skills. They have learned to take the eagle's perspective, get the big picture, motivate others, take decisions and come up with and try out innovative ideas. They are supported by specialists who possess the necessary technical knowledge.

The roots of these differences are sociological and lie in the German education system. From an early age, children learn facts according to a structured plan. They learn the importance of detailed knowledge and to think analytically. They are not trained to be innovative or question the status quo. They also learn that they have to speak up for themselves if they want to get noticed in class and get good grades: self-assertiveness. The system trains young people to realise the importance of personal success but does not train them to work together.

The German management press frequently speaks of the *Ellenbogen-gesellschaft* (the elbow society), in which advancement and success come with assertiveness. Hard work is considered a must and it is not uncommon for a leader to place a higher priority on his profession than his family. This, however, cannot be generalised. The pressure to work hard and produce results is immense and this pressure will be passed down through the ranks.

Security is valued greatly in Germany. Not only do people need to feel financially secure, managers also need to feel secure in the knowledge that tasks they have delegated are carried out appropriately; they are responsible for the success of any project under their leadership. They tend to exercise a great deal of control over subordinates, demanding regular interim progress reports, but generally hand over responsibility for the approach taken to the task.

Until relatively recently, motivational skills were not considered significant. Money and the satisfaction of carrying out a task successfully were considered sufficient motivation. Success is expected and praise is rare. Failure and mistakes, on the other hand, are not tolerated. They not only reflect on the person who made the mistake, they reflect on the manager responsible. Two responses are common. One is criticism of the culprit (which may also be in front of colleagues). The other is to sweep the problem under the carpet, protect the culprit from outside influences by keeping him or her busy with tasks that will not be too challenging, in order to protect the reputation of the manager responsible.

This has been changing in recent years as people have become better off and more able to take advantage of a wide variety of leisure activities. They are demanding more from life than job security (which they are slowly beginning to realise no longer exists) and at work are demanding more responsibility and fulfilment. The realisation that undermotivated employees cost a company a great deal of money has also played a significant role in this development. Many in-company training pro-grammes now stress the need for managers to develop the ability to motivate employees.

Authority

A German manager derives his authority from his position, which he probably will have attained having proved his professional competence, either technically or commercially. Whether or not he possesses the necessary people skills to motivate subordinates, he expects personal and professional respect to be shown *because* he is a manager. He has earned this respect with the promotion that has given him his position.

Respect for authority is a German value. Authority is automatic. This manifests itself in the way decisions are reached in meetings. Open discussion is accepted. Anyone can contribute as long as they have something to add to the theme under discussion – otherwise they are not expected to participate actively. The manager will weigh up the arguments, make his decision and delegate tasks. For him, there is no question that his decisions will be implemented regardless of whether the person chosen to carry them out agrees. An employee will accept the decision and does not expect to participate in the decision-making process. Only senior people are in a position to question a manager's competence and decisions.

British and American managers in charge of German employees frequently express frustration at their subordinates' seeming inability to take decisions for themselves: they are simply not accustomed to doing so as the responsibility lies with the manager.

German managers responsible for joint groups containing British or American employees are sometimes overcome with disbelief and frustration when they find their decisions are not being carried out, failing to understand that respect for authority is not automatic, that consensus is the order of the day. Furthermore, they may not realise how qualified British and American employees expect to share in the decision-making process before being asked to implement the results.

Decision making, problem solving and security

Risk avoidance and thorough analysis are the main concepts here. German managers tend to feel uncomfortable with situations over which they have no control (hence their control over decisions in meetings). As taking risks implies less than complete control, they attempt to control the risk by analysing all potential new projects thoroughly before making decisions. Why?

The reasons are historical, psychological and economic. Germans associate risk with the possibility of failure: something they have learned to avoid since their school days. Young people grow up in a system where mistakes are punished by negative grades and failure is punished by making children resit a school year. They learn to fear making mistakes and it is not uncommon, when presenting a new idea to Germans, to hear the response: 'What if it does not succeed?' They enter working life taking a low-risk strategy of avoiding undertakings which are not 'guaranteed' to achieve success. Before achieving their current status, they will have learned how to balance risks and potential benefits conservatively.

This is done by objective analysis. Written documentation assists Germans in feeling more secure about unknown entities. A document is generally considered objective proof that thought has been given to the idea, which does not of course indicate that people will believe everything that is put on paper. Having read an analysis, they normally like to sit on the idea for a while and consider it in peace. Decisions take time, longer than in Britain and much longer than is standard in the United States. However, once Germans commit themselves, they do not generally turn back.

There are also significant historical and economic factors explaining the German aversion to risk taking. The rampant inflation of the 1920s, with its immediate economic and later disastrous political consequences, has taught Germans to be ultra careful when investing, as well as to place faith in the status quo as long as it is serving them well. Having embarked on cooperation, they tend to remain loyal as long as they feel secure about the quality and conditions of the business relationship; which does not prevent them from attempting to renegotiate terms.

They like to seek long-term agreements which give them the security of being able to plan for the next few years. This has its roots in the structure of German industry, with family-owned medium-sized companies which have grown over a period of decades by continuously reinvesting profits as the powerhouse. The relatively small number of incorporated companies are owned predominantly by the banks and other financial institutions. Their interest lies in perpetuating a system in which the company can continue to operate. Here again, surpluses are pumped back rather than distributed to shareholders. Contrast this with Britain and the United States where the proportion of private shareholders, who expect results and dividends every year, is far higher. Planning periods therefore tend to be shorter.

The German approach to problem solving is similar. If a unit ceases to work or a device under development is not functioning as expected, all components which might possibly be connected with the malfunctioning piece are analysed in detail until the cause is found. People can then feel secure in the knowledge that their solution is right. This is in stark contrast to the pragmatic 'get the unit working again as soon as possible' approach which tends to be favoured in Britain and America. It is hardly surprising that these differences result in countless, enormously expensive conflicts in American–German and British–German projects each year. A recent co-operation between German and American engineers developing a telecommunications chip was almost abandoned, not for technical reasons or because of challenges in meeting the tight delivery deadline, but because both sides could not come to terms with each other's approach to solving the technical problems. The Americans would try to get over hiccups by finding a solution that worked, did not necessarily rule out future problems and did not get to the root of the original problem. The Germans would immediately stop further development until they had found and solved the cause of the problem. Both sides traded insults and allegations and both were convinced that theirs was the only approach – until they became aware that they were simply using different approaches which could be combined to good effect to produce a better solution.

This craving for security and 'objective' information also displays itself in other ways. Employers and potential partners demand documents confirming one's qualifications for the task. Just as it is inconceivable for a company to employ someone without having seen degree and diploma certificates as well as testimonials from previous employers, a potential business partner will want to see documentation about your company and products to help him feel more secure with a new, unknown and therefore risky undertaking.

The tightly woven social security net is highly valued throughout society, providing the necessary security for survival in old age or in case of misfortune. High quality is a must, as it guarantees reliability. This is not merely a matter of pride in producing a quality product, it is the security of knowing that it will function as and when needed. Safety standards and emission controls are extremely tough. Germans like to be secure in the knowledge that the risk of accidents is minimised and that the quality of their descendants' lives will not be compromised by environmental damage.

Presenting and negotiating

The key concepts are clear organisation, thorough analysis and serious, reputable argumentation. Thorough analysis includes a historical overview to add credence to your experience as well as detailed analysis of the path you have taken to reach your conclusions. The bottom line is important, but is only persuasive if the audience can see that it has been reached scientifically by carefully weighing up all possible alternatives. Presenters persuade by demonstrating their credibility through their *Fachkompetenz* (professional abilities) and proving their mastery of the complete situation. Presentations tend to be formal, which does not mean that there is no place for humour. However, the humour should be relevant to the theme and not laid on too thickly.

Although the relationship plays a significant role in negotiations, Germans tend to be more impressed with quality, reputability and reliability. Relatively little time is spent on small talk, the motto being 'let's get on with business'. Formality and a respectable distance to your counterpart are expected. This distance takes the form of recognition of his status (Herr Dr Peter Schmidt is to be addressed as Herr Dr Schmidt, not Herr Schmidt and certainly not Peter) and not appearing to push too hard for a close (he has the authority to make a decision and will expect this to be explicitly recognised).

Teamwork

Unlike people in Anglo-Saxon countries, Germans do not learn to work together from an early age. The German concept of a team is more often than not a group of experts who work together on a specific task to reach a specific goal. Working together may imply adding their input following individual work on the topic of their expertise.

Only recently have they begun to take the Anglo-Saxon concept on board: working together, jointly coming up with creative solutions to new challenges. Although belonging to and having the security of a group is very important to Germans, at higher levels of management they tend to work alone.

Communication style

German verbal communication patterns are one of the greatest sources of confusion to others. In brief, they are very direct, short and to the point and can thus appear to be abrupt and demanding. The content of the message is more important than the means by which it is transmitted. The word *muß* (have to) is used much more frequently than in English. Germans whose command of English may be very good, but who lack an understanding of the undertones of communication styles with English-speaking people, tend to translate directly, producing English expressions using German communication patterns (see section below on language).

While Britons and Americans tend to value their independence and consider being asked rather than ordered to carry out a task as a sign of respect, Germans accept authority more readily and, although they may prefer to be asked, they will do something despite being ordered to. When faced with the German pattern of getting straight to the point, many non-Germans, and especially Britons who are accustomed to receiving instructions put in the form of a request, feel put upon and talked down to. Understatement will generally not be understood.

In German, the 'please' may be replaced by an acceptable friendly tone. They are also prone to forget it when speaking English.

The American anthropologist Edward T Hall uses the concept of high- and low-context cultures to explain these differences in style. In low-context cultures, people have a need for information to be transferred in great detail and very explicitly. High-context cultures, on the other hand, favour inference more than explicitness. Germany is a very low-context culture requiring explicit, to-the-point information. The United States is medium to low context, whereas Britain is medium to high context.

Make allowances for non-native speakers of the language. If faced with this seemingly abrupt communication style, it is useful to check back on what your counterpart really meant to say before making a value judgement.

Small talk plays a less significant role in building a business relationship than it does in the United States and is far less important than in Britain. It is normal to get down to business very soon after meeting a new prospect for the first time.

HIDDEN DIFFERENCES

Time

Punctuality is absolutely essential in business dealings with Germans. A 9 o'clock appointment means precisely 9 o'clock. To arrive late (without genuine extenuating circumstances, which are of course understood) is unacceptable. To arrive earlier than 8.58 might be interpreted as an infringement on your counterpart's time. This also applies to social appointments.

Business in Germany tends to be highly organised and regulated. Business people generally work under a great deal of pressure and organising their diaries helps them relieve this. It may be difficult to get an appointment at short notice, so it is advisable to plan ahead. It is also not unusual to arrange specific appointments for telephone calls. Germans like the security of knowing what will happen when and prefer to plan their day in sequence, dealing with one thing at a time.

Punctuality is also considered an indication of reliability and reputability. Deadlines exist to be adhered to. Once fixed, they are only changed if circumstances make it impossible to meet them. Elaborate excuses for failing to meet a deadline only exacerbate the problem.

Language

This precision is also a feature of the language. It is structured and contains an abundance of rules stipulating sentence structure. This naturally mirrors German communication patterns.

Germans who speak English are also prone to succumb to a number of language pitfalls (known as false friends), which may lead to misunderstandings if both parties are unaware of them. Some of the most common are:

- *muß* (have to), which can give the impression that the speaker is giving orders;
- *Problem*, which literally means problem but is also used in place of theme, topic, issue, matter, due to the German habit of concentrating on possible difficulties;
- *aktuell* (current, up to date), which, if translated as 'actually', can give the impression that the speaker is stating his or her view of the real position very forcefully;
- *eventuell* (possibly), which, if translated as 'eventually', can give the impression that the speaker is trying to delay making a decision;
- *seriös* (reputable), which is often mistakenly translated as serious and may leave the impression that the speaker doubts your intentions.

Barriers

Germans are often perceived as distant and hard to get to know. They are not; it simply takes longer to get behind the barrier of the real person. They value their private sphere and draw a clear line between business and pleasure. They require time to come to terms with new people who enter their lives and will slowly search for ways of getting to know you. If they feel that a stranger is trying to get too close too quickly, they feel threatened and may block. In their own time, they open up and will begin to talk about their family and interests. First names and the familiar *Du* form will follow. Once you have been permitted to enter someone's life, a deep meaningful friendship, which is valued greatly, will follow. We can liken the German approach to building relationships to a pineapple – a relatively hard outer surface which takes a while to penetrate, but a welcoming rich interior behind it. The Anglo-Saxon approach is more akin to a peach – a soft, welcoming outer surface which goes relatively deep, but an extremely hard core which it is very rare for outsiders to penetrate.

Humour is often said to be out of place in German business. Nothing could be further from the truth. It is true that business is taken very seriously and that meetings tend to be formal, but this does not mean that people are humourless. They do not appreciate humour for its own sake and slapstick in business is out of place. However, a humorous remark that is relevant to the situation at hand is more likely to break down barriers than to create them. Outside the office, Germans like to laugh as much as anyone else.

Recognition of personal space is a matter of etiquette and status. In the office, doors are more often kept closed than open. This does not mean that nobody may enter, but generally expresses a preference for working undisturbed. It is expected that colleagues and visitors will knock before entering. Managers generally prefer visitors to enter via the secretary's office. The importance of a person in the hierarchy can often be recognised by the size and position of the office. The larger the office, the higher the rank. Corner offices and those on the top floor are generally reserved for those having the greatest amount of responsibility.

Status symbols

Germans take great pride in their achievements and are not ashamed to demonstrate their success. The most obvious status symbol is the car, which is frequently used to judge the degree of success a business partner is having. Mercedes, BMW and Audi are the three so-called noble brands driven most frequently by successful business people. If you wish to create a positive impression and you hold an appropriate position in your organisation, it might be advisable to hire one of these brands from the airport. If you are not a senior manager, take a car further down the range.

The size of one's house as well as the location are also indications of status. Not so obvious are vacation destinations. Many top managers, however, are content to spend their time off at a quiet location in Germany or one of the neighbouring countries.

CONCLUSION

With the increase in the volume of business globally and the improvement in communication technology, outside influences on

German business practice are growing. The merging of the eastern and western German cultures, greater participation in international projects with the resulting exposure to other successful ways of doing business, increasing competition from low-wage, high-technology countries abroad, the rising cost of maintaining the social security system and increasing demand for quality leisure time by employees are some of the significant changes that are slowly beginning to cause a shift in the mindset of German managers and employees. Cultures can be seen as paradigms – which shift.

Doing business in Germany is a challenge. Like all successful countries, Germans possess a firm conviction that their way of doing things is the best way. This by no means indicates that they are unwilling to accept alternatives or to try out new ideas. It does mean that you need to present very convincing and solid arguments in order to persuade them to change. To be successful (ie to obtain the optimum results from a business relationship with a German company), thorough preparation is essential. This includes research, preparation of documentation in a manner that will appeal to them and learning to communicate with them at their level. It means accepting their idiosyncratic behaviour and avoiding the trap of judging their procedures and standards on the basis of your own. Above all, it requires the will to succeed and patience.

Part Two

Business Practice and Development

8

Länder Profiles

Federal state / English translation	Baden-Württemberg / Baden-Württemberg	Bayern / Bavaria	Berlin / Berlin	Brandenburg / Brandenburg	Bremen / Bremen	Hamburg / Hamburg	Hessen / Hesse
Area (sq km)	35,751	70,546	889	29,053	404	755	21,114
% of Germany	10.00	19.80	0.20	8.10	0.10	0.20	5.90
Capital	Stuttgart	Munich	Berlin	Potsdam	Bremen	Hamburg	Wiesbaden
Population ('000)	10,272	11,992	3,478	2,533	679	1,704	5,981
% of German population	12.60	14.60	4.30	3.10	0.80	2.10	7.30
Working population ('000)	4,744	5,771	1,625	1,096	294	910	2,696
Unemployment rate (1995 average %)	7.40	7.00	14.20	15.30	14.00	9.80	8.20
% employed in agriculture and forestry	2.90	5.40	0.60	1.34	0.30	0.70	0.70
manufacturing	43.80	39.20	28.70	23.76	27.30	21.70	38.30
trade & transport	15.70	17.30	21.60	17.90	27.50	25.40	21.50
other services	37.60	38.10	49.10	57.00	44.90	52.20	39.50
GDP total (DM billion)	484	565	141	58	39	134	328
GNP per capita (DM)	47,000	48,000	42,500	24,500	58,000	79,000	57,000
Foreign direct investment 1994 (DM million)	32.80	22.50	10.20	0.70	2.10	24.20	55.60
% of German FDI	13.37	9.17	4.16	0.29	0.86	9.87	22.67

Federal state / English translation	Mecklenburg-Vorpommern	Niedersachsen Lower Saxony Westphalia	Nordrhein Westfalen North Rhine Palatinate	Rheinland Pfalz Rhineland	Saarland Saarland	Sachsen Saxony Anhalt	Sachsen-Anhalt Sachsen-Holstein	Schleswig-Holstein Schleswig	Thüringgen Thuringia
Area (sq km)	23,170	47,659	34,075	19,846	2,570	18,408	20,446	15,739	16,171
% of Germany	6.5	13.30	9.55	5.56	0.72	5.16	5.73	4.41	4.53
Capital	Schwerin	Hannover	Düsseldorf	Mainz	Saarbrücken	Dresden	Magdeburg	Kiel	Erfurt
Population ('00)	1,823	7,715	17,816	3,952	1,084	4,607	2,759	2,708	2,518
% of German population	2.30	9.30	21.72	4.82	1.32	5.66	3.36	3.31	3.07
Working population ('000)	796	3,341	7,300	1,708	347	1,867	1,167	1,247	1,062
Unemployment rate (1995 average %)	17.00	10.70	10.70	8.40	12.10	15.20	17.60	9.00	16.50
% employed in agriculture and forestry	5.30	4.20	1.90	5.80	0.40	2.60	3.60	4.18	4.10
manufacturing	29.30	32.70	36.90	41.10	45.90	40.30	36.00	29.07	25.60
trade & transport	17.30	20.60	18.60	17.00	18.00	17.50	18.50	21.14	32.00
other services	48.40	42.50	39.80	36.10	35.70	39.60	41.90	45.61	38.30
GDP total (DM billion)	42	291	742	148	41	109	65	99	59
GNP per capita (DM)	23,500	39,500	43,000	38,000	39,500	24,000	23,500	40,000	23,500
Foreign direct investment 1994 (DM million)	0.90	14.90	66.50	5.70	2.80	0.90	1.40	3.30	0.80
% of German FDI	0.37	6.07	27.11	2.32	1.14	0.37	0.57	1.35	0.33

Map 1 The *Länder* of Germany

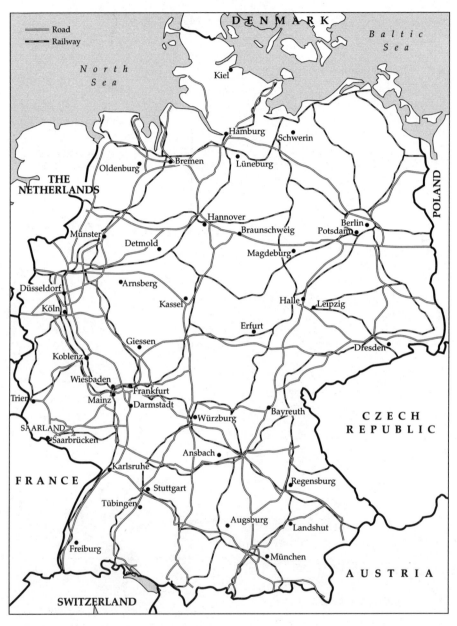

Map 2 The infrastructure of Germany

Rheinland-Pfalz. Investing in the heart of Europe means running pulsating profit.

Right at the heart of the European Community a German State is developing into one of the most important economic centres of the future: Rheinland-Pfalz.

A new founded institution now makes this place even more attractive for investors: ISB. A partner, that helps you to promote your business plans in the most effective way. In any question concerning site selection, incentives or financing, we are coming up with assistance. Just contact us for further information.

Rheinland-Pfalz. The German State for Investors.

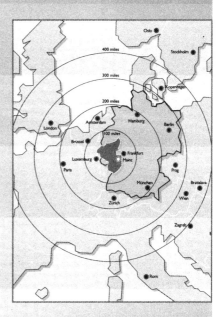

 ISB Economic Development
RheinlandPfalz

ISB GmbH · Wilhelm-Theodor-Römheld-Str. 22
D-55130 Mainz, Germany
Telephone (+49-61 31) 9 85-0
Telefax   (+49-61 31) 9 85-2 99

9

The Structure of German Industry

Prof Dr Peter Oberender, University of Bayreuth[1]

In Germany more employees work in the industrial sector than in other countries. This is mainly due to the high percentage of exports in German industry. Even though there has been a reduction in recent years, still about 26 per cent of total employment is in industry, creating 27 per cent of the total gross value added. The share of employment in industry in the old *Länder* (former West Germany) is rather higher than it is in the new *Länder* (former East Germany).

In international comparisons the industrial competitiveness of Germany shows some weaknesses. Yet with an export quota of around 29 per cent in 1995 Germany must face this challenge. Taxation of businesses has reached a high level. There are severe legal restrictions to promote ecologically sound production, licence requirements are strict and licensing takes a long time for some industrial sites. Moreover, costs per working hour are the highest worldwide. An important factor in rising costs per working hour is constituted by the additional personnel costs, which in 1995 amounted to 80.1 per cent of the total cost per working hour. The greatest share of these additional personnel costs is taken up by insurance contributions to the German statutory social security scheme which have to be paid by employers.

[1]I would like to thank Mr. cand. rer. pol. Matthias Sander for his qualified research assistance and my assistant Dipl. Volkswirtin Birgit Wezel who kindly agreed to translate this paper into English.

In Germany the statutory social security scheme is organised with social insurance on a pay-as-you-earn basis, in contrast to an insurance on a fully funded basis. This means that today's employees and employers pay into an insurance fund. The money that is collected is not used to build up a stock of capital but is paid out immediately for old-age pensions, unemployment benefits, health care and old-age care.

Because of the disadvantageous demographic development, increasing insurance contributions are to be expected for the future. With increasing insurance contributions, the burden on employers will also grow because they have to pay parts of the contributions for their employees.

Yet Germany as an industrial location also has important competitive advantages, e.g. a good infrastructure, highly qualified employees, a large investment in research and development, political stability, few strikes and high technological standards. Together these are factors which ensure high productivity and a high quality of products.

Overall one may say that the importance of industry for the German economy will remain great in the future, even if there will be a slight decline.

TYPES OF ENTERPRISES AND CAPITAL STRUCTURE

Three main categories of enterprises can be found in German industry: sole proprietors, partnerships and corporate enterprises.

With a sole proprietor only the owner has the legal right of management. The owner alone is liable for the company's liabilities, for business and private capital. The creation of additional business capital is limited by the owner's personal assets. About 74 per cent of all industrial companies are sole proprietors, employing 16 per cent of all industrial employees.

Partnerships are *Offene Handelsgesellschaften* (OHG: general commercial partnerships with an unrestricted liability of its partners for debts), *Kommanditgesellschaften* (KG: limited commercial partnerships) or GmbH & Co KG which is a limited partnership (KG) formed with a limited liability company (GmbH, *Gesellschaft mit beschränkter Haftung*) as general partner and the members of the GmbH, their families or outsiders as limited partners.

An OHG has at least two partners. All partners have unlimited liability for the partnership's debt. Management can be delegated or would otherwise be the joint responsibility of the owners.

A KG has one partner who is liable with all his or her private and business property (unlimited partner) and at least one partner who is only liable up to his or her share in the company but not with private property (limited partner). Only the unlimited partner is by law entitled to top management. Four per cent of all German industrial enterprises are KGs or OHGs employing 8 per cent of the total workforce. On average, each such enterprise has 49 employees.

A GmbH & Co KG is a typically German form of enterprise. The characteristic feature of this type of enterprise is that in the end all partners are limited partners only. Five per cent of all enterprises are GmbH & Co KGs, encompassing 18 per cent of total industrial employment.

There are also three types of limited liability companies: GmbHs (*Gesellschaft mit beschränkter Haftung*: limited liability company; roughly comparable with a UK limited company), KGaA (*Kommandit-gesellschaft auf Aktien*: commercial partnership limited by shares; no UK equivalent) and AGs (*Aktiengesellschaften*: joint-stock companies).

In the GmbH top management is in the hands of a manager who is appointed by the partners. The liability of the partners is restricted to their interest in the company. Sixteen per cent of all companies are GmbHs, comprising 34 per cent of total employment. On average GmbHs have 54 employees. During recent years more and more general partnerships have been transformed into limited liability companies.

For the AG top management is in the hands of the executive board, the board of directors and the general meeting of shareholders. Financing capabilities are exceptionally good for this type of enterprise. On the one hand creditability is high because of the distinct protection of creditors; on the other hand the possibility of raising new capital by issuing additional shares is good as well. Additionally, there is a high level of protection for shareholders.

Only 0.2 per cent of all enterprises are AGs and KGaAs. On average they employ 3000 people, 24 per cent of total industrial employment.

In comparison to other highly industrialised economies, in Germany joint-stock companies are of minor relevance only. In 1994 a special law, the *Finanzmarktförderungsgesetz* (a law to help develop financial markets), was passed to make the founding of a joint-stock company more attractive and to encourage the transformation of existing enterprises into joint-stock companies. This law introduced legal simplifications, especially for small joint-stock companies.

While in an average German enterprise only 18 per cent of the total capital is equity capital, the share in industrial enterprises is 23 per cent. Taking methodological differences into account one finds that in comparison to other European enterprises German industry does not have a significantly lower share of ownership capital, even though empirical research has quite often emphasised the opposite. The 77 per cent share of loan capital consists of 37 per cent short-term liabilities, 13 per cent long-term liabilities and 27 per cent reserves (among which are 13 per cent pension fund reserves).

In industrial sectors the share of equity differs greatly. In the chemical industry it reaches 37 per cent, in electrical engineering 26 per cent, while it only amounts to 15 per cent in textile and wood-based industries.

COMPARISON OF INDUSTRIAL SECTORS

Motor vehicle construction

In 1995, motor vehicle construction, with a turnover of 259.6 billion deutschmark (DM), was the most important German industrial sector (12.8 per cent of total industrial turnover).

Even though there has been a decline in employment in this sector of over 200,000 employees during the last five years, the sector still has about 671,800 employees, 10.2 per cent of all employment in the industrial sector. The export quota of 47.5 per cent is extraordinarily high. Thanks to extensive rationalisation, profits have improved again recently after their drastic decline during the 1993 recession. In Germany the motor vehicle construction sector is highly concentrated. Half of total employment in this sector is with the three leading companies: Mercedes-Benz, Volkswagen and BMW. For the years to come it can be expected that motor vehicle construction will be a growing sector.

Mechanical engineering

In 1995 the turnover of mechanical engineering reached DM253.3 billion, which accounts for 12.4 per cent of the total industrial turnover. The number of employees has declined during recent years to a total of 1,063,700 (or 16.1 per cent of total employment in industry). Because of its high export quota (43 per cent) this sector is strongly affected by international competition, the unfavourable exchange rate of the deutschmark and high German production costs. The sector comprises 14.6 per cent of all the enterprises in industry and is, with its 160 employees per enterprise, a typical sector of medium-sized enterprises. In the medium term, prospects for growth will be about average. Therefore, the engineering sector will remain of great importance for German industry in the future.

Electrical engineering

Electrical engineering and the manufacturing of office machines were responsible for 14.2 per cent of total industrial employment which amounts to 938,700 employees, generating a total turnover of DM242.3 billion (11.9 per cent of total turnover). This sector is also highly dependent on exports with its export ratio of 35.4 per cent. In 1994 the enterprises in this sector reached profits slightly above average with a profit–turnover ratio of 1.6 per cent (after tax) and a return on equity of 7.5 per cent.

Electrical engineering is also a highly concentrated sector (major companies being Siemens and Bosch). Additionally, there are numerous medium-sized businesses.

Prospects for growth in this sector are good, but enterprises have to face strong international competition.

Chemical industry

Total turnover in the chemical industry was DM234.6 billion (11.5 per cent of total industrial turnover). The sector employees 538,000 or 8.2 per cent of the total workforce. The export quota was 39.2 per cent. Profits and net creation of value were above average. The profit–turnover ratio was 2.3 per cent (after tax) in 1994.

The German chemical industry is also a highly concentrated sector, averaging 314 employees per enterprise. Dominant companies are BASF, Hoechst and Bayer. The industry's share of total industrial production will remain stable in the medium term.

Food-processing industries

With 524,000 employees (7.9 per cent) the food-processing industry has a total turnover of DM220.8 billion (10.9 per cent). The sector has an extremely low export ratio of only 9.8 per cent. Profits are average and the profit–turnover ratio was 1.5 per cent in 1994.

This industry is less concentrated, with an average of 103 employees per enterprise. Prospects for growth are below average, though the sector is somewhat cyclical.

Manufacturing of metal products

The manufacturing of metal products comprises steel and light metal engineering as well as the manufacturing of ironmongery, tinware and metalware. There were 591,000 employees (9 per cent). Turnover reached DM124 billion (6.1 per cent). The export quota was 17.6 per cent and profits were positive. In 1994 a profit–turnover ratio of 2.8 per cent was realised.

The sector mainly consists of medium-sized enterprises employing an average of 92 employees per enterprise. Prospects for growth are average.

Paper-manufacturing, publishing and printing industries

This sector realised a turnover of DM122.6 billion (6 per cent) with its 419,000 employees (6.4 per cent). The profit–turnover ratio was above average (2.3 per cent in 1994). The sector is dominated by medium-sized enterprises (on average 104 employees per enterprise) and prospects for growth are average.

Production and primary processing of metals

Metal production and metalworking comprise the iron and steel producing industry and non-ferrous metal production. The 300,300 employees of this sector (4.6 per cent) achieved a turnover of DM102.4 billion (5 per cent). Exports make up 32.5 per cent of the sector. Prospects for profits have been and will continue to be negative. Prospects for growth are also negative. The branch is highly concentrated (on average 260 employees per enterprise).

Rubber and plastic industries

This sector employs 354,600 employees (5.4 per cent) and achieves a turnover of DM86.5 billion (4.2 per cent). The profits of the mostly medium-sized businesses are good. In 1994 a profit–turnover ratio of 2.4 per cent was realised. On average there are 122 employees per enterprise. Future prospects are positive for the plastic industries. The rubber industry, on the other hand, expects a below-average growth rate.

Glass manufacturing, ceramics and manufacturing of stones and non-metallic mineral products

This sector has 281,600 employees (4.3 per cent) and had a total turnover of DM73 billion (3.6 per cent) in 1995. The profit–turnover ratio is relatively high, but only 8 per cent of all German industries are in this sector. Enterprises are smaller than in most sectors, employing only 75 employees on average. Prospects for growth are average.

Textile and clothing industries

This sector has a turnover of DM55.4 billion (2.7 per cent) with 255,800 employees (3.9 per cent). In 1994 the profit–turnover ratio was 2.5 per cent. Medium-sized enterprises are the characteristic feature of the sector. Average employment per enterprise is 95 employees. Prospects are negative because of strong competition from very cost-efficient competitors abroad, especially in the clothing industry.

Overall one may note the great importance of the motor vehicle industry, mechanical and electrical engineering and the chemical industries. These four branches alone make up 49 per cent of total industrial employment, accounting for 49 per cent of the total industrial turnover with a 65 per cent share of total industrial exports.

THE GOVERNMENT'S INFLUENCE ON INDUSTRIAL DEVELOPMENT

To ensure the efficiency of markets and to safeguard competitive market processes against the abuse of economic power, an anti-cartel and anti-trust law has been passed (*Gesetz gegen Wettbewerbsbeschränkungen*). The law first and foremost forbids cartels (though exceptions are possible, mainly on request). Furthermore, the law provides for the federal cartel office (*Kartellamt*) to implement measures to control businesses with major economic power in their specific markets.

The state also intervenes in the economy through regulations that interfere with businesses' contractual and economic freedom. In Germany, industry complains about the growing bureaucracy, too many restrictions on environmental matters compared to foreign countries, many restrictions regarding production technologies and extremely lengthy licensing procedures. Furthermore, entrepreneurs have to face disadvantages because of far-reaching employee rights, high personnel costs (wages and social security contributions) and a high level of taxation. An intense discussion has arisen in Germany about the necessity for deregulation. Progress is still slow, especially because of the strong influence of pressure groups. State-owned or state-run enterprises are only of minor importance in the German economy. Under the chancellorship of Helmut Kohl, governmental interests in e.g. Volkswagen, VIAG, Veba or the Industrieverwaltungsgesellschaft have been reduced or sold off altogether.

A major part of governmental influence comprises subsidies. Subsidies occur as financial assistance or as tax reductions and tax exemptions. Subsidies' share of gross domestic product is 2.5 per cent (for the former West Germany), of which one-fifth goes to manufacturing industries. In the former East Germany subsidies made up a quarter of domestic product.

Subsidies aim at the preservation of existing structures, a reduced pace of adjustment to new circumstances and supporting new branches which are expected to be of high potential for future economic development. These receive subsidies because they are thought to carry high risks and to cause extremely high costs which cannot be borne by private enterprises alone. Additionally, subsidies are supposed to increase incentives for investment, research and development, to help someone start in business and to revitalise disadvantaged regions.

There is a high concentration of subsidies in manufacturing industries. Sectors that gain specifically from these subsidies are the mining industries, shipbuilding industries, the very capital-intensive tobacco and mineral oil industries, the iron and steel industries and the aircraft and aerospace industries, because of their high potential and promising future outlook. During recent years the share of subsidies used to support research and development has fallen dramatically. Therefore, subsidies now have more of a conservational character, e.g. for specific industries, structures and regions.

Considerable influence on subsidies for the former East Germany was exercised by the Treuhand (the agency responsible for privatising East German industry). Its explicit aim was to safeguard employment, especially in industry, by giving subsidies. Subsidies were given in different forms: the assumption of losses and financial assistance for investment projects, loans to form equity capital and allowances by ensuring low prices when privatising companies. A major incentive for investment in the former East Germany came from new forms of tax relief, especially financial assistance for producers' durable equipment and extraordinary depreciation of up to 50 per cent of the total investment sum.

The chapter on Grants and Incentives will exemplify some possibilities of assistance for enterprises and those wishing to go into business.

NATIONAL PLAN FOR BUSINESS PROMOTION

There are special federal promotional measures for medium-sized businesses. First of all, general financial assistance is available, e.g. the European Recovery Programme and the programmes of the German Reconstruction Loan Corporation (*Kreditanstalt für Wiederaufbau*). Prerequisites for this assistance are investment in new businesses, the enlargement of existing businesses or job-creating investments. Loans are generally long term and are characterised by extremely low interest rates and redemption-free periods.

On behalf of the federal or the *Länder* governments, banks also give guarantees for loans. These loans are to be used to improve a company's competitiveness. Within the tax legislation, special forms of depreciation and depreciation on savings to help small and medium-sized enterprises are available.

Moreover, federal financial assistance is available for research and development, e.g. a programme for innovation by the Reconstruction Loan Corporation (*Kreditanstalt für Wiederaufbau*) or the programmes of the Ministry for Education, Science and Technology for specific projects in these fields.

The *Gemeinschaftsaufgabe Verbesserung der regionalen Wirtschafts-struktur* (joint task force for improvement of the regional economic structure) gives, for example, regional investment grants to those companies investing in disadvantaged regions. Specifically for medium-sized enterprises there are programmes for the improvement of the environment, for encouraging advice on business and to support information and training.

In addition to special programmes for medium-sized enterprises there are programmes for those willing to start a new business. The federal government offers a programme to help create equity capital. There are also programmes from the European Bank for Reconstruction and the Deutsche Ausgleichsbank specifically for those starting a business.

Additionally, there are programmes by the European Commission for medium-sized enterprises. These programmes primarily offer loans from the European Investment Bank and financial assistance for venture capital.

The German *Länder* also offer assistance. Regional business promotion occurs in the form of reductions in business tax or by giving subsidies when offering property to set up businesses. In the case of investments in the former East German *Länder*, the federal government offers additional assistance, e.g. grants for investment, special forms of depreciation, assistance for innovation projects and job-creating programmes.

IMPORTANT INSTITUTIONS OF THE GERMAN SOCIAL AND ECONOMIC SYSTEM

A peculiarity of the German social and economic system is the existence of quasi-governmental institutions. Chambers of Commerce, Chambers of Handicraft and Chambers of Agriculture are corporations under public law (*Körperschaften des öffentlichen Rechts*). They are institutions exercising sovereign powers and are organised by direct self-administration. Their sovereign powers include, for example, arbitration in disputes between competitors, the offering of expert opinions and participation in the area of professional education. They influence economic policy by offering comments and giving advice and they inform their members about current issues in economic policy. The Chambers encompass all entrepreneurs since there is compulsory membership.

Another set of quasi-governmental organisations are the associations of employers and the trade unions, both called *Sozialpartner* (social partners). Both are 'partners' in the labour market. They arrange agreements on working conditions, especially wages, working hours and additional voluntary social security for their members. Furthermore, they are representatives in the self-governing boards of the German statutory social security system. Trade unions organise external and internal co-determination (employee participation: *Mitbestimmung*).

Another representative in internal employee participation is the local employee council (*Betriebsrat*). An employee council can be elected in all enterprises having at least five employees. The council is elected by the employees of that enterprise. According to law, co-determination of the employees' council is possible in social matters (e.g. social institutions within the company, beginning and end of working hours), in personnel matters (e.g. hearings in the case of dismissals) and in economic matters (e.g. information and advice when internal changes in the company are being planned).

Apprentices face a dual system of training in Germany. This encompasses a period of theoretical training in school for two or three years while at the same time taking part in practical training within a company. The legal foundation for the training of apprentices is the

Berufsbildungsgesetz (law on professional training) and the *Handwerksordnung*. German industry offers more than 100 different courses for apprentices. At the end of an apprenticeship the apprentice has to pass an examination and receives a diploma from the Chamber of Commerce, the Chamber of Handicraft or the Chamber of Agriculture, depending on the kind of apprenticeship completed.

REFERENCES

Bundesministerium für Wirtschaft, *Jahresbericht der Bundesregierung '96*.

Bundesministerium für Wirtschaft, *Das ERP-Programm*, Bonn 1972–84.

Bundesministerium für Wirtschaft (ed.), *Wirtschaftliche Förderung in den neuen Bundesländern*, Bonn, 1991–4.

Bundeszentrale für Politische Bildung (ed.) (1991) *Informationen zur Politischen Bildung 175, Wirtschaft 2, Arbeitnehmer und Betrieb*, reprint 1991, Bonn.

Deutsche Bundesbank (1994) *Monatsbericht Oktober 1994*, 46. Jahrgang, No. 10, Frankfurt am Main.

Hohe Subventionen in Ostdeutschland – Wenig Abbau in Westdeutschland, in Deutsches Institut für Wirtschaftsforschung, *Wochenbericht 1995*, 62. Jahrgang, pp. 106–117.

Lampert, H, (1980) *Volkswirtschaftliche Institutionen*, München.

Lampert, H, (1992) *Die Wirtschafts- und Sozialordnung in der Bundesrepublik Deutschland*, 11th edition, München.

Oberender, P. (ed.) (1984) *Marktstruktur und Wettbewerb in der Bundesrepublik Deutschland - Branchenstudien zur deutschen Volkswirtschaft*, München.

Oberender, P. (ed.) (1989) *Marktökonomie – Marktstruktur und Wettbewerb in ausgewählten Branchen der Bundesrepublik Deutschland*, München.

Schierenbeck, H, (1993) *Grundzüge der Betriebswirtschaftslehre*, 11th edition, München.

Weiß, J.-P. (1993) *Wirtschaftliche Entwicklung Deutschlands bis zum Jahr 2000*, Wiesbaden.

STATISTICS

Bundesministerium für Wirtschaft (ed.) *Leistung in Zahlen*, Bonn.

Deutsche Bundesbank, *Monatsberichte der Deutschen Bundesbank*.

Institut der deutschen Wirtschaft (1996) *Zahlen zur wirtschaftlichen Entwicklung der Bundesrepublik Deutschland 1996*, Köln.

Statistisches Bundesamt, *Fachserie 4, Produzierendes Gewerbe.*
Statistisches Bundesamt, *Statistische Jahrbücher der Bundesrepublik
Deutschland*, Stuttgart/Mainz.

10

Small and Medium-Sized Enterprises and their Trade Associations

Bernhard Wingenbach, General Manager, British Chamber of Commerce, Germany

Company names associated with the German economy are Daimler-Benz, Siemens, Volkswagen, Deutsche Bank, Allianz and a few more. This does not, however, explain the structure of the German economy. These world-renowned large companies are significant for their total turnover but not when it comes to the number of enterprises and the number of employees. More than 99 per cent of German companies fall into the category of small and medium-sized enterprises.

The Federal Ministry for the Economy defines size classifications as in Table 10.1. With a total of around 2.6 million entrepreneurs (500,000 of whom are in the new federal states) and with more than 60 per cent of all employees, the many small and medium-sized enterprises and entrepreneurs achieve a share of over 50 per cent of Germany's total turnover. At the same time, the superior strength of the large companies

Table 10.1 *Size classification for German companies*

	Number of employees	Turnover in DM
Small enterprises	to 49	to 1 m
Medium-sized enterprises	50 to 499	1 m–100 m
Large enterprises	over 500	over 100 m

– generally known around the world – attracts attention. Less than 1 per cent of German companies fall into this category, although these enterprises employ 40 per cent of employees and achieve nearly half of total turnover.

In the European Union, 99.8 per cent of companies fall into the category of up to 250 employees; they represent 66 per cent of all jobs and achieve 65 per cent of the EU's turnover. For countries such as Portugal or Greece these figures are not surprising; however, they are surprising when they also apply to Germany.

In practice, Germany has an unusual economic system, which has also undergone a long development.

In Germany, some small and medium-sized enterprises are also called *Mittelstand*. This term does not only apply to the enterprises counted in accordance with these criteria, but also describes a class of the population, with its origin dating back centuries. It is based on the changes in the population from the feudalistic middle ages up to today's, modern state. The middle class, situated between the aristocracy and the rural population and which particularly concentrated on trade and crafts, achieved documentation and extension of rights in the various constitutions, applicable to the appropriate region, through joining guilds, associations and other organisations.

The up and coming *Mittelstand* also exercised influence through being elected as councillors in the existing administrations at the time. The guilds also stated the requirements for training and for joining the respective trades.At the same time, a regulatory framework was created which guaranteed its members, in addition to social security in the future, a certain social and financial status.

Centralisation of the various areas, which were divided into many small parts, did not take place until relatively late. The striving *Mittelstand* had its heyday in the nineteenth century. The state was also interested in participating in the social shaping of working relationships, in a regulatory function. The intention was to illustrate to the entrepreneurs their responsibility towards their employees and society as a whole.At the same time, during the industrial revolution, entrepreneurs in factories were able to lay foundations for measures which were exemplary for the employees in terms of social security.

A comparison of trade statistics illustrates historical trends. Figures from the *Statistical Handbook of the Prussian State* dated 1883, in respect of the results of enterprises counted in 1882, can be compared to the *Statistical Year Book of the Federal Republic of Germany* dated 25 May 1987 (roughly 100 years later).

As a sum of all economic areas, the data is as follows. For 1882, 1,650,806 main companies, of which:

- 1,594,725 'Main companies with a maximum of five employees';
- 56,081 'Main companies with more than five employees', with a total of 4,209,535 employees as a yearly average.

for 1987, 2,097,853 companies, of which:

- 1,829,890 with up to nine employees;
- 156,253 with 10 to 19 employees;
- 108,353 with 20 to 499 employees;
- 3,357 exceeding 500 employees, with a total of 21,915,838 employees as a yearly average.

Then, as today, the 'micro enterprise' is dominant, generally the 'one-man band' with few employees.

On the other hand, the aim during the first half of the twentieth century was the agglomeration of enterprises into huge companies, ie the reduction of small and medium-sized enterprises through mergers and forceful fusions into large companies, with the basic idea to be market leading and to increase efficiency through synergy. The foundation of the I.G. FarbenindustrieAG in 1925, as a joint venture through merging chemical factories, illustrates this well. In 1938 this economic giant had a staff of 218,090 and a profit of 667 million Reichsmark. In the Federal Republic of Germany after the Second World War, there followed the destruction of these large conglomerates into individual companies which remained as large companies, but were now legally independent and turned into competitors.

With the introduction of the social market economy, the individual responsibility of the entrepreneur followed. The state creates the framework, in which the market determines the life and survival of companies through the balance of supply and demand. Here the entrepreneur is solely responsible for adjusting supply and services in accordance with the market situation.

A large proportion of small enterprises – despite the extreme competitiveness among them – are more capable of meeting these requirements than are large companies. This competitiveness, in particular, creates a rapid response to market forces.

This co-existence has its advantages, both for the many small enterprises and the few large companies The small enterprises have an infrastructure which is oriented to the requirements of the large companies. They can take advantage of the powerful system of financial institutions and road infrastructure. The large companies, in return, have a large selection of individual suppliers with whom they can co-operate. The danger of being dependent on an individual supplier is therefore not so prevalent.

The historically conveyed term *Mittelstand* and its history continue to be a backdrop for these enterprises, its mentality being important for fruitful co-operation.

Mittelstand enterprises are characterised by various factors, which can either be to their advantage or disadvantage. One entrepreneur or a small group can make decisions quickly, flexibly and in the short term. On the one hand this allows them a high degree of flexibility and adjustment to market requirements, but on the other hand they are dependent on the decision maker's sole perception of a situation.

The entrepreneur's role of an 'all-round-person' for *all* areas of the company has also to be considered. His (or her) private connection to the family aggravates the situation, which often leads to stress.

A further problem for small enterprises is the lack of opportunities for (investment in) research and development or market research, which is also due to obstructed access to capital markets for these companies. As a general rule, the only option for the entrepreneur is self-finance or (bank) credits; finance through issuing of stocks or shares is not usually a possibility.

On the employment market, *Mittelstand* enterprises compete with large companies. Very often they are at a disadvantage in respect of prestige, the salary available or (voluntary) social contributions. In the past, however, during the recession, they have proven to be safe companies for employees. It is also important that *Mittelstand* enterprises contribute significantly to training opportunities. Around 80 per cent of the training contracts for various professions are signed with these enterprises.

Another phenomenon, which must not be underestimated, is the family business. Many *Mittelstand* enterprises are family businesses, ie various family members, family branches or generations share responsibilities in the company. This can be an advantage, but it can also lead to considerable tension in respect of private and business life. In some cases it may lead to ruptures within the enterprise.

At the same time, the question of the company's continuation beyond the current owner or managing director has to be considered. Around 700,000 *Mittelstand* entrepreneurs will be looking for a successor for their businesses within the next 10 years. In around 300,000 cases the question of a successor will have to be solved by the year 2000. Every fifth enterprise in Western Germany will therefore see a change at the top of the company. According to a survey, 43 per cent of all change of management cases is secured through a family member (mainly of the younger generation). In respect of succession, 30 per cent of the enterprises will be managed by a company member or will be sold to a third party. In 27 per cent of these companies the boss's chair will remain empty. The company is threatened with shut-down or split-up because no suitable successor is in sight. Especially for small enterprises, the problem of finding a successor is extremely significant; nearly one in two entrepreneurs of the founder generation, in companies with an annual turnover of up to DM250,000, has no successor.

Another aspect pertinent to the organisation of the family business and the question of a successor is the legal form of the business. Every business is faced with the question of which type of company is best suited in view of economic, tax or inheritance aspects. A statistical census carried out in 1987, in respect of the number of work places, reports that of the 2.1 million companies of the then Federal Republic, 1.6 million (77 per cent) were sole traders, employing 6.1 million people. This most simple legal form, under which all corporate decisions and responsibilities are with the owner, who also carries the full risk, is especially popular among smaller enterprises. Here the entrepreneur is also the proprietor of the enterprise.

Besides this legal form, the *Gesellschaft mit beschränkter Haftung (GmbH)* (limited liability company) has become more popular over recent years. It is chosen mainly for small and medium-sized enterprises whose proprietors wish to limit their liability risk. According to this census of work places, 220,000 enterprises (around 10 per cent) were already trading as GmbHs, with 5.7 million employees. Here the enterprise is a legal entity in its own right, which is represented by third parties.

Typical types of business for a large company are the *Aktiengesellschaft (AG)* (private limited company) or the *Kommanditgesellschaft auf Aktien (KGaA)* (partnership limited by shares). In 1987 there were 2780 companies of this category in the Federal Republic, employing 3.2 million staff.

Altogether, the *Mittelstand* enterprises represent an important pillar of the German economy. The federal government and the EU especially support these *Mittelstand* enterprise structures with special grants.

THE CHAMBERS OF COMMERCE AND OTHER TRADE ASSOCIATIONS

Because of the split into many small enterprises, bringing interests together and representing them to other groups is particularly difficult. In Germany various official institutions are given this task, such as the chambers of industry and commerce or the individual trade associations.

Foreign business people will certainly find it strange that membership in the regional chamber of industry and commerce, or an appropriate organisation or association responsible for a particular trade sector, is not voluntary for a company but that it is compulsory and chargeable.

The regional economy's mouthpieces are the 83 chambers of industry and commerce. Companies of all sizes have to be members of the respective regional chamber of industry and commerce. These offer advice and help to their member companies in many fields, be it questions relating to production and sales, vocational training, economic and patent law, environmental protection or the provision of information. The chambers of industry and commerce also collect information on grants for businesses and advise their member companies on availability. They also maintain a co-operation exchange for their members, intended to facilitate co-operation among individual businesses.

The umbrella organisation of these chambers of industry and commerce is the *Deutscher Industrie- und Handelstag* (DIHT). Its task is to ensure and support co-operation among chambers, to provide regular opportunities for exchange of experiences, to safeguard trade interests and to lobby the trade's interests to authorities and political powers.

At the same time, the DIHT also looks after the *Delegierten der Deutschen Wirtschaft* (delegates of the German economy) and the *Repräsentanzen der Deutschen Wirtschaft* (representatives of the German economy), which were initiated to sponsor foreign trade relations in 22 countries, in all parts of the world, as well as the foreign chambers of commerce.

The foreign chambers of commerce are alliances of German and foreign traders, businesses and trade associations, intended to sponsor economic co-operation between Germany and the relevant partner country.

Currently there are more than 50 recognised German chambers in 46 countries on all continents. Foremost, they are service providers for German and foreign businesses. Their information, advice and agency services are tailored to the practical requirements of businesses involved in foreign trade. They are especially prepared to deal with small and medium-sized companies. They assist, *inter alia*, with setting up business relationships and dealings with authorities, they gather market intelligence and provide information on investment opportunities or general legal matters.

Further representation of interests is through affiliation of individual craft trades in guilds and regional craft associations. Nowadays, the guilds are a free association of self-employed craftspeople of the same or similar craft, with the aim of sponsoring their mutual business interests within a region. The guild is a body of public law, under the supervision of the chamber of commerce. Its main tasks are, among others, to regulate vocational training and to hold examinations. Identical guilds within a state are joined in a *Landesinnungsverband* (state guilds association). The *Bundesinnungsverband* (federal guilds association) is the organisation for state guilds associations on a federal level.

In Germany, the 56 chambers of trade are the lobbying bodies and administrative organisations of the tradespeople in a region. The chamber of trade, as a public legal body, has the following tasks besides lobbying: regulation of training, examinations for skilled workers and foremen, issuing of trade certificates, management of the trade register and supervision of guilds. Only people who are registered are allowed to follow a trade; this registration requires them to pass a foreman's examination in this particular trade or to show proof of a similar foreign training, according to the trade regulations.

There are 128 common professions which come under the heading of trade, with 6.1 million employees in over 550,000 trade companies. Their share of 17 per cent of all work places in Germany is not far from a turnover of DM800 billion, representing a tenth of total production, according to the trade census of 1995. However, a structural change has also taken place here. Since the last trade census in 1977, the number of companies in the garment, textile and leather industry has reduced by nearly 60 per cent; in the electrical and metal industry, however, a business increase of 22 per cent was recorded. Regional differences also apply: in the new federal states, more than half of trade employees work in the building industry, compared with 39 per cent in the old federal states.

Further interest groups in the way of associations also exist for the so-called free professions, such as doctors, architects, notaries, solicitors, tax advisers. Again, it is the associations' task to represent the communal interest in economy and politics, to check that the professional regulations are adhered to and to organise a training framework for each profession.

In addition, there are also organised interest groups with various intentions. From trade associations to employers' and professional associations, there is a wide spectrum of more than 20,000 associations, which reflects the variety of interests of a diverse society.

In these cases, membership is voluntary. All associations – large or small – have a common goal: to be heard and to have their own interests reflected in the political decision-making process. As subject knowledge and experience are gathered within associations, which are also drawn on by authorities, the influence of these associations in terms of law preparation is considerable. The political parties also have an interest in getting to know and considering the associations' opinions because the associations have financial power, means of information and mobilising potential. In other words, trade associations play a vital role in daily politics. *Mittelstand* enterprises have the opportunity to air their wishes and requirements with considerable potential; at the same time, the possibility is offered of meeting a specialist in one's own field of experience, and to tap into selective trade information.

One has to note, however, that the trend is towards internationalisation of interest groups beyond national boundaries. Again, representation for the *Mittelstand* is important, especially if one talks about companies which are represented not only in one's own country.

In this case, an interesting point of contact for *Mittelstand* companies is the respective bilateral chambers of commerce such as the British Chamber of Commerce in Germany in Cologne, or the American Chamber of Commerce in Frankfurt. Here, regularly occurring problems due to trade between two countries are classed as daily business; a pool of experience gained by other members can be accessed.

An important resource for companies is provided by the relevant employer associations, as a counter balance to the trade union organisations of the workers and employees. They are affiliations of employers from different branches of the economy, with the aim of influencing working conditions, especially in terms of signing tariff contracts between employers and employees. Together with the trade unions, they represent the so-called social partners and have the power to shape employment law. Although the employer associations are manned mainly by representatives of the large companies, their decisions are widely influential because, as a rule, tariff agreements apply to all enterprises. An affiliation of employer associations is the *Bundesverein-igung der deutschen Arbeitgeberverbände* (Federal Organisation of Employer Associations).

Of equal importance and influence is the *Bundesverband der Deutschen Industrie* (BDI) (Federal Association of German Industry). Its task is the perception and sponsorship of all mutual interests of industry sectors belonging to it. For this reason, the BDI works together with other top organisations representing entrepreneurs.

Due to this multitude of information channels it is difficult for the individual business to find the right contact immediately. Advisory organs such as the chambers of commerce or the respective trade associations often assist their individual industry sectors. There are other associations for economic sponsorship or the *Mittelstand*. Many of these associations also publish their own trade journal, which addresses possible partners in the way of advertising or a possible co-operation exchange.

Despite these umbrella interest organisations, it is difficult for the individual *Mittelstand* enterprise to step out of the shadows and to get in touch with a person in a managerial position – at whatever level of importance. A recently published survey[1] investigated this phenomenon in more detail and came to the conclusion that very often it is a case of highly specialised companies and the interplay of various aspects. According to this study, 'little giants' or 'hidden champions' exist in every sector. The machinery industry is the most represented, the second largest segment is the group 'Others', followed by the electronics, metal finishing, chemical, print and paper, food and textile industries.

Of the companies investigated in this study 76 per cent are family businesses; 50 of the 500 German companies investigated are listed on an exchange. Some are well known through their products (eg Haribo, Bonn, Gummibärchen), others are less well known because, as component suppliers for a product, they are seldom named (eg Laukhuff Orgelteile (organ parts), Weikersheim).

Professor Simon, in his study, has identified certain criteria that are common to the *Mittelstand*'s 'hidden champions'. Success begins with a

[1]Hermann Simon, (1996) *Die heimlichen Gewinner* (Secret Winners), Campus Verlag, Frankfurt/Main.

clear and sophisticated goal: to be the best or number one. In order to achieve this, a long-term plan, qualified staff and strong determination are required. Markets need to be clearly defined and the company's activities should be concentrated on a core activity, because specialists very often beat a Jack-of-all-trades.

Success, however, will only be achieved with global marketing; this is the only way that even the smallest market niches can grow. Foreign language and culture skills and the earliest possible occupancy of market positions build the foundation for global success. An important aspect of being close to the customer is excellent customer care, which is often characterised through 24-hour service and 48-hour response time for spares. Thus the customer's service requirements are met, wherever they are. Market-leading smaller enterprises' competitive advantage is qualitative supremacy, rather than price.

Business culture, a significant aspect in long-term success, is very often underestimated. It appears to be based on 'old-fashioned' values such as performance and diligence. At the same time, employees' motivation and creativity are above average. Specific characteristics apply to the founders or management of these enterprises; very often they have been working for the company for a long time and have developed their own style of management, which can be described as squire-like. They frequently ask as much of their employees as they ask of themselves, they can be authoritarian but can also motivate and propel the specialists within the company to top performance. They do not think much of modern management methods and gurus.

As the introduction has already shown, the German economy is certainly not only limited to large companies – size alone does not guarantee success in the economy. A diverse and versatile *Mittelstand* made up of small and medium-sized enterprises, which are often more adaptable and open to risk and which therefore have their 'noses in front', round off the business mixture with which Germany asserts itself in international competition.

11

The Role of Multinational Companies within Germany

Gabriele Hintzen, BDI General Economic Policy Department

MULTINATIONAL COMPANIES – A RESULT OF THE WORLDWIDE GLOBALISATION OF MARKETS

Multinational companies accelerate the process of globalisation because their activities go beyond national boundaries and seek the location with the best conditions. They therefore tighten worldwide competition among potential host countries which, through attractive conditions such as taxes, low additional labour costs or flexibility in the workplace, want to attract investment, in order to secure or increase growth and employment.

As international investors, multinational companies not only play an increasingly important role in world economies but, in the 1990s, have also become an important factor for world economic growth and development. They are responsible for the interstate transfer of financial capital, technology and management skills, and also influence the international division of labour through their product, marketing and procurement strategies. Last but not least, they contribute considerably to the restructuring of national economies through their entrepreneurial decisions.

Anglo-Saxon countries play a particular part in this. Among the world's 25 largest multinational companies, five are from the UK, seven from the USA, a further seven from Japan and only one from Germany, Siemens.

The oil, automotive and electronics industries are at the top of the list. With direct investments multinational companies network many national economies and build an integrated international production system, and are therefore the productive heart of world market globalisation. In the recipient countries, foreign capital contributes considerably to the broadening and modernisation of capital stocks.

WHERE DO MULTINATIONAL COMPANIES INVEST?

Since the beginning of the 1980s the environment for direct investments has changed dramatically. With the liberalisation of capital flows, the opening of national markets for foreign direct investments, the abolition of restrictions on foreign companies' activities and therefore the discrimination between domestic and foreign companies, conditions for direct investment have improved.

Worldwide, the USA, UK, the Netherlands and Belgium/Luxembourg are emerging as the main magnets for direct investment. The Asia-Pacific region is also gaining increasing importance for international direct investment. The most important investor is Japan which, due to its high production costs and the necessity for physical presence in the dynamic markets, has forced the establishment of production networks.

For some time, foreign investors have avoided Germany. Over a number of years Germany's balance of direct investments with abroad has been negative: in the 1980s, the split between capital withdrawals to other countries and investments into Germany dramatically widened. In the 1990s the distance has decreased because the dynamics of German investment abroad have considerably eased as a result of the recession.

In 1995 a mere DM13 billion moved into Germany from abroad; in the same year German companies invested nearly DM50 billion. In the Federal Republic of Germany, foreign investments represent only 1 per cent of home investments. This is the penultimate position in the league table; traditionally, only Japan scores worst. Over the last few years US investors have even reduced their corporate capital in Germany, although the USA still owns the largest share of corporate capital in the country. The Netherlands follow. These two countries own half of the directly invested capital in Germany.

MOTIVES FOR ENTREPRENEURIAL ACTIVITIES ABROAD

Direct investment takes place for a number of reasons. They cannot be explained with one single motive. Basically, multinational companies' direct investment provides a country with foreign know-how.

In terms of a company's investment calculation, the decisive argument is the expected return from a material investment. Following the assessment of local conditions, a company will only decide to invest abroad if a sufficiently large premium is expected to be earned.

Market and cost orientation and other aspects of corporate strategy can be defined as motives for direct investments:

- Securing sales markets and the exploitation of new markets, but also the avoidance of import barriers, are of major importance when it comes to market orientation. Here, direct investment is a medium for international division of labour and strengthens the export position of a country, resulting in employment security for the export-intensive sectors.
- Taking advantage of local input and infrastructure benefits for the strengthening of a company's entire competitiveness is the consideration in terms of cost orientation. Here, the costs for labour (wages and social costs) and the strain on capital, including taxes, play particular roles.
- Diversification of exchange risks, the creation of internal competition or the shifting of R & D activities and production into technologically friendly regions can represent strategic aspects.

Good communication and transportation facilities, quality human resources and services are the necessary requirements for investment in respect of technologically sophisticated production. Generally, these requirements are only fulfilled in national economies with a high degree of development and present a case for multinational companies to move into Germany.

WHAT ROLE DO MULTINATIONAL COMPANIES' INVESTMENTS PLAY IN GERMANY?

It is interesting that foreign direct investment in Germany has always been restricted to a small circle of countries: at the end of 1993 the share of the six most important capital providers – USA, Netherlands,

Switzerland, Japan, France and UK – in respect of the total value of indirectly and directly held capital was 80 per cent.

In 1993 international capital providers' most important target sectors were the chemical industry, the oil-processing sector, machine and vehicle production, the electronics and the food trade. Overall, one can observe that in the Federal Republic, the existence of foreign direct investments is distributed more evenly than Germany's relative position abroad. In line with the Federal Republic's high income level, resulting in the corresponding size of the market, sale-facilitating investments have great importance: at the end of 1993, 22 per cent of capital invested in German trade and production came from abroad.

It is worth noticing not only that the foreign manufacturing industry invests less in Germany, but also that there is a tendency to withdraw from Germany altogether. In five of the last seven years the foreign manufacturing industry has withdrawn more capital from Germany through dissolution of capital investments than has been raised through direct investment in Germany. Even the extensive stimulation of indust-rial investment in the new federal states has not reversed the tendency for foreign companies to disinvest in Germany. Looking at the balance, no positive employment effects resulted from foreign investment in the industrial sector.

In Germany foreign industrial companies are mainly represented through sales outlets, with production in second place. Around one in three manufacturing companies undertakes research and development in the Federal Republic. In the past the majority of foreign construction and industrial companies effected direct investment, above all for the exploitation of the market. For industrial companies in particular, wage costs are important. For companies in the manufacturing industry the tendency will be for awareness of labour costs to increase. Tax arguments are also of relevance. The aim of reducing transport costs and related resources through direct investments is an important factor for indust-rial companies. Similar aspects apply for the evaluation of state investment programmes. They are mainly taken up by industrial companies as a positive factor.

While German companies have been successfully investing abroad for a number of years, have extended their product range through acquisitions of foreign companies, have reduced their costs and enforced their market presence, foreign direct investment in Germany has increased less. One reason is that 'hostile takeovers' are very difficult to achieve in Germany because of the concentration of share ownership. In addition, friendly takeovers are also uncommon. This seems to be changing, however. 'Shareholder value' is a new buzzword. Restructuring is aimed at reducing costs and increasing efficiency.

In the first place large companies are under pressure to sell subsidiaries. The selling fever however, has not yet taken over the *Mittelstand* companies. Here, a sale still represents failure, although this point of view should change with a change of generation. While the company founder is emotionally involved with his or her company, successors see the alternatives in a much more objective light. They know that in order to keep the company competitive through 'global sourcing' they need to work together with foreign companies.

Compared to Anglo-Saxon countries the German takeover market is still underdeveloped. Only recently has a takeover code been introduced which, although not legal, is intended to strengthen Germany as a financial market. In the meantime it has been accepted by a majority of quoted companies and broad acceptance is expected. Transparency in the event of takeover offers, equal treatment of all shareholders and minority protection are its essential elements. In future, foreign investors will also have to obey the fairness rules of this code.

WHAT CONDITIONS DO MULTINATIONAL COMPANIES FIND IN GERMANY?

In Germany companies view the role of multinational corporations quite positively. A survey by the Munich based Ifo-Institute has shown that multinational companies' investments in Germany are regarded as positive, including the employment aspects. Two-thirds of the companies surveyed believe that below the line, foreign subsidiaries and company takeovers in Germany will create additional employment opportunities. Over half of the companies consider the import of technologies to be more important than the danger of being exposed to theft of ideas. Forty per cent of the companies surveyed welcomed the fresh view of corporate culture; scepticism about foreign customs existed in only a quarter of companies.

However, conditions for companies within Germany have to be further improved. Due to the state of development in industrial nations, structural differences in individual areas, such as the organisation of companies and markets, the extent of state intervention and regulation density and the tax and social system, gain particular importance. They illustrate artificial comparative advantages or disadvantages of a nation's economy and, at the same time, they are important parameters in terms of a location's competitiveness.

Compared to other industrial nations, Germany shows structural deficits in a growing number of these areas. Keywords are inflexibility of the employment market, long-term planning and approval times and procedures, high tax burdens for companies and high employment costs.

For a number of years the BDI has been pinpointing these structural deficits. In the meantime, much has happened within Germany: The federal goverment's 'saving package', passed in autumn 1996, contains a number of important measures to move the rudder and steer the ship in the right direction. It represents a basis for sensible budget policies in terms of unemployment, illness and old age pension insurance policies. It ensures more flexibility within the employment market through the easing of dismissal protection for smaller companies, and it provides extended opportunities for temporary employment. Employment barriers are therefore lifted and new employment is facilitated. Positive results for the employment market are expected. Through restrictions in the continued payment of wages in the event of illness, employment costs are intended to be reduced. Many companies will save immediately; other companies, depending on the clauses concerning continued payment of wages anchored in tariff agreements, will eventually save a total of DM70 billion which is paid annually in respect of continued pay, following cancellation or newly created agreements.

The BDI welcomes the federal government's 'saving package' as the first step on the long, hard road towards elementary and lasting reforms. Further steps will have to be taken to make Germany more attractive for foreign companies in order to ensure growth and employment. Extensive corporation tax reform and reform of the old age pension and health insurance system are also required. If these intentions are consistently planned and introduced, they will be of benefit to the investing companies, the employees and Germany as a whole.

12

The Dual System of Vocational Education and Training in Germany

Hermann Schmidt, President, the Federal Institute for Vocational Training, Berlin / Bonn (BIBB), and Laszlo Alex, Director, BIBB

BACKGROUND

Vocational education and training (VET) in Germany continues the tradition of medieval guild training, as practised all over Europe. However, in contrast to other countries, this system of practical and theoretical learning was adapted for the purposes of industry in the nineteenth century. Systematic on-the-job training was provided in workshops and was complemented by general education and occupation-related theory in colleges. In the course of the twentieth century, practices across different industrial sectors were brought together into a modern vocational training system, and were codified in the 1969 *Vocational Training Act (Berufsbildungsgesetz)* and *Education Acts* for VET in the *Länder* (regions).

At present, companies train 1.6 million young people between the ages of 16 and 22 in more than 300 recognised training occupations. This means that two-thirds of the age cohort are covered by this form of transition between school and work, of whom 58 per cent are young men and 42 per cent are young women.[1]

Note: [1]*In 1950 the equivalent figures were 75 and 25 per cent*

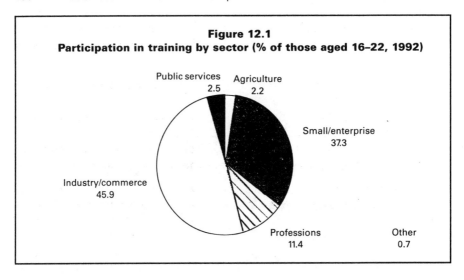

Figure 12.1
Participation in training by sector (% of those aged 16–22, 1992)

Public services 2.5 — Agriculture 2.2 — Small/enterprise 37.3 — Professions 11.4 — Other 0.7 — Industry/commerce 45.9

Figure 12.1 shows their national distribution across the half million accredited training companies, by occupational sector.

THE BASIC STRUCTURE OF GERMANY'S EDUCATION SYSTEM

There are 3.5 million pupils in primary schools in Germany. From there, pupils go on to a number of different types of secondary schools:

- *Hauptschule* (equivalent to a secondary modern school);
- *Gymnasium* (equivalent to a grammar school);
- *Realschule* (in between a secondary modern school and a grammar school);
- Comprehensive school;
- Special school.

The first three types each cater for around 1.5 million pupils.[2] Most of the 16 *Länder* have introduced comprehensive schools as an additional type of school, catering for 0.4 million pupils; 250,000 pupils attend special schools.

At the level of upper secondary education (after 15), the *Gymnasium* prepares young people for higher education and the Dual System prepares young people for work in particular occupations. It is 'dual' in the sense that it combines employer-provided training with part-time

Note: [2]*Source: BMBW, Basic and Structural Data 1993–4*

education at vocational schools *(Berufsschulen)*. In addition, a large number of full-time vocational schools offer 1–3 year programmes which have three functions:

- preparing young people for higher education in a *Fachoberschule* (vocational sixth forms);
- improving the chances of school leavers obtaining the most sought-after places in the Dual System;
- offering a broad foundation in areas such as technology or commerce, designed to facilitate the transition to work.

Participation trends in upper secondary education between 1975 and 1992 show increased percentages of the 16-19 age cohort in all of the various routes. In fact, adding up the figures for 1992 gives a total of 137 per cent, showing that many young people in Germany use more than one opportunity during these three years to improve their competence, after leaving compulsory education and before taking up work. This is one of the explanations for the relatively low rate of unemployment among young people.

ACHIEVEMENT AND PROGRESSION

Over the last 30 years Germany has seen changing attitudes towards education, with important implications for the flow of learners through the education and training system.

While the typical craft-level trainee in the 1960s came from a *Hauptschule* (more than 80 per cent), such trainees are in the minority today (40 per cent). In the 1960s, fewer than 3 per cent of trainees had achieved the *Abitur*, mainly in some selected commercial training occupations (eg banking, insurance). Today 15 per cent of all trainees (over 200,000) start with the *Abitur* behind them, in technical, commercial, craft and agricultural occupations, and also in SMEs (small and medium-sized enterprises).

The growth in education and training in the Dual System has contributed to the overall trend of rising educational achievement. Today, about two-thirds of young people start their training in the Dual System, while just 15 years ago it was less than 50 per cent.

Roughly one-third of young people study at some point for the *Abitur* at a *Gymnasium Oberstufe*, and 6 per cent attend a *Fachoberschule* leading to a *Fachabitur* (equivalent to vocational 'A' levels). A further 10 per cent of an age cohort attends other full-time vocational schools for the *Berufsvorbereitungsjahr* (a year of vocational preparation) or the

Berufsgrundbildungsjahr (a year of full-time education and training in an occupational training field). These two programmes aim to help young people make a start in the Dual System or in work. It is worth noting that full-time vocational schools have *increased* in importance as a result of the growth of the Dual System. Moreover, increasing participation in education and training over the last 20 years has made attendance at consecutive programmes of advanced-level secondary education commonplace, for example two year full-time vocational schooling followed by training in the Dual System.

The growth in participation in education and training for each generation has brought about a considerable improvement in the structure of qualifications and competence among the working population. Those holding vocational or professional qualifications have grown from 65 per cent to over 80 per cent in the last 15 years. By 2010 this percentage is expected to be 90 per cent of the working population.

ASSUMPTIONS AND CHARACTERISTICS OF THE DUAL SYSTEM

The Dual System is founded on close links between public and private training organisations, between statutory provision and provision governed by collective agreements, and between public training policy and private training investment. Its most significant characteristics are as follows:

- participation of companies is voluntary;
- standards and content of three-year training are agreed by employers and trade unions and then legally codified;
- co-operation between employers and trade unions at various levels supports and renews the system;
- independence of the system is preserved through corporate bodies (chambers);
- the system is financed mainly by corporate training providers, with supplementary funding coming from government;
- the provision of further education includes both general and occupation-related theoretical study.

A number of factors, many of them specific to Germany, contribute to the notably positive response of young people to the Dual System.

The dual system is successful because:

1. A vocational qualification confers high standing in Germany, where it is recognised that the nation can succeed in international competition only with as competent a workforce as possible.

2. In the mid-1980s, employers and trade unions placed the ability to act independently at the centre of all training programmes. The aim was for all young trainees to be able to plan, carry out and manage their own work tasks.

3. Skilled blue- and white-collar workers and SME craftsmen enjoy a high status in society. Contributing factors are the attitude of the trade unions, which see themselves as a community of skilled workers, and the important role which SMEs play in the German economy. By the 1980s the prestige of the Dual System had increased to the point that a significant proportion of all *Abitur* holders participated in it.

4. VET is a primary political concern. Since the 1970s, the government has prepared an annual report about the state of VET, including any shortcomings which have appeared. An adequate supply of accredited training places has long been a concern of the prime minister, employer organisations, trade unions and the media.

5. The Dual System is not questioned by any major political party as the most suitable system of VET. Likewise, both employers and trade unions regard it as the stable basis of their VET policy relationship, whatever other differences of outlook they may have.

6. Two large research and development institutes, the Federal Institute for Vocational Training (*Bundesinstitut für Berufsbildung*) and the Institute for Labour Market and Occupational Research (*Institut für Arbeitsmarkt- und Berufsforschung*) offer a database and advice to employers, trade unions and the government. They provide a platform for joint planning and for the improvement and adaptation of vocational training.

7. A substantial infrastructure of 385 authorised institutions manage and regulate vocational training. Most of these are the professional chambers such as those of industry and commerce, of SMEs [*Handwerks-kammer*] and of medical practitioners and of lawyers. Membership of the chambers is a statutory obligation, and they accredit organisations for training, register all training contracts, assess trainers, and conduct intermediate and final tests with the aid of tripartite examination commissions (employers, trade unions and FE teachers).

8. When planning VET (eg duration, content and level of training occupations), the government acts on the consensus principle, by building on the agreement of employers and trade unions.

Note: [3]*Of the 370 odd training occupations about 100 are hardly used, though are still nominally inforce*

9. Employers and trade unions provide on-going renewal of the training content and the examination syllabus. They are supported in this task by the Federal Institute, which continually observes changes in work processes, conducts research and collaborates with specialists of the 'social partners' in revising the training regulations.

10. Each year 34–40 training regulations (of the 370 occupations) are revised.[3] These are frameworks and do not prescribe methods or procedures, so can be implemented by the most modern means available to training providers.

THE *BERUFSSCHULEN* IN THE DUAL SYSTEM

The *Berufsschulen* (equivalent to FE colleges for initial vocational craft/technician level education) work in tandem with companies in three-year programmes of VET for young people in the Dual System. They operate under the jurisdiction of the *Länder* and, with schools, are within the portfolio of their Minister of Education.

Teachers in *Berufsschulen* are civil servants of the *Land*. They have a university degree (eg in economics or engineering) and a teaching diploma in a vocational field. They teach on part-time or full-time courses in initial or further vocational education and are expected to keep in touch with problems of industrial practice on a continuous basis. Instructors, on the other hand, teach workplace practice in workshops or laboratories. They are qualified as technicians or *Meister* (qualified supervisors).

Given the wide range of their tasks, *Berufsschulen* have remarkable achievements to their credit, but they are often the target of criticism. For example, changes in companies' work organisation, technology and personnel practice take place at widely different rates, but *Berufsschulen* are expected to be at the forefront at all times. Their standards are frequently compared with those of leading-edge companies, despite the limited resources at their disposal. Meanwhile, many companies, especially those with out-of-date production methods, cannot see any need for *Berufsschulen* because they fail to appreciate the importance of underpinning theory.

The Education Ministers of the *Länder* oversee the development of syllabuses for the *Berufsschulen*. These are aligned with current training regulations, and with the actual training given in companies at the local level, subject to agreement between the *Berufsschule* teachers and trainers.

In most of the *Länder*, weekly release from the company is legally fixed at 12 hours. The task of *Berufsschulen* is to foster the personal development of young people by means of general education (mother tongue, early stages of foreign languages, politics, sport and religion) and through an understanding of the theoretical basis of the occupation. These requirements have grown considerably in the last 20 years. Moreover, during this period the *Berufsschulen* have catered for an increasingly broad variety of students, from those without a leaving certificate up to those with the *Abitur*. The curriculum of one group may take 3.5 years while that of another takes only 2 years, although, given good performance, training contracts between trainee and company may be shortened by six months. Finally, there also remains the obligation to teach those young people without training contracts, since young people are obliged to undertake vocational education until they have reached the age of 18.

Taking into consideration the exceptionally complex tasks of the *Berufsschulen* today, they achieve their technical and pedagogical aims to a high degree.

COSTS AND BENEFITS OF VOCATIONAL TRAINING

The costs of in-company training vary widely and depend on:

- trainee wages, which are negotiated through collective agreements and depend on occupation[4] (and represent 49 per cent of the gross cost of company training);
- the extent to which training is on the job or in a training workshop;
- the use of full-time professional trainers (about 40,000), part-time qualified trainers (about 700,000), as well as a large number of 'training-qualified' blue- and white-collar workers. The cost of training personnel is 39 per cent of total costs;
- costs of management, examinations, teaching and learning materials (12 per cent of total costs).

As a result, the gross costs per year vary, according to occupation, between DM5000 and DM50,000. The Federal Institute has estimated the 'average annual gross training cost' at DM30,000. However, trainees also contribute to production, which reduces this sum by an average of DM12,000. Hence, the average net annual cost per trainee is DM18,000. In many enterprises, particularly small ones, trainees can contribute a

Note: [4] *In 1993 they varied between DM680 and DM1870 per month, with an average of DM1055; [5] the trainee quota is the ratio of trainees to the total employed in the company*

great deal to production, with the result that their output at least covers the cost of their training.

There are other benefits for companies which, while often recognised, are rarely measured in cash terms. For example, training companies save recruitment and personnel costs, reduce the risks of bad selection, and save induction and socialisation costs. It is therefore not surprising that many companies attribute great advantages to training and train more young people than they need, often considerably more than the 'trainee quota'.[5]

During the latest recession, many companies, particularly large ones, drastically reduced their training effort to save expenditure.[6] Politicians, employer organisations and trade unions started a campaign to increase further the number of available training places. This campaign is already having positive effects.

The amount of trainee wages is negotiated between the employers and trade unions for each sector of industry (for example, the engineering or chemical industries). The actual amount reflects the supply of and demand for young people in the different labour markets; it averages, for example, DM700 a month for hairdressers and DM1800 for bricklayers.

The development of key capabilities

Learning through working is the fundamental principle of vocational training. It offers the most favourable conditions for the development of so-called key capabilities. These capabilities are in great demand in all forms of work because of the uncertainties and the rate of change which are a characteristic of our era. Key capabilities include the ability to take responsibility for achievement of occupational tasks, the ability to work and communicate effectively with colleagues in teams, the ability to think in terms of systems, and to learn how to learn.

However, such key capabilities are an empty shell without occupation-related skills and theoretical knowledge. The dual education and training system in companies and colleges can link practical application and experience in the workplace with underpinning theory and reflection.

Time is a key factor in the development of key capabilities. This is one of the important reasons for the relatively long duration (three years) of the dual training system. It is significant that unemployment among

Note: [6]*eg in engineering the trainee quota fell from 6.5 to 3.5 per cent*

Dual System 'graduates', especially in the younger age groups, is persistently below national average figures.

Environmental protection in vocational education and training

Since the early 1980s, VET objectives for environmental protection have become part and parcel of curricula in in-company training and further education. Right from the start, the principle was established that VET in all training occupations should be committed to environmental protection.

In the established training occupations, the following aims are pursued with varying intensity:

- awareness of environmental issues and development of an environmental conscience;
- environmentally conscious behaviour at the workplace, especially efficient use of resources, avoidance of waste, and recycling;
- environmental protection as an occupational competence, eg in chemical occupations.

Over the last 15 years, and in pursuit of these aims, a number of concepts and measures have been developed in initial and continuing training. They now play an important role in the final tests and examinations.

PUBLIC INVESTMENT IN VOCATIONAL TRAINING

In the Dual System, enterprises bear the costs of practical training while the *Länder* pay for the further education component. The federal government and *Land* governments subsidise, or sometimes pay in full, specific areas of special interest to the nation. Some examples are discussed below.

Research in vocational training at the Federal Institute for Vocational Training

In 1996 the cost of this work was DM50 million. It was completely financed by federal government.

Promotion of group training centres

Two-thirds of all trainees are in firms with fewer than 50 employees. The federal and *Länder* governments subsidise the training efforts of these companies through group training centres, usually managed by the chambers. In 1994, subsidies for building and equipment investment costs, as well as running costs, amounted to around DM700 million.

Innovation in vocational training

The Secretary of State for Education and Science offers incentive grants for innovative developments in in-company vocational training. These amounted to 75 per cent of the costs of pilot projects, around DM15 million, in 1996. They covered such areas as the development of new methods, adaptation to technological progress, and special needs training.

Supply deficiencies in the Dual System

The Dual System does not oblige employers to train. As a consequence, several factors affect the availability of training places:

1. Since employers bear the cost of training, the general economic situation is of special importance.
2. The geographical distribution of 'training companies' results in regional differences.
3. What training is available depends on the structure of different industrial sectors, eg mechanical engineering, care manufacture and repair, building and construction.
4. The present lack of a sufficient number of medium-sized companies in former East Germany has created a special regional problem.

However, the Federal Constitutional Court, the highest German court, ruled in 1980 that the government is responsible for ensuring that sufficient training places are provided when companies cannot secure an adequate supply of training.

Lack of in-company training places in East Germany

The national training system is spreading into the new private company structures in former East Germany. In practical terms, this means building a new Dual System in East Germany. Public funds are being used to rent additional training facilities, engage training personnel and subsidise training places in companies. The Federal Labour Office (*Bundesanstalt für Arbeit*) finances around 15 per cent of the 280,000 training places in special training facilities at an approximate cost of DM900 million in 1996. Meanwhile, the new *Länder* encourage new enterprises to provide training by offering them special grants costing in excess of DM400 million.

The training of those with special needs

It is an agreed policy to train as many young people with special needs as possible in the Dual System. This is reflected in the fact that each year there are between 30,000 and 40,000 young people without a certificate of secondary education, or coming from special needs schools, who gain access to the Dual System. There is also special provision for both young people and adults so severely handicapped that they cannot be placed in ordinary employment. Initial and continuing training facilities have been put in place by the Secretary of State for Employment and Social Services in which such people with special needs (more than 90,000 in 1995) are trained and cared for. This is funded by the Federal Office for Labour to the extent of DM2500 million in 1995.

OUTLOOK

During the coming decades, an increase in the popularity of school leaving examinations, especially the *Abitur*, is likely, widening access to further and higher education.

A survey of secondary school pupils early in 1995 showed that the modest decline in demand for training places in the Dual System has come to an end or is reverting to slow growth. Therefore, we can anticipate a general increase in participation in learning activities, with further increases in the demand for educational provision in *Gymnasia*, vocational full-time schools and in the Dual System, at the expense of the *Hauptschulen*.

ACKNOWLEDGEMENT

This article first appeared in the National Commission on Education's March 1995 bulletin.

13

The Role of Trade Unions and Works Councils in Germany

Wolfgang Lecher, Lecturer in Sociology, Economics and Philosophy, Tübingen and Frankfurt / Main

THE CORE OF THE GERMAN INDUSTRIAL RELATIONS SYSTEM: WORKS COUNCILS AND COLLECTIVE BARGAINING

Industrial relations in the Federal Republic of Germany are defined by the dual system of representation of interests embodied in 'collective bargaining freedom and participation'. (Possibly the best introduction in English to the German industrial relations system is given by Jacobi *et al.*, 1992.) In the German collective bargaining system, the institutions are separated into trade unions and works councils. There is a corresponding separation of trade union collective bargaining policy and works council policy on internal agreements; and there is a separation of the right to strike at the collective bargaining level, and peace in industrial relations at the works constitution level. In this structure of representation, collective bargaining freedom and (participatory) rights which are provided by law play the predominant role; a fact which clearly indicates the very high level of statutory regulation of industrial relations in Germany compared to the situation in many other countries. But these rights merely establish the basic outline. How industrial relations are organised in concrete terms depends on many different circumstances, such as the industrial relations climate between state, employers' associations and trade unions (which is determined by the political climate); on the state's informal moves to intervene in collective bargaining disputes; on the strengths and weaknesses of the contracting parties in collective bargaining; and on the varying impact of participation at workplace, plant, group, macroeconomic and, more recently, also European level (European works councils).

Collective bargaining freedom in Germany is determined by the only 'group right' in the German Constitution and safeguards what is known as coalition freedom, coalitions being trade unions and employers' associations. The actual collective bargaining policy pursued within the framework of the Constitution is not determined by the trade union or employer umbrella organisations but by the individual unions and the sectoral employers' associations. Legally, the state has no right to intervene in their collective bargaining freedom and there is thus, for example, no compulsory arbitration by the State in the event of a strike. This, however, does not preclude possibilities of bringing influence to bear indirectly through targeted information, media policy, public pressure by the government, etc.

As is the case in other countries, collective bargaining policy relates primarily to wages, working conditions and working time. These are negotiated by collective bargaining parties, and any government regulations have to come second. The trade unions are not subordinate to political parties; the principle of the non-partisan, united trade union precludes such indirect government or party influence on trade union policy and thus on collective bargaining policy such as occurs in countries with factional trade unions. On the contrary, the parties are assessed by the trade unions and gauged according to the extent to which they are geared to working people. This is done regularly in elections by means of what are termed trade union electoral touchstones. The trade unions are thus non-partisan but by no means non-political.

The right to strike is an important trade union instrument in the context of collective bargaining freedom and an important means of exerting pressure in order to achieve the conclusion of collective agreements; its employer counterpart is the lockout. This is where bargaining freedom becomes practical, although the trade unions take the view that the possibilities for lockouts in Germany, which, compared to other countries, are very extensive, violate equality of weapons. As a result, the fight against lockouts is a constant topic of debate in industrial relations in Germany.

Some figures will give a general idea of the dimension of collective bargaining (discussed in detail in Bispinck, 1993): there are currently some 35,000 collective agreements in effect in Germany covering 90 per cent of the labour force. The subjects of these agreements are wages and salaries, fringe benefits (holiday bonus, insurance contributions, employers' contributions to tax-deductible savings schemes, etc.), working time, qualification and further training; in other words, working conditions in the broadest sense of the term. The terms of the agreements and terms of notice are laid down in each specific agreement. Employers and unions are then committed to refraining from industrial action during those periods. Both sides must belong to associations which are authorised to bargain collectively. Where this is not the case, the collective agreement is void and its obligations are not liable to penalty by law. If a strike is to be called when the commitment to refrain from industrial action expires, a strike vote must be held by secret ballot and a vote must likewise be held on termination of the industrial action.

Improvement of the collective agreement on individual points may be, and indeed is, achieved in company agreements concluded between the works council and the management. This is one of the most important functions of works council participation and it thus constitutes one of the links between collective and company bargaining policy. One of the major objectives of the trade unions is thus to achieve a system of representation, i.e. a system where elected representatives (from trade unions as far as possible) carry out the function of participation, and thus can carry through their own ideas on economic and social policy as distinct from those of parties and the state. The struggle for participation in the narrower sense is thus always also a struggle to extend trade union rights. The current participatory institutions cover various levels, various forms and varying prospects of exerting influence (see Lecher and Naumann, 1991). These levels include:

- the workplace: efforts are being made to develop this level further, particularly since it has been becoming increasingly clear that the workplace level is gaining considerable significance as a result of the introduction of new technologies and new modes of work organisation in companies, and the providing of qualifications which this requires (further details below);
- the plant/company: the *Works Constitution Act* applies here, laying down the rights of works councils. The same applies in the case of the public services with their *Staff Representation Act* and staff committees;
- the undertaking: the statutory rules on supervisory board participation apply here for supervisory boards on which the parties have different ratios;

- and finally, the macroeconomic level: there are as yet no arrangements governing participation at this level. Regional co-ordination (in the context of European structural aids, for example), which is becoming increasingly important, has been carried out to date without any appreciable trade union influence.

The various participation possibilities are as follows:

- systems of representation: these cover works councils and supervisory boards, where the same persons are sometimes members of both bodies;
- sectoral collective agreements, which, both qualitatively and quantitatively, have always been, and still are, the most important field of action in the German industrial relations system;
- informal corporate arrangements between the management and the works council on possibilities for participating in efforts to resolve company problems; these arrangements are not safe-guarded by legislation and thus depend on the readiness of both parties to negotiate. They include, in particular, arrangements on the introduction of new technologies and the changes in the organisation of work which this necessitates. This is a possible field of action for the participation of works councils in decisions concerning the workplace, and for the prospective action of European works councils at group level.

And finally, participation rules have varying prospects of exerting influence, for example:

- the right of initiative and the right of veto, particularly in the context of the *Works Constitution Act* and, here again, on personnel issues and questions of working time. Works councils have a right of veto, for example, with regard to the approval of overtime;
- monitoring rights, which are granted to supervisory boards in particular. These rights have recently been a subject of debate, however, because trade union and/or company supervisory boards generally do not have the same level of information at their disposal as do providers of capital, and their rights can therefore only be exercised to a limited extent;
- the consultation rights, which works councils hold primarily in economic questions and which are exercised much more frequently;
- the information rights to which the works council and the supervisory board are entitled in economic and social issues. These also form the crucial field of action of the European works councils.

As regards the various levels, forms and prospects of influence, it can thus be concluded that statutory participation rights differ widely from relative strength on the one hand, as far as personnel and social measures are concerned, to relative weakness on the other in the case of economic decisions.

TRADE UNIONS: STATE AND PERSPECTIVES

How has this industrial relations system with its two fundamental components of 'collective bargaining freedom' and 'participation' (and, above all, the combination of the two) – a fairly original system compared to those prevailing in other countries – stood the test of time in the past few years? At first sight, the German trade unions are quite impressive. Membership density is about 40 per cent and 35 per cent of the membership are organised in DGB (German TUC equivalent) affiliates. In absolute figures in 1995 9.35 million employees were organised in DGB unions. Compared to the drastic drop in membership figures in many other European countries and the situation in the United States and Japan, one can talk of relative stability as far as Germany is concerned. Membership structures, however, are corresponding less and less to employment structures. Whereas the proportion of white-collar employees has now increased to over 50 per cent of the total number of employed persons, now only 23 per cent of the members of DGB unions are white-collar workers. The proportion of women members is also 23 per cent, whereas almost 40 per cent of the total number of people in work are women. The trend is even less favourable when it comes to young workers; only 13 per cent of young workers are members of a trade union, and the number of young members has been on the decline for years in the majority of DGB affiliates. There is also a shift in the ratio of full-time employees to part-time employees, the unemployed and retired workers. These structural shifts are reflected not least in the growing financial difficulties experienced by the trade unions, whose membership as a whole is decreasing due to rising unemployment, part-time work and the disproportionately low percentage of highly skilled and thus well-paid workers.

If we attempt in conclusion to assess the trade union situation in comparison with the other EU countries, the following comments can be made:

- In the German Federal Republic the instrument of free collective bargaining as the free negotiation of working conditions between employer associations and trade unions, in particular at the sectoral level, has proved to be productive, progressive and also flexible. Trade union membership density is (still) sufficiently high to enable the unions to use this instrument to counter government deregulation measures (which, it is true, have in most cases merely been announced, but have by no means resulted in such extensive intervention as in the United Kingdom, for example).

- The separation of political parties and trade unions as different pillars of the worker movement is likewise firmly established and has stood the test of time. Throughout Europe, trade unions with definite political leanings have, without exception, greater problems of acceptance in society than do unions which are independent of political parties. When parties and trade unions are too closely linked, this is evidently harmful for both organisations in the long run.

- Although the dual system of representation of employees' interests through trade unions (collective bargaining policy and the right to strike) and works councils (company agreements involving the commitment to refrain from industrial action) now runs smoothly on the whole and is productive, there is the constant latent problem of the council members becoming independent of the trade unions. These problems are liable to become intensified as ideas of participation in decisions relating to the workplace become more definite. But the system does have the capacity to deal with problems flexibly as well as great capacity for compromise, owing to the fact that the authorisation bases of the two pillars on which it rests are different.

- The participation system which has been established by law in Germany is thus geared mainly to plants/companies and undertakings. In view of the growing need for employees to have a say in the introduction of technological innovations and new forms of work organisation, the demand for constant further qualification and the intensifying debate on a collective bargaining capacity which is co-ordinated at the European level, the German industrial relations system needs to be revised on at least two points. These are direct participation (participation at the workplace) and the introduction of European works councils.

SOCIAL PRODUCTIVITY AND DIRECT PARTICIPATION

The German trade unions have been considering a change of outlook in the past few years aimed at taking an active role in the planning, introduction and control of new technologies and the flexibility this involves regarding the organisation of work, qualifications and wages. Roth and Kohl (1985) pioneered trade union adoption of the topic, particularly in the largest German union, IG Metall. Cf. Lecher (1991) for further orientation of this discussion towards the flexibility and productivity potential of participation in decisions concerning the workplace.) This change has far-reaching consequences for the trade unions and their relations with employees and the structures for representing their interests in the company (and thus for the industrial relations system as a whole).

The company and the workplace are tending to become the most important context for taking a critical look at, and shaping, technology-induced work processes involving new forms of work organisation, even if it must be borne in mind that the company or plant is incorporated into the higher-level central planning and management system of the undertaking or group of undertakings. Within the framework of the dual system in Germany, works councils are becoming more significant than the trade union organisations operating above the company level. At the same time, however, they have to deal with the possibilities of non-representative, direct employee participation in decisions concerning the workplace. Trade union bargaining policy is tending to become a framework policy for differentiated company agreements between works councils and company management. The determination of wages, for instance, should no longer be linked only to the current job activity and performance of the individual, but should also be commensurate with the qualifications held and system-related (group) performance potential. Through participation at the workplace, which has hitherto been omitted to a large extent in the German system, it is now to become possible to achieve decentralised flexibility, social productivity and the humanisation of work.

The move to open industrial relations systems and downwards towards direct participation is, incidentally, to be observed in all highly indus-trialised countries. (The problems of efficient coordination of indirect and direct participation which inevitably ensue and are crucial for works councils and trade unions are discussed in the European context by Krieger and Lange (1992).) In 1986, there were already four million quality circles involving some 40 million employees, and there has meanwhile been a tremendous increase in the United States, the 'Small Tigers' of East Asia and in Europe in particular. But it is not only the fact that the system has spread that clearly indicates that the participatory concept is successful; the fact that the quality circle concept has been developed further into new forms of production and work organisation, such as total quality management (TQM) – for example, approximately 1.8 million employees were involved in TQM at the beginning of the 1990s – is further proof of its success. When one considers further elements of group work (up to 8 per cent of the people employed in automobile production including the subcontracting

industries were recorded in Germany in 1992) and financial participation in the results of the undertaking (just under 20 per cent of all
workers in France are involved), then the trade unions are clearly facing
a massive challenge to provide constructive answers. This means that
they themselves and/or the traditional representative structure at the
company level must join these new participation models, in order to
avoid the situation where only the workforce is reduced under the
fashionable slogan of 'lean production', but also in order to be able to
play a role in the shaping of humane working conditions.

The (re)discovery of the subjective factor of productivity – which has
always been predominant with British classicists as living work as
opposed to dead work (capital) – is, however, only one aspect of the issue.
Further aspects which are at least as interesting and important are the
market-related technical and qualification-related innovations which
meanwhile rank high in the developed industrialised countries and the
relevant multinational subcontracting firms. These factors are as
follows:

- the growing need for flexibility as the result of changing market
  requirements (keywords: diversified production of quality goods
  in small series);
- changes in the employment market owing to the growing supply
  of qualified and well-trained workers;
- the scope for rationalisation, organisation and flexibility offered
  by the new microelectronically aided technologies;
- the counter-productive elements of the classical Taylorist system
  of organising work (keywords: extremely short task cycles and
  excessive fragmentation of tasks);
- experiments and empirical examples of possibilities for linking
  individual employee interests with a new style of work organisation in the company (keywords: production islands, partially
  autonomous groups, team and group work).

The last point in particular refers to a concept of workplace participation
as the point of departure for achieving 'alternative' quality circles. The
following aspects could be quoted as essential points of such a model of
work organisation which is geared to workers and socially oriented: the
employees concerned should be represented through a combination of
direct participation and (classical) representative participation, since
it is not possible, particularly in the case of major projects (such as the
introduction of CAD/CAM in the plant), for all of the persons concerned
to participate in all tasks and decisions to the same extent. The
representation should be carried out by union-oriented employees so
as to ensure there is a link between participation in decisions concerning
the workplace and the trade unions and works councils. As a general

principle, individual participation must be integrated into the existing (works council/trade union related) system of collective representation of interests so as to avoid a situation where groups with varying involvement are played off against one another (rationalisation winners against rationalisation losers, the regular workforce against the fringe workforce). This will be one of the most difficult tasks of the trade unions and in particular of works councils.

Those affected by the introduction of new technologies, and thus by the work organisation and qualification measures this entails, must as a fundamental principle be given the opportunity also to meet the management and the people in charge of developing the technology and work organisation systems in their own working groups, in addition to and independent of joint project groups, with a view to discussing and organising their objectives. A co-ordinated participation infrastructure must thus be built up within the company, the fundamental element being the participation of those concerned in decisions concerning the workplace. And finally, this complex model of participation must be regulated in some sort of binding form (e.g. through a company agreement between the management and the works council, where possible on the basis of a collective framework agreement between the trade unions and the employers' association). This would guarantee continuity and a habitual pattern of conduct, since these are the preconditions for the long-term success of such decentralised participation in decisions concerning the workplace.

These requirements entail both effects in the field of performance-related pay, which has predominated hitherto, and new problems for the trade union representation of interests:

- With the introduction of new integral work activities and the organisation of work in groups, the subjective aspect is likely to be enhanced. This will bring a departure from quantifiable performance scales relating solely to results (time-related piece-work systems, bonus pay, Motion Time Measurements). On the other hand, subjective performance criteria related to an individual's conduct and motivation will become more important. This includes willingness to co-operate, loyalty to the company, identification with company objectives and other virtues which are deemed positive, i.e. social qualifications which are not related to any specific process and/or extra-functional social qualifications.
- This at the same time involves a development from result-related individual performance to group-related system performance. Labour qualifications which are not related directly to individual tasks are gaining importance.

- Time-related, performance-controlled forms of remuneration (prescribed time to be worked on standard pay) will become more significant. Performance requirements will be prescribed for the fixed hourly wage; these requirements will no longer apply to the individual worker but will be calculated for entire groups and departments as system-related production reference numbers (relating to production targets).

- With these trends the negotiation of agreements between employees and/or works councils and management, as a perform-ance programme which is accepted by both parties, will become more important than the traditional and often pseudo-scientific registration of quantified individual performance. Fairness standards and concepts of fair pay will become more important than the quantification of work performed, which has prevailed hitherto.

- If the traditional elements of performance registration and the corresponding assignment of pay lose significance, new forms of participation in the negotiation of the performance compromise must be implemented through collective bargaining and at com-pany/plant level. New tasks facing trade unions and works councils are thus to shape this process of negotiation and to standardise the rules of the system accordingly. The essential factor is now to transform the piece-rate policy which has prevailed hitherto into a real performance policy for integral tasks and group work, within the framework of a collective bargaining policy geared to working time and technology. The requirement for trade unions and works councils to shape that policy actively is growing in comparison to the performance control activity which has prevailed hitherto.

Participation at the workplace will thus play an important role in the future as a socially oriented model of participation which complements, but also contrasts with, the relevant social techniques employed by management. What is important for trade unions is to combine these possibilities for direct participation sensibly and effectively with the representative participation which has prevailed hitherto.

THE FUTURE POSITION OF EUROPEAN WORKS COUNCILS IN THE GERMAN INDUSTRIAL RELATIONS SYSTEM

In addition to developing direct participation, the second challenge for the German industrial relations system is presented by the process of internationalisation, which has been institutionalised through the enactment of the European Commission Directive on European works councils (EWCs). Obtaining information from the transnational group of undertakings in question for the body representing employees' interests in the respective national sections of the group, however, is not the sole function of a European works council. These councils are just as much a channel through which knowledge of the various industrial relations and trade union representation systems in the different countries can be acquired, and the national industrial relations systems gradually integrated Europe-wide. Rehfeldt (1994) points expressly to this dual aspect, which is extremely important for building up a future European industrial relations structure.) The establishment of European works councils (EWCs) thus also affects the trade unions. The following comments give a brief description of the directive and a critical assessment from the trade union point of view, as well as proposals for linking and/or integrating the future EWCs into the future decisive articulations of the industrial relations system: extended participation in decisions concerning the workplace and the ability to bargain at supranational level.

After many years of debate and after the failure of the 'compensatory social dialogue' of the two sides of industry at the EU level, the directive on the establishment of European works councils was adopted by the EU Council of Ministers of Social Affairs in September 1994 and should be nationally implemented two years later. (Blanpain and Windey (1994) give the best and most complete survey of the vicissitudes of the history of the directive right through to its adoption.) It lays down procedures for informing and consulting employees' representatives for the approximately 1500 undertakings currently operating on the European scale. To fall within the field of application of the directive, a group of undertakings must have a total of 1000 employees in the 11 EU Member States (except for the UK, which has opted out of these issues by declining to sign the Maastricht Social Protocol) and 150 employees in each of at least two member states.

Where this is the case, negotiations are held between the central management of the undertaking and a special body of employees' representatives on the forming of the EWC, provided, however, that this is requested by at least 100 employees and/or their representatives from at least two establishments in at least two different member states. The tasks, composition, term of office, frequency and length of sessions and, not least, the financial and material resources to be made available for the establishment and operation of the EWC are laid down by this negotiating body. Employees can consult trade union representatives, who act as experts. The cost of these negotiations is borne by the undertaking.

The German trade unions welcome the establishment of EWCs. The EWC directive will also stimulate the debate on the inclusion of the trade unions and thus, in the final analysis, of collective bargaining policy for crossfrontier undertakings. This applies especially to monistic systems (apart from the UK, the Scandinavian countries in particular and also Italy), where trade union bargaining policy takes place at the plant/company level and there is thus a direct combination of information and consultation rights deriving from the directive and the exercise of those rights for collective bargaining policy at the company level. But it is also clear that with the establishment of EWCs, the trade unions will be directing their attention not only to the supranational level, but also to the possible changes at the company level in the various groups of undertakings falling within the field of application of the directive.

The practical implementation of this directive in dual representation systems, such as the system in the Federal Republic of Germany, could also lead to the information possibilities thus acquired being used at two levels. On the one hand, the European works councils could try to reach a sort of European group company agreement with the management. The EWC level would probably play the weakest part in the works council/national works council/group works council/EWC hierarchy to begin with, and the employers' associations are still absolutely against the directive being used in that way. But it is by no means to be ruled out in the future, particularly in the context of the promotion of corporate identity. Arrangements of this nature would, however, have an inherent tendency to corporate trade unionism, which would mean a certain amount of exclusivity of industrial relations within the group as far as the national industrial relations environment is concerned. A mechanism of this nature could result, in the long term, in exclusion from the national industrial relations system.

However, it would also be conceivable, and most desirable for the trade unions and for the standardisation of industrial relations systems at the European level, if the national trade unions operating in the respective groups of undertakings would co-ordinate their activities and make the information received from the European works councils the basis of real collective bargaining talks and agreements with the competent employers' associations. But the precondition for this would be that the trade unions concerned collaborate constantly on group-related issues and that the employers' associations agree to this type of negotiating system. (It was the Head of the International Department of the Dutch trade union confederation FNV, J. van Rens (1991), who made this interesting forward-looking proposal, which has also been taken up in the programme of the European Trade Union Confederation.) Both prospects seem unreal for the time being, but they should not be ruled out completely given the novelty and openness of the EWC instrument.

A final aspect of the possibilities of EWCs results from the dual development of contemporary economic and production logic towards greater decentralisation (decentralisation down to the plant/company level, direct participation, participatory management) and at the same time greater globalisation (internationalisation, trans-border business structures, corporate identity, the development of European identity under the pressure of world market competition, particularly in the triad). In a forward-looking EWC model, the attempt should at least be made to bring these opposite poles closer together, primarily according to the three criteria of the structure of the institutions to be created, the procedure for electing the representative body and the good flow of information desired between the various levels: plant/company, undertaking, national group management (sub-group) and transnational group management.

The following problems have been identified on the basis of the limited experience gained to date with voluntarily agreed EWCs in several transnational European groups of undertakings (based mainly on the research fundings of Streeck and Vitols (1993) and Marginson (1994):

- the fact that the institutional rules depend on the goodwill of the management (there is no entitlement guaranteed by law);
- the fact that the quantity and quality of information is left to the discretion of the management (here again there are no legal guarantees);
- the uncertainty about one's own position, i.e. on the one hand mainly 'national identity' and thus national co-operation between the management and the body representing employees' interests, particularly in the relationship of parent companies and subsidiaries; and, on the other hand, the predominance of the international collaboration of European works councils over national interests;
- language-related communication problems and major problems in the building of confidence at supranational level between the various bodies representing employees' interests;
- familiarisation with the different respective national representation structures, their working methods and mentalities (e.g. German works council members' problems with the positions of British shop stewards and the non-organised members in France);
- assessment of the significance of information provided by the management, and the difficulties in disseminating this down to the plant/company level.

OUTLOOK

The dual system of employee representation through trade unions (collective bargaining, backed up by the right to strike) and works councils (workplace agreements and the obligation to maintain industrial peace) has proved to be effective both as a system of representation and in terms of economic efficiency. However, there are latent problems related to the issue of the autonomy of works councils, and their scope for pursuing localised and special interests, especially when placed under economic pressure. This issue has now emerged as an acute difficulty for the unions (and, in fact, for employers' organisations) in eastern Germany, where local managements and works councils have sought to be exempted from the wage rates specified in industry agreements. Moreover, this question could also take on greater significance in the longer term should hopes for enhanced co-determination at workplace level come to fruition. But the system does provide a relatively flexible mechanism for resolving problems and a relatively high capacity for achieving compromise, as each of the two components of the respective systems derives its legitimacy from different roots.

The existing system of statutory co-determination is primarily concerned with the individual establishment and the firm. Given the greater need for employee co-determination at the immediate workplace, on issues such as technical and organisational innovation and the need to develop regional and structural policies at European level, there is both scope and some imperative for the extension of co-determination to these, as yet untackled, fields of activity. Meeting the need and aspirations for individual and collective co-determination, and thus contributing to industrial peace and social harmony, requires a structure of employee, works council and trade union influence at all these levels.

Looking to the future, complex and highly industrialised societies, such as Germany, still have to grasp the full implications of the fact that their system of industrial relations, with its associated impact on employee motivation, represents a central, productive social force which is no less important than the customary technical and economic components of productivity. The crucial issue for the trade unions in the short and medium term is whether they can link the related issues of economic efficiency and social progress in a form which benefits working people and does not exclude unemployed and whether they can reach a European organisation and bargaining level. In view of German economic strength within the European Union, how these issues are resolved within Germany will also have a major impact on the rest of Europe. At the moment, the employers have accumulated years of experience in wielding the 'soft technologies' of quality circles, user involvement and corporate culture, and the internationalisation of capital is unequivocally predominant.The trade unions still have much ground to make up.

REFERENCES

Bispinck, R. (1993) 'Deutschland' in Bispinck, R. and Lecher, W. (ed.) *Tarifpolitik und Tarifsysteme in Europa* (Collective bargaining policy and collective bargaining systems in Europe), Cologne: pp. 48–79.

Blanpain, R. and Windey, F. (1994) *The European Directive on European Works Councils Information and Consultation of Employees in Multinational Enterprises in Europe*, Louvain:

Jacobi, O., Keller, B. and Müller Jentsch, W. (1992) 'Codetermining the future', in Ferner, A. and Hyman, R. (ed.) *Industrial Relations in the New Europe*, Oxford/Cambridge, MA: pp. 218–69.

Krieger, H. and Lange, R. (1992) 'Der "New Deal" für die neunziger Jahre: die Verzahnung repräsentativer und direkter Arbeitnehmer-beteiligung in Europa (The new deal for the nineties: Dovetailing representative and direct employee participation in Europe), *WSI-Mitteilungen*, 12, pp. 788–99.

Lecher, W. (1991) 'Den Tiger reiten Soziale Produktiviät und direkte Partizipation' (Riding the tiger: Social productivity and direct participation), *Gewerhschaftliche Monatshefte*, 2, pp. 103–109.

Lecher, W. and Naumann, R. (1991) 'Bundesrepublik Deutschland' in Däubler, W. and Lecher, W. (eds) *Die Gewerkschaften in den 12 EG-Ländern Europäische Integration und Gewerkschaftsbewegung.* (The trade unions in the 12 EC countries, European integration and the trade union movement), Cologne: pp. 24–31.

Marginson, F. (1994) 'Freiwillig vereinbarte Europäische, Betriebsräte: Voraussetzungen und Probleme für Management und Gewerk-schaften' in Lecher, W. and Platzer, H. W. *Europäische Union Europäische Arbeitubeziehungen? Nationale Vorraussetzungen und Internationaler Rasmen* (European Union European industrial relations? National preconditions and international framework), Cologne.

Rehfeldt, U. (1994) 'Die "europäischen Konzernräte": Bilanz der französischen Initiativen' (The European 'group councils: a survey of initiatives in France) in Lecher, W. and Platzer, H. W. (eds) *Europäische Union Europäische Arbeitsbeziehungen? Nationale Voraussetzungen und internationaler Rahmen* (European Union European industrial relations? National preconditions and inter-national framework), Cologne.

Roth, S. and Kohl, H. (eds) (1988) *Perspective: Gruppenarbeit* (The group-work prospect), Cologne.

Streeck, W. and Vitols, S. (1993) *European Works Councils: Between Statutory Enactment and Voluntary Adaptation*, Discussion paper WZB.

Van Rens, J. (1991) 'Europa-weite Bündelung der Kräfte in gewerkschaftlichen Joint-Ventures' (Pan-European concentration of forces in trade union joint ventures), *Die Mitbestimmung* B, pp. 291–3.

14

The German Market Research Market: Descriptions, Developments, Information

Walter Tacke, MBA, Management Consultant

THE DEVELOPMENT OF THE GERMAN MARKET RESEARCH MARKET

In Germany market research is a market which over the last few years has grown by around 9–10 per cent annually. However, for 1996 the business outlook is more restrained.

In 1995 German market research institutes turned over around DM1.6 billion. Germany therefore leads in terms of turnover figures for the European market research institutes (ESOMAR, *Market research industry turnover, Trend Report 1990–1994*, March 1996).

The market research institutes' most important sponsor was the consumer and durable consumer goods industry. In 1995 the total turnover was distributed as in Table 14.1.

In 1995 the share of sponsors from abroad reached a new peak at 31 per cent of total turnover.

Table 14.1 *Turnover distribution for 1995 according to sponsors*

Sponsor	Turnover distribution (%)
Consumables industry	63
Media and publishers	12
Other sponsors (associations, service providers, authorities, etc)	25
Total	100

The number of staff in market research institutes also grew. This positive trend is substantiated through growth in the area of consultancy, which is labour intensive.

SPECIFIC MARKET DEVELOPMENTS AND THE NEED FOR INFORMATION

At present, the development of the German market is characterised by a number of important demographic, economic, social and consumer trends. Market research is accountable for these developments in a variety of ways.

The following are the main trends:

- Population decrease and change in the population structure (increasing ageing of the population, advanced education, proletarisation of academics, large share of foreigners (guest workers), war refugees, escalation of one-person households, etc).
- Economic development is held back by a number of restraints (extreme tax burden due to the excessive state quota, increasing debts of public-owned industry, high payments to East Germany, East Europe, the EU and third world countries, Germany as expensive production location).
- Social development is increasingly determined by the following factors:
  - Society is becoming more complex and individualisation is increasing.
  - Changes in values become more dynamic, resulting in intensified changes in consumers' opinions, attitudes and actions.
  - Consumers' needs are diversifying but are also influenced by irrational, unpredictable and unexpected factors.
  - Effects and consequences of social, state and economic measures, such as laws, regulations, reforms and social requirements, are much more difficult to forecast.

    – The information surplus available to the population leads not only to increasing selection but also to loss of orientation.

Despite all this there are so called megatrends. Characteristically these dominate the market for a long time. They can be described as follows:

- Everything is becoming increasingly more 'glocal', ie on the one hand electronic media turn the world into a village and on the other the motto 'All business is local' prevails.
- Regionalisation is coming to the fore. In particular, this is illustrated by the advancement of regional cooking and recipes.
- Geographically oriented target group concepts (microgeographic analyses and market segmentation) are up and coming.
- We are confronted with a growing adventure and leisure movement while maintaining strong economic and rational behaviour.
- Faith Popcorn's 'cocooning' trend (to hibernate in one's own four walls) has affected 40 per cent of the population, as discovered through an extensive empirical examination (*Das Kundenbarometer* 1994, page 79).
- And as consumers think they have less and less time they demand more and more convenience. Railway station services, garage shops, corner shops/off licences, bistros and coffee shops are the modern docking stations, especially for younger and older singles and for young couples without children.
- Differentiation of mass products can also be observed, resulting in gourmet food for cats, an increasing array of varieties of tomato soup, for example, and soups for children.

The identified trend developments have a positive influence on market research because the consumers' market behaviour of today is partly a reflection of tomorrow.

Consumer closeness and the requirement to be constantly up-to-date with changing behaviour characterise current developments and lead to the increasing importance of market research in Germany.

The consequence is a large requirement for information which should not be theoretical but much more oriented to consumers' current behaviour.

THE STRUCTURE OF GERMAN MARKET RESEARCH INSTITUTES

Market research practitioners are diverse and various. The diversity is characterised by undertaking different and sometimes highly specialised tasks. One should differentiate between market research institutes, field organisations, market research advisers, studios and EDP (electronic data processing) service providers.

They can be itemised as follows:

- 228 market research institutes;
- 30 field organisations;
- 49 market research advisers;
- 87 test studios;
- 31 other service providers (EDP evaluation).

In respect of market research institutes, they are mainly so-called mixed institutes, ie most of the time they conduct all common types of market research:

- all methods which serve the purpose of evaluation and collection of information, facts, opinions, attitudes and behaviour;
- study of principles for consumer goods, durable consumer goods and for industrial goods in some areas of the market;
- analysis of wishes, needs and expectations, apprehension etc against producers or service providers, brands, products (so-called motive studies);
- investigation of number of users, buyers' share and their change as well as market fluctuation;
- investigation of brand and company awareness, measurement of goods and brand or producer image;
- product, price, packaging, market and advertising tests;
- advertising media/communication tests;
- analysis of reader structures;
- advertising effectiveness control, etc.;
- measurement of the flow of goods from the producer through wholesaler/retailer to the consumer, with the assistance of various parameters (sales, turnover, market share, distribution, stock turn and others).

Some institutes have specialised and either deal exclusively with panel research (Nielsen, IMS, GfK-Panelforschung) or they concentrate on certain sectors (agricultural research, metal or retail research).

More detailed descriptions of the institutes mentioned can be obtained in the *BVM-Handbuch der Marktforschungsunternehmen 1996* (BVM Manual of Market Research Companies 1996), Deutscher Fachverlag, Frankfurt am Main, page 515.

In addition, there is a further manual: *asw-Handbuch Marketing-Forschung in Deutschland 1995, Unternehmen-Adressen-Daten* (asw-manual Marketing Research in Germany 1995, Companies-Addresses-Data), Schäffer/Poeschel, Stuttgart.

PRIMARY RESEARCH – COSTS AND DURATION

The institutes mentioned in this chapter are mainly primary research institutes, whereas secondary research (desk research) is mainly undertaken by in-house, corporate market researchers.

Costs for primary research depend on a number of parameters which can be illustrated as follows:

- extent of the work prior to market research (size of inquiry, production of questionnaire, identification of target group, etc);
- type of survey (written, personal or telephone survey);
- size of sample;
- methodology of the survey (quota or random);
- normal survey, fixed date or lightning survey;
- number of questions asked;
- difficulties in reaching target persons and conducting interview;
- intensity and methods used to evaluate the survey results;
- commentary concerning results (yes/no) and possibly presentation.

It is easier to identify costs for so-called multiple-topic surveys (omnibus). They merely depend on the type of survey (open, closed), the method (personal, telephone, CATI) and the size of the sample.

In addition, average prices for group discussions (*Context*, issue 13/96, page 11) can be illustrated as follows:

- Provision of participants only approx. DM10,000 + VAT
- With leader approx. DM15,300 + VAT
- With report approx. DM23,000 + VAT
- With simultaneous interpreter approx. DM25,300 + VAT

The prices in Table 14.2 indicate current charges.

Table 14.2 *Current charges for group discussions*

Method used	Selection method	Number	Costs closed question	Costs open question	Duration
CAPI*	Random	1000	1200	2000	2 weeks
Phone	CATI** random	1000	900		2–3 days
Face to face	Random	1000	1300	1800	3 weeks
Face to face	Quota	2500	2300	2900	3 weeks

* CAPI = Computer assisted personal interviews
** CATI = Computer assisted telephone interviews

OFFICIAL AND COMMERCIAL SECONDARY RESEARCH

The following can be named as sources for secondary research (desk research) in Germany:

Official statistics

- Statistical year book for the Federal Republic of Germany (annually)
- Statistical year book for the states
- Statistical year book for German communities
- Statistical year book for large towns

Commercial statistics

Quellen-Lexikon der Marktforschung für Marketing, Kommunikation, Vertrieb und Einkauf aller Branchen (desk research, Source-Encyclopaedia of Market Research for Marketing, Communication, Sales and Purchases for all Sectors), München 1994/95. This encyclopaedia contains all official and commercial secondary sources.

HOW TO FIND THE RIGHT MARKET RESEARCH INSTITUTE

For a company, finding the right working relationship with a suitable market research institute can be compared to a person looking for the right doctor.

The last statement is all the more apt when it comes to cross-boundary market research. No matter how the organisational side is defined (immediate contact with a foreign market research institute or working relationship with a home institute which maintains the relevant contact abroad), it is imperative to find a reliable institute.

There are three ways to get hold of reliable market research partners, either abroad or in general:

A direct working relationship with a foreign institute

If one chooses a direct working relationship with a foreign institute one should check, with the help of a checklist, whether or not the conditions for a beneficial working relationship exist. Such a checklist is included at the end of the chapter.

Some of the most important quality characteristics should be additionally explained:

- An institute's familiarity and the time it has been established are certainly not sufficient alone to judge its performance. However, a successful impact on the market is proof of quality.
- An institute's legal form and its membership of associations and international market research chains expresses a great deal about its reputation and the compliance of its standards, eg concerning confidentiality in respect of working relationships.
- In market research great emphasis is placed on the professional quality of the institute's staff. This can be measured by examining their lecturing posts at universities and polytechnics, at publications and adviser activities.
- One should not neglect appraisal of technical standards (CATI-telephone studio, EDP equipment, interviewees etc) because they ensure that contracts are speedily and methodically processed.
- Because the time of standardised market research is over and specific sector and target group information is always in demand, special sector knowledge can denote sound technical briefing.

All in all one can say that the German institute environment has been safe, so far, from so-called black sheep.

Choosing a domestic institute

A different situation arises when one chooses a domestic institute to undertake foreign market research. Most of the larger German institutes are members of dependent and independent chains. These memberships are illustrated in the *BVM Handbuch der Marktforschungsinstitute 1996* (BVM Manual of Market Research Institutes 1996) previously mentioned.

This type of approach has the following advantages:

- only one communication partner;
- minor communication losses;
- no language difficulties;
- identical survey methods;
- comparable results through standard demographics;
- identical survey period;
- simultaneous presentation of results;
- cost savings;
- clear legal accountability;
- evaluation and use of existing experiences.

Obtaining information from select institutes

The third option concerning quality assurance and reliability of surveys in Germany is to obtain relevant information from the following institutes. *Arbeitskreis deutscher Markt- und Sozialforschungs institute e.V.* (ADM) (Working Group of German Market and Social Research Institutes), Langer Weg 18, 60489 Frankfurt am Main (Tel. 0049 69 97843136, fax 0049 69 97843137). Only companies with several years of continued work in the field of market, opinion and social research and which have more than five employees (without interviewers), amongst them at least one person with a completed university education, can become members of this institute.

Berufsverband deutscher Markt- und Sozialforscher e.V. (BVM) (Association of German Market and Social Researchers), Frankfurter Str. 22, 63065 Offenbach (Tel. 0049 69 8001552, fax 0049 69 8003143). Qualification of BVM members is secured in two ways through its statutes:

- A professional register exists in which personal BVM members are listed who have proven to an acceptance committee that they have three years' (in the case of university graduates this time reduces to two years) work experience in the field of market and/ or social research.
- The federal executive committee can expel members if the reputation or the interests of the BVM have been damaged.

As most of the institutes are either members of the ADM or BVM, whether personal membership or as an institute, the accuracy, merit, quality and reliability of the work undertaken by German market research institutes are guaranteed.

In Germany there is no accepted or known association for the protection or safeguard of the interests of market research sponsors.

FURTHER IMPORTANT INFORMATION ON MARKET RESEARCH

Data protection is of significance beyond the new version of the IHK/ESOMAR international code for the practice of market and social research of 1994, because in Germany there are binding laws which are not contained in the IHK/EOMAR code.

To meet these additional requirements a declaration for the practice of market and social research in the Federal Republic of Germany was added to the IHK/ESOMAR code, which also applies when research is commissioned from abroad or if it is undertaken abroad.

Furthermore, the ADM, BVM and also the Arbeitsgemeinschaft sozial-wissenschaftlicher Institute e. V. (ASI) (Association of social science institutes) have worked on and issued a number of guidelines or principles which directly or indirectly apply to domestic or foreign sponsors/institutes, if research is undertaken in Germany.

The guidelines are the following:

- Guideline for telephone surveys.
- German market research associations' guideline concerning peculiarities of pharmaceutical market research.
- German market research associations' guideline concerning group discussions and quality individual interviews.
- German market research associations' guideline concerning observation methods and observations in respect of demoscopic research.
- Guideline for interviews with minors.

Additional guidelines are being prepared.

For further investigation into the field of market research a list of German language market research literature will be useful. The same statement applies to the most important German language trade magazines, detailed below.

CHECKLIST FOR THE EVALUATION OF MARKET RESEARCH INSTITUTES

1. How well is the institute known?
2. What is its general reputation (image) within the trade and in the eyes of the general public?

3. For how long has the institute been in existence?
4. What is its legal status and who is financially involved in the institute?
5. Does the institute, either as a subsidiary or as a member, belong to an international group of market research institutes?
6. To what trade organisations does the institute or its head belong?
7. Does the institute have a brochure?
8. Are there any regular or *ad hoc* publications which the institute or its leading employees produce?
9. What qualifications does the institute's head have?
10. What qualifications does the manager responsible for the project have?
11. How well is the institute equipped with staff?
12. How well is the institute equipped with resources?
13. Is the institute specialised in any way or does it concentrate on any activities?
14. For what trade sectors, companies or other sponsors has the institute worked in the past (references)?
15. What is the institute's turnover?
16. How many interviewers does the institute employ?
17. What is the standard of the interviewers?
18. How are the interviewers trained and controlled?
19. Is the institute prepared to let the sponsor attend interviews from time to time?
20. Are the interviewers paid adequately and promptly?
21. Does the institute do any principal research of its own accord?
22. Has it developed any particular research methods?
23. Is it keen to experiment?
24. How does the institute respond to enquiries or requests to supply a quotation for a specific research project?
25. How flexible is it in respect of specific client requirements?
26. How do the institute's fees compare to the competition?
27. What is communication like between the institute and the sponsor during a research study?
28. Are agreed deadlines generally kept?
29. How does the institute respond to unexpected difficulties in fieldwork or during the evaluation?
30. In general, what do the institute's reports look like (presentation, clarity, coherence)?
31. Is the institute's head or the project manager able to present research results coherently and convincingly even for market research laypeople?
32. Are client information and specific research results treated with sufficient confidentiality?
33. Does the institute have any connections with science?

TRADE PUBLICATIONS

Planung und Analyse (planning and analysis), Deutscher Fachverlag, Frankfurt am Main.

Marketing-Journal, Verlag Marketingjournal, Hamburg.

M & M, Marktforschung und Management (market research and management), *Zeitschrift für Forschung und Praxis* (magazine for research and practice), Verlag Schäffer und Poeschel, Stuttgart.

15

Agents and Distributors

Ute Sellhorst, Lawyer, Central Organization of Commercial Agents and Brokers

COMMERCIAL AGENTS – PREDOMINANT MARKETING FORCE

Commercial agents are modern service organisations. They perform a selling function, on contractually agreed terms, on behalf of other companies.

Selling is the decisive factor in business. Every item produced is worthless until it is sold. Sales must be effected in a highly competitive and constantly changing market situation. Only efficient and flexible selling ensures sufficient and balanced employment in production. This is the job of commercial agents. In the Federal Republic of Germany, they account for annual sales worth DM400 billion on behalf of their principals.

Commercial agencies are the predominant marketing force in the Federal Republic. According to an investigation carried out by the IFO-Institute for Economic Research, the majority of German manufacturers sell their products through commercial agents. In other words, the majority of German manufacturers assign the selling of their products, customer cultivation and the winning of new customers to trained specialists with particular local knowledge – to commercial agents.

The commercial success of any agency business is closely linked to that of its principals. A commercial agency can only achieve long-term success through obtaining regular orders for its principals from satisfied customers. The hallmark of a successful commercial agent is a range of agencies tailored to meet customers' requirements. Only a commercial agent is in the advantageous position of being able to offer customers such a range of goods.

More than 50 per cent of all commercial agencies have three to six represented firms, 30 per cent represent one or two firms and nearly 20 per cent are engaged in seven and more firms. Even more firms abroad choose the way of distribution by commercial agencies to gain a foothold in the German market: nearly 40 per cent of commercial agencies also represent foreign firms.

The buyer is offered a range of complementary goods by the commercial agent and is therefore able to carry out purchases more rationally with few business partners.

The range of complementary goods constitutes an advantage for the companies represented due to the fact that selling products from one company positively influences sales of another company. Through having several agencies, the commercial agent obtains a general view of the market situation and the solvency of customers. This is to the distinct advantage of the principals.

Irrespective of the level of turnover, principals have well-equipped and efficient sales organisations in every area in which they are represented.

INCREASED SALES THROUGH PERSONAL EFFORT

For the principal the commercial agent is 'Our man in . . .'. To the customer it is the local subsidiary of the firm he or she represents, solving problems of time and distance.

The link between supplier and customer is never broken. The fact that it is not only a technical link but also a human one is of added importance in this highly technical age. The vital factor in even the largest agency firm is the personality of the agent, his or her personal involvement and personal advising of both principals and customers. This does not change the fact that commercial agencies are also scooping out all chances for rationalization and increasing working efficiency. Modern technologies and new media are being used on a wider scale. Using these, order transactions can be effected more economically and in less time.

In addition, modern commercial agencies utilise the manifold opportunities for rationalising through co-operation. The practice of several agency firms establishing their offices and storerooms in the same building reduces their individual overheads and is convenient for customers.

The commercial agency provides a local sales office, which is always ready for action, for all its principals. Many agents in the capital equipment field have their own consultancy and project-planning departments.

The commercial agent arranges his or her own sample displays or presents sample shows of principals' products in collaboration with fellow agents. He or she co-operates in the settling of complaints and in examining the credit-worthiness and solvency of customers, and is always ready to intervene.

For many commercial agencies, the provision of warehousing and distribution facilities has come to be an indispensable supplementary service to principals and customers. More than 41 per cent (and in some branches up to 60 per cent) of all agents have delivery warehouses of varying size and importance.

Sample stockrooms inside commercial agencies are a valuable sales aid to represented firms, and enable customers to examine the principal's complete ranges in detail with a minimum of inconvenience and in the shortest possible time.

Increasing technical advances are producing a growing demand for servicing facilities. This demand is being met by commercial agents, 12 per cent of whom now provide a technical advisory service to their customers.

Technical servicing facilities are particulary important in the capital equipment sector, in which more than 25 per cent of commercial agents provide servicing workshops for their customers.

Sales-related services

- customer recruitment, cultivation and visiting;
- written and telephone offers, sampling;
- advice to customers and suppliers;
- a staffed office, correspondence, follow-up of orders, appointment programmes;
- market studies and market reports;

- processing of complaints;
- sample showrooms;
- collaboration at trade fairs;
- planning and statistics.

Examples of additional services

- warehousing and storage;
- supervision and instructions to warehousing distributors;
- deliveries;
- invoicing, debt collection;
- servicing workshops;
- technical consultancy and project planning;
- sample shows;
- sales promotion by demonstrators and retail merchandisers;
- shelf servicing and delivery service;
- ordering and use of sales aids;
- evaluation of advertising.

ESTABLISHING CONTACTS WITH GERMAN COMMERCIAL AGENTS

The best chance of finding a suitable commercial agent would be a request to the Central Federation of Commercial Agents and Brokers (*Centralvereinigung Deutscher Handelsvertreter- und Handelsmakler Verbände* CDH), Geleniusstr. 1, 50931 Cologne, Germany, *Tel* 0049 221 51 40 43, *Fax* 00 49 221 52 57 67. This federation is the central organisation for commercial agents in Germany. There are 14 regional associations under the auspices of the CDH. These cover the whole of the Federal Republic including 'Eastern' Germany. The regional associations look after their members locally, dealing with business, legal, tax and other issues which are important for the running of a business.

In addition to this, CDH is organised into 20 trade associations, which help the commercial agents solve problems specific to their trade. The trade associations cover most product areas, for example machines, electro-technology, furniture, clothing, food and semi-luxuries etc. There are approximately 19,000 commercial agents and brokers organised within the CDH. These solely concern those companies which mediate between one business enterprise and another, for example between one industrial enterprise and another, or between an industrial enterprise and the wholesale and retail trade. Commercial agents who sell direct to consumers are not members of the CDH.

CDH is a member of the International Union of Commercial Agents and Brokers (IUCAB) which has its headquarters in Amsterdam in the Netherlands (De Lairessestraat 158, NL-1075 HM Amsterdam, Tel. 0031 20 470 01 77, Fax 0031 20 671 09 74). This membership provides very close contact with the other commercial agent associations in Europe.

The tasks of the CDH as a national federation include:

- representing members' interests at relevant ministerial level in the government for all economic policy, tax policy and legal issues;
- representing members' interests on panels of the European Union;
- co-operation with other central organisations from the spheres of industry and commerce, and the Chambers of Commerce and Industry;
- public relations;
- economic studies;
- information on member companies;
- provision of further training courses;
- offering services which are of use to commercial agents.

The CDH publishes a magazine (*HV-Journal* – Commercial Agents & Brokers). Companies looking for an agent may announce their agency offer in an advertisement by describing the product in detail and thus appealing specifically to those commercial agents into whose range their product would fit. Commercial agencies which are interested in the offer will then contact the company directly.

THE COMMERCIAL AGENT AS A MARKETING PARTNER

The commercial agent is the partner of both parties to a sales transaction – seller and buyer. The agent assumes the selling function on behalf of his or her principals. A prerequisite of success is recognition by customers that the independent agent is the most acceptable kind of salesperson.

Parallel to the contractual relationship of the agent to the principals, there exists their common interest in retaining and widening their range of customers and in increasing sales.

The agent as well as employees also has a close and often friendly relationship with customers. This is based on mutual trust, the essential foundation on which successful sales are built.

As a result of his or her all-round activities, the commercial agent is in a position to inform and to advise both principals and customers. This is, in itself, an additional and valuable sales impulse.

More than 90 per cent of all commercial agency firms represent manufacturers; 10 per cent represent wholesalers, mainly importers. The spectrum of agents' customers is wide and varied. A major group of agency firms sells to manufacturers, predominantly agency firms for representing capital equipment and component producers.

A large number of agents co-operate with wholesalers and retailers on the customer side. Examples of other important categories of customers are the craft trades, hotels and restaurants and public authorities.

So-called export agents represent domestic manufacturers for sales to export houses, which are mainly located in Hamburg and Bremen.

Irrespective of the different customer groups, the task of all types of commercial agency firms is the same: to ensure the turnover of their principals and to retain a satisfied range of customers.

Commercial agencies are a branch of commerce in which small firms predominate; 21 per cent of all commercial agencies operate as one-person firms. The holder undertakes every function. Half of all commercial agencies employ up to three employees, 20 per cent work with three to six and 8 per cent employ more than six persons. The commercial agent engages representatives at his or her own financial risk.

The personality of the owner of a commercial agency is the driving force behind it and the guarantor of its successful performance . This applies equally to one-person firms and to agency businesses with a large sales organisation.

THE REMUNERATION OF THE COMMERCIAL AGENT

Normally, the companies represented pay for the services of the commercial agent in the form of a commission, whereby the commission is determined by turnover. Since remuneration is only made when orders are brought in and the relevant business has been carried out successfully, the businesses represented can, from the outset, reckon on a fixed percentage for distribution costs. The commercial agent bears the expenses which occur in the normal course of the business, such as staff, office, keeping a car on the road.

It is also possible that the commercial agent receives remuneration in another form in addition to commission, above all a fixed commission. This particularly applies in the launching of foreign products on to the German market for a set period of time. In addition there is often a special remuneration greater than the normal sales commission for extra services which are rendered in the sales function and for looking after a sales territory assigned to an agent (eg customer service, repairs).

It must be pointed out here that there is no general commission percentage rate which is the basis for all commercial agency contracts. The percentage commission is negotiated between the company represented and the commercial agency on an individual basis. For this reason it is not possible here to give figures for commission rates negotiated in practice. Commission percentages are agreed between 1 per cent and 25 per cent, for example. The basis for calculation is the extent of the services which are to be performed by the commercial agency and the costs incurred in conjunction with this.

LEGAL BASIS

The law on commercial agency is recorded in Germany in sections 84–92c of the German Commercial Code. The rights and obligations of the commercial agent and of the principal, commission entitlements, termination of the agency contract, claim for indemnity and other points are regulated here.

In spite of the fact that all EU member states implemented the prescriptions of the European Directive relating to self-employed commercial agents (86/653/EEC), national laws still differ. False implementation, indefinite terms and the scope of discretion give reason for the different legal positions.

The following describes the main prescriptions of the German Commercial Law:

Form of the contract

The contract between the commercial agent and the principal does not require a particular form, which means it can be concluded orally, in an exchange of letters or as a conclusive act (eg after repeated mediation in business deals). However, each party to the contract can demand that the contents of the contract be recorded in a document signed by the other (section 85 of the German Commercial Code).

Specimen contracts can be ordered at CDH Wirtschaftsdienst-GmbH, Geleniusstr. 1, 50931 Cologne, Germany, Tel. 0049 221 51 40 43, Fax 0049 221 52 57 67.

Commission

The usual remuneration for the commercial agent is commission, ie he or she receives in recompense for activity a specified percentage of the sales revenue accruing to the principal as a result of his or her mediation. In accordance with section 87, paragraph 1 of the German Commercial Code, a prerequisite for the right to commission is that the commercial agent's activity has led to the conclusion of a transaction between the principal and the customer. The commission is, therefore, a form of remuneration dependent on success, so that the principal can expect variable sales costs. He or she only incurs costs if the commercial agent is successful in his or her mediation, whereas he or she must pay fixed costs with other modes of selling and distribution even if the efforts to gain orders are unsuccessful.

However, the commercial agent does not receive the commission until the principal has fulfilled the order. If the transaction is not executed as concluded or only partly so by the principal, the right to commission ceases to apply if and in so far as the non-execution arises from circumstances beyond the principal's control.

Commission must also be paid for repeat and supplementary orders from customers whom the commercial agent had already recruited for similar transactions. If a particular district or group of customers is assigned to the commercial agent, he or she has a right to commission for transactions concluded with persons in this district or among these customers even in dealings where he or she has not been directly involved.

The rate of commission is negotiated on an individual basis. If there is no such agreement, the usual rate is assumed by act of law (section 87b, paragraph 1 of the German Commmercial Code) to be acceptable to both parties. The commercial agent may receive a fixed allowance or another form of remuneration in addition to the commission and by virtue of an agreement to that effect.

Termination

The agency contractual relationship is terminated:

- by time if the contractual relationship was agreed for a fixed period;

- by bankruptcy on the part of the principal, but not when the commercial agent is bankrupt, however;
- by rescindment by mutual agreement (cancellation agreement);
- by dismissal with notice. The law provides that the following minimum periods to terminate the contract be observed (section 89, paragraph 1 of the German Commercial Code):
  - in the 1st contract year, 1 month;
  - in the 2nd contract year, 2 months;
  - in the 3rd contract year, 3 months;
  - from the 6th contract year on, 6 months.

  Notice of termination is only admissible at the end of a calendar month. It is possible to extend the periods to terminate, but the period for the principal may not be shorter than for the commercial agent.
- by termination without notice if there is just cause (section 89a of the German Commercial Code) so that the party terminating cannot be expected to wait until the contract can be ended by ordinary notice of termination;
- by the death of the commercial agent. Where a company or partnership acts as an agency – OHG (general commercial partnership), KG (limited commercial partnership), GmbH (limited liability company) – the continued existence of the contractual relationship is not fundamentally affected by the death of one of its members. Nor does the death of the principal automatically terminate the contractual relationship.

Claims for indemnity

When the contractual relationship is terminated, the commercial agent is entitled to claim for indemnity under the conditions specified in section 89b of the German Commercial Code. This constitutes a claim for compensation for the regular customers established and cultivated by the commercial agent and relinquished to the principal when the contractual relationship expires.

The claim for compensation requires:

- termination of the contract;
- considerable advantages for the principal. The principal must also enjoy substantial advantages after the contract has been terminated from business connections with new customers established by the commercial agent;
- commercial agent's loss of commission. Once the contract expires or is terminated, the commercial agent must lose the claims to commission which would normally be his or hers if the contract had continued to exist. A forecast must be made to predict the

extent of repeat and supplementary orders which can be expected
from the regular customers established and cultivated by the
commercial agent;
- equity. The payment of compensation must be based on principles
  of equity, taking all circumstances into account. First to be
  considered are factors reducing compensation (eg pension scheme
  funded by the principal, activities on the part of the commercial
  agent which were in violation of the contract, particularly
  favourable terms of contract). Reduction of compensation can be
  offset by other factors however (eg unexpected termination, grossly
  inappropriate reasons for terminating the contract, increased costs
  in introducing a product, behaviour of principal which is contrary
  to the contract, below average commission);
- raising of the claim.

Limitation period

All claims arising from the contractual relationship become prescriptive
after four years (section 88 of the German Commercial Code). A
contractual reduction of the limitation period is admissible, but not
unilaterally to the disadvantage of the commercial agent (principle of
equal treatment). The period begins with the end of the year in which
the claim was due.

CONCLUSION

There is no generally applicable recommendation as to whether a
company should work together with a commercial agent or whether it
is advisable for a company to set up its own external sales function. This
decision can only be taken from the perspective of a particular company,
whereby the criteria of cost, success and risk have to be taken into
consideration.

When making a comparison of these systems, the commercial agent is
often assessed as being the more efficient distribution channel, in
particular for foreign suppliers. This assessment is also supported by
the continually rising demand of foreign companies for German
commercial agents. Important reasons for this in addition to advantages
of cost are: the entrepreneurial commitment of the commercial agent;
his or her personal involvement for the company represented and the
customers to be looked after; knowledge specific to the trade and of the
customers in that trade; as well as, in most cases, the years of business
experience behind him or her.

DATA ON THE COMMERCIAL AGENCIES BRANCH

- Commercial agencies in Germany – est. 64,000.
- Total value of merchandise sold on commission basis – est. DM400 billion.
- Market share of domestic sales – est. 30 per cent.
- Commercial agencies with foreign representatives – 40 per cent.
- Average number of products/firms per commercial agency – five.
- Average sales volume per commercial agency – est. DM7.1 million ($4.4 million).
- Average gross commission revenue per commercial agency – est. DM290,000 ($181,000)
- Total cost as a percentage of total revenue – est. 96 per cent.
- Average number of employees – four.
- Customer base
  - retail: 54 per cent;
  - wholesale: 52 per cent;
  - industry: 47 per cent;
  - gastronomy: 7 per cent.

16

Technology Transfer

Brian Padgett, Managing Director,
The Technology Exchange Ltd

The term 'technology transfer' encompasses a wide variety of activities, both formal and informal, which enable new developments, inventions and know-how to be passed from one organisation, individual or institution to another.

METHODS OF TRANSFER

The formal methods include the licence agreement; a design, research or development contract in which the rights are assigned; and a business franchise where the know-how is transferred as part of the business package.

Informal transfers occur through publication in scientific and technical journals by university researchers and others, through training programmes and educational courses, and frequently illegally by reverse engineering or redesigning of products purchased on the open market to avoid conflict with protected intellectual property or by industrial espionage during the pre-launch phase of a new product or process. The published patent itself is a prime source of information on a new development and this will be scrutinised by competitors to see if there are any loopholes which may not have been covered and which allow use of the idea without infringement of the patent, or if the result can be achieved in a better or cheaper way.

This chapter will focus, of course, on the more formal methods of transfer, but it is important to be aware of the informal methods since they represent a threat which must be countered by careful protection of intellectual property rights through patent, registered and unregistered design, copyright and trade mark protection. Informal methods also represent a potential leakage of intellectual property before the rights are fully protected and this has been particularly true in the case of papers describing the results of university research published in scientific journals. The number and quality of such papers from an individual researcher have been major factors in determining future academic advancement, and it may be a disadvantage to delay such publication until patent protection has been granted since there is a risk that by this time the research results may have been superseded and hence would not be accepted for publication.

ACADEMIC SOURCES OF TECHNOLOGY

In the UK, most universities regard the intellectual property generated by both staff and students as the property of the university where this has been generated out of work conducted on projects within the university. The more enlightened universities have appreciated a need to share the rewards with the researcher up to 50 per cent of the total, and some universities even cover the cost of IPR protection and licence negotiation out of their share of the rewards.

In most UK universities industrial liaison offices have been established as separate departments, and in some German and UK universities institutes have been established for the purpose of commercialising intellectual property arising out of university research and for sourcing research contracts from industry. In Germany these UN-institutes generally take the form of a partnership of public and private interests in which the professors and senior researchers can gain their reward from the commercialisation of their research results, whereas in the UK these bodies are usually wholly owned by the university (personal communication from Peter Wolfmeyer, Deputy Managing Director, ZENIT GmbH, Mülheim).

The result of this difference in approach has been that in Germany the academic researchers have tended to focus their work on the application of their research results, including the development of manufacturing processes to ensure that commercial advantage can be delivered through both product quality improvements and increased manufacturing efficiency.

It is not uncommon for German professors to have served a craft apprenticeship at the start of their careers, whereas in the UK it would be rare indeed to find even one who has achieved academic distinction from such a background (personal communication from Prof. M. E. Cooley, Member of Advisory Board, Institute of Work and Technology, University of Bremen).

IMPORTANCE OF TECHNOLOGY TRANSFER TO INDUSTRY

The concept of technology transfer has assumed a greater importance in industry due to the growth in number of small and medium-sized enterprises, which has to some extent compensated for the downsizing and restructuring of many major companies over the past couple of decades.

Trading technology was, up the late 1960s, an activity which took place mainly between universities, research institutes and large organisations or between the large organisations themselves.

The method usually involved direct confidential introduction preceded by a minimum of promotional activity. This generally resulted in an exclusive or sole licence to a non-competing organisation which enabled it to utilise a specific piece or a portfolio of intellectual property from a university, research organisation or resulting from the internal R&D activity of the licensor firm where this did not correspond to its own immediate market interests.

Much of this surplus R&D arose at the time when major firms were being seriously advised to 'stick to the knitting', in other words to concentrate on their principal product strengths. This advice was given by consultants who were employed to improve industrial competitiveness in the face of competition from the USA, Germany and increasingly from the Far East and especially from Japan.

Such spin-offs of non-core technologies and activities to other firms who were better placed to exploit them were common up to a few years ago, when R&D activity was scaled down and refocused onto mainstream objectives to improve short-term results and increase share values.

More recently this displaced research and development activity from industry has resulted in a large crop of high technology small and medium-sized enterprises (SMEs) who have developed good new products from a modest resource base and who have recognised the need to involve outside partners in their manufacture and commercialisation. This strategy has particularly been applied to overseas markets which the SME's own marketing plans would not otherwise have allowed it to reach before its technology developments had been superseded. This is particularly true for fast-moving fields such as micro-electronics and biotechnology.

The approach which The Technology Exchange has recommended to these firms involves, where possible, the offer of a non-exclusive licence to a range of potential partners who could actively manufacture and market for their own applications or territories. To recover the investment in research and development and the costs of intellectual property protection in all the countries where the product can be marketed from a network of licensees can result in low up-front costs, which would be more attractive than pursuing alternative lines of development even where the licensees have the resources to undertake this.

This strategy can be vital if the technology development needs to be widely adopted to ensure compatibility between systems and products. A prominent example is the Dolby system of noise reduction in hi-fi systems where tapes and records may be transferred from recording machines to a number of different models of reproduction equipment.

In a similar way, the outcome of the battle for supremacy between the VHS and Betamax video systems depended essentially on the number and importance of the manufacturers licensed to use these systems.

SELECTING YOUR PARTNERS

Before embarking on a search for partners, either as a source of technology or as an aid to commercialisation outside your own markets, you must first of all determine the role which you wish to play in the total business activity as this develops into the future.

The type of partner chosen should then ideally have complementary skills and strengths if the relationship is to prove a lasting one.

You might, for example, consider as a partner a major multinational firm which can provide volume manufacture and immediate global distribution of your product. But such an organisation could easily undertake any of the complementary roles which you might wish to retain, with the exception, perhaps, of your existing intellectual property.

A smaller firm could be chosen as a partner which may not have access to resources on the same scale. But, if it has products of its own which overlap with your own products, it may be possible to cross-license complementary products, thus adding significantly to the product range of both organisations without involving any additional research and development cost or initial licence payments.

In comparison with the appointment of distributors and agents, licensed manufacture can avoid import duties and a partner who has invested significant sums in the manufacture and marketing of your product alongside its own is much less likely than a distributor or agent to be persuaded to leave you in order to market the product of a competitor attracted by a higher sales commission. Such desertions normally occur, of course, with those agents who have proved most successful in establishing and developing a new market for your product.

STAGES IN THE LICENSING PROCESS

For smaller licensees who may not be able to shoulder the financial risk of market failure, the licensing process frequently commences by distribution of the partner's product in order to establish the level of market demand and price sensitivity.

This, of course, only applies where the product is already in manu-facture, either by the licensor or by an existing licensee, and delays the requirement for investment in manufacture, although some modifi-cations may be required to suit local standards and legislation.

The need for low-risk market testing tends to rule out the acquisition of early-stage developments or research results from a university, research organisation or even from a private inventor, unless the cost of manufacture is low because the technology is well known and the product is uncomplicated. The royalties required by the licensor may be higher for products at an advanced stage of development. They present a lower risk for the licensee and both market price and manufacturing cost may be more easily established.

Even large organisations who want to license a complex product are very reluctant to start the new project from a patent which requires them to produce the drawings, manufacture the tooling, source the bought-out parts and materials, then develop and test the prototype followed by pre-production, production and marketing. All of this represents a considerable investment, a high risk and can occupy several years before success or failure in the marketplace can be assessed. During this period, of course, the development of technology has moved on and product improvements by competitors can easily outdate the technology involved in the product which has been licensed. This will reduce both its market potential and sales value and may eliminate them altogether.

Most complex products are in fact transferred by a process known as gradual import substitution and commence by importing the product on consignment, possibly relabelling under your own logo or by local assembly from knock-down kits of parts. This has the advantage of enabling the licensee to become familiar with servicing the product, which may be required even before local manufacture has commenced.

Local manufacture usually starts on a part-by-part basis and the investment in tooling and manufacture can then be structured to match the income generated from profits on product sales. Usually the process starts by local manufacture of the heavier, lower-technology parts, investing in the production of more parts as the market demand grows until finally the higher-technology or quality-critical parts are being manufactured.

During this process it may be necessary to involve your suppliers in the technology transfer process, since some specifications of materials and special fasteners or seals etc may not be locally available. The transfer of the manufacture of some proprietary items to your suppliers will involve separate licence deals between third parties or sub-licences from your principal licensor partner.

From the point of view of the licensor, the continued supply of even one critical component or secret ingredient simplifies the calculation of royalty payments, since this gives the licensor a means of measuring the number or quantity being manufactured by the licensee. Some licensors may require the return of any faulty or damaged components supplied in this way if disputes are likely to arise regarding production output for royalty calculation.

EVALUATION OF TECHNOLOGY AND CALCULATION OF ROYALTY RATES

This is a broad topic which could justify a whole book to itself, but for our purposes there are some simple rules which, if not definitive, at least provide a starting point for the negotiation between licensor and licensee.

There are usually two forms of payment to be negotiated within a licence agreement.

Initial payment on signature of agreement

This payment covers at least the cost to the licensor of transferring the technology and know-how to the licensee in order for the licensee to be able to commence manufacture. This may also include the opportunity cost to the licensor of the staff time and resources required to assist the licensee in recruiting and training the staff, selecting, purchasing and setting up the plant, specifying and ordering the materials and in the manufacture, testing, marketing and servicing of the product. It may also include the cost of modifying the product design to meet the licensor's obligations to comply with national standards of safety, performance and environmental legislation. Professional indemnity insurance of the licensor and staff may also be required.

Some allowance for the recovery of R&D cost may be included, but this is normally recovered from later royalty payments.

Royalty payments

These payments are usually fixed at a percentage of the arm's-length selling price of the product being licensed. It is calculated on the basis of sharing the profit margin between the licensor and the licensee from the contribution which each is considered to have made to the generation of that profit.

As a rule of thumb, it is frequently considered that between 10 and 33 per cent of the profit margin may be due to the efforts of the licensor and the most frequently quoted figure is 25 per cent. Thus if the profit margin on the product is 20 per cent this would result in a royalty rate of 5 per cent on the arm's-length net selling price of the product which would be payable to the licensor. By 'arm's-length' we mean the sale to a third party who is unconnected to the licensee, i.e. not to a company's subsidiary or from an internal company transaction.

This rule of thumb is interpreted very widely from industry to industry and, during royalty rate negotiations, reference will usually be made to the royalty rates which are commonly used within the industry. However, information on royalty rates is notoriously difficult to obtain, since such information is normally regarded as a commercial secret shared only by the parties to the agreement. Royalty information may only become publicly known when disputes over royalty rates arise and are decided in court.

As a general rule, however, a high-technology, state-of-the-art product for which R&D cost has been high and where the life of the product may be short due to rapid changes of technology would justify a higher royalty rate and this may reach 12 or even 15 per cent of the net selling price. Conversely, a long-life low-technology product which can continue to be sold for the full life of the patent may justify a much lower royalty rate of even 1 or 2 per cent of net selling price.

Royalty rates on patents which relate to only one aspect or part of the end product or process are difficult to determine unless the part in question has its own independent market value. But the royalty rate may be applied to the whole product in cases where the patent or development has been the factor which was responsible for the success of the product as a whole.

Sometimes the value of the patented development may represent a different contribution to the individual selling price of a range of products produced using the patent. An example in which The Technology Exchange was involved several years ago was a microprocessor-based control system for electric motors where the microprocessor was a fixed value element in control systems costing from £200 to £400,000. In this case the royalty was a fixed sum in pounds or dollars linked either to inflation or to the total cost of the parts covered by the patent.

Minimum royalties

The grant of an exclusive licence usually includes a performance clause which requires the licensee to use its best endeavours to promote and exploit the technology. To enforce this, the contract usually includes a minimum royalty guarantee which operates after a certain period to allow time for manufacturing preparations to be completed. Minimum royalty levels in years 2, 3 and 4 etc may be payable by the licensee whether sales have been generated or not. The minimum royalty guarantees are usually based on a fixed proportion, e.g. 50 per cent of anticipated sales levels.

Sources of technology and licensees in Germany

Germany benefits from a large number of very active and professional licence agents who both source technology for their clients and can promote licence opportunities to German manufacturers. A number of Regional Development Agencies and Chambers of Industry and Commerce – the Industrie und Handels Kammer (IHK) network throughout Germany – also have developments from their members or from firms in their region available for exploitation.

The Technology Exchange has worked successfully for a number of years with several organisations, notably ZENIT of Mülheim in Nord Rhein

Westphalia, TVA in Berlin and more recently with VDI/VDE, the professional engineering institutions in Germany, in networks involving similar organisations in other European countries who assist industry to adopt new technology developments from universities and encourage cross-border co-operation between enterprises in their own regions.

Intellectual property protection in Germany is taken very seriously indeed and there are around 900 patent agents; their professional association is the Patentanwaltskammer in Munich.

Much of the independent research in Germany is conducted by the Fraunhöfer Institute, comprising around 50 separate divisions mainly located close to universities and concentrating on specific areas of technology. All concentrate on applied research and operate mainly under contract to industry, but are part-financed from public funds. The Fraunhöfer Institute in Karlsruhe has a role in technology forecasting for industry similar to the role performed in the UK by the DTI's Technology Foresight Panels. A number of independent research institutes are run and owned by large companies, e.g. Krupp of Essen. Fundamental research is carried out by organisations such as the Max Planck Institute (personal communication from Peter Wolfmeyer).

All of the publicly funded research institutes are, like similar UK research organisations, seeking to reduce their dependence on public funding and are willing to perform contract research for non-German firms and to license research and development results outside Germany. A list of useful addresses is given in the Appendix.

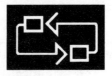

17

Joint Ventures in Eastern Europe through Germany

Michael Harms, Bureau for East-West Co-operation

THE FEDERAL REPUBLIC OF GERMANY'S BILATERAL BUSINESS RELATIONSHIPS WITH CENTRAL AND EASTERN EUROPEAN COUNTRIES

Business relationships with the 10 East-Central and South-Eastern European countries with which the European Union has signed association treaties (ratified and therefore legal with Poland, Hungary, Czech Republic, Slovak Republic, Romania, Bulgaria; signed with Estonia, Latvia, Lithuania and Slovenia) have developed particularly dynamically. In 1995 goods traffic with these countries increased by 22.3 per cent, while Germany's total foreign trade only grew by 4 per cent. German exports to countries with EU membership amounted to DM43.4 billion, an increase of 21 per cent. Imports from these countries amounted to DM41.1 billion, representing an increase of 23.8 per cent. The German trade surplus reduced to DM2.3 billion compared to DM2.7 billion in 1994.

In 1995 trade with former Soviet countries only increased by 0.1 per cent. This can be traced back to the reduction in German exports to Russia by 4.3 per cent to DM10.3 billion and the reduction of German exports to Kazakstan by 50 per cent to DM409 million. In 1995 the trade volume with former Soviet states amounted to DM30 billion. German exports of DM14.6 billion (−3.1 per cent) were matched with imports to

Germany of DM15.5 billion (+3.3 per cent). The trade surplus of DM905 million is due to a negative balance amounting to DM3.3 billion for Russian trade movements, whereas in respect of trade movements with all other former Soviet countries Germany achieved export surpluses.

With a trade turnover of DM25.1 billion, Poland was for the first time Germany's largest trading partner among the Central and Eastern European countries. In second place was the Russian Federation with DM23.9 billion, followed by the Czech Republic with a turnover of DM22.4 billion.

Developments among East-Central and South-Eastern European countries in terms of market economy restructuring and increasing economic networking with the EU and with Germany are also evident in the development of the goods structure. For 1995, 44.7 per cent of exports to Germany were made up of machinery, electronic, mechanical and optical products and vehicles, ie industrial goods, which can be used directly for industrial modernisation purposes. The international competitiveness of these countries has increased further. This is illustrated through the exports to Germany of industrial finished products, of the above categories, which have risen to 25.7 per cent.

The industrial restructuring process in the former Soviet countries made less progress, as the structure of the bilateral goods traffic illustrates. In 1995, 51.4 per cent of German exports to the former Soviet countries were made up of industrial finished products, of the above categories. German imports, however, were mainly raw materials and semi-finished products. It is a characteristic that among Russian exports to Germany in 1995, finished products had only a 10 per cent share, while technological goods such as vehicles, machines and electronic products only accounted for 2.1 per cent.

CO-OPERATION AND DIRECT INVESTMENTS

Direct German investments, in the shape of establishing companies, branch offices and joint ventures, are becoming increasingly important for both sides. For Eastern European countries this means long-term engagement: they increase the productivity of the investment and they are the basis for long-term employment. Through production in Eastern Europe German companies reduce their costs and are therefore able to work more effectively in the growing markets of this region.

At the end of 1993 the volume of direct German investments in the Central and Eastern European countries amounted to DM5.5 billion, at the end of 1994 it was around DM8.0 billion and at the end of 1995 it was already above the DM10 billion level, measured with the help of the so-called transfer performances of direct German investments, ie new investments minus returns. In 1994 in excess of DM2.7 billion net filtered into Central and Eastern Europe; in 1995 this amount was roughly DM4.3 billion.

On the whole, Central and Eastern European reform countries have gained in popularity in the eyes of the German investor. The intensive involvement of the German economy, however, has developed quite differently. The different investment conditions and motives of German businesses contribute to this situation.

Some 70 per cent of all German capital investments concentrate on the Czech Republic, Hungary and Poland. These countries have made reforms and have realised them consistently. Economic development is positive, they have traditionally had close economic relationships with Germany and have acknowledged that they share certain attitudes. However, the markets in these countries (except perhaps Poland) are relatively limited. When it comes to investments through German companies in these countries, cost reduction is the principal consideration.

Direct German investments in the successor countries of the former Soviet Union were very low in 1995 – compared with the potential of these countries – at around DM150 billion (net transfer performance). Of these figures, Russia's share alone was around DM120 billion. In the other countries of the former Soviet Union, as in the other South-Eastern European states, direct German investments play only a minor role. Investment conditions in these countries are sometimes very difficult and the economic crisis has certainly not been overcome. If one considers the potentially huge market volume of these countries, German engagement is decided on considerations relating to the shaping of the market and market protection.

GERMAN INSTITUTIONS FOR ADVICE AND CONTACT SEARCH IN EASTERN EUROPE

In Germany there are a number of institutions which sponsor the deepening of economic co-operation with Eastern Europe. Their service portfolio is mostly geared to suit the German economy, but to a large extent it can also be used by British companies (preferably with a German partner). Addresses can be found in the appendix. The most important institutions are mentioned below:

Ost-Ausschuß und Kooperationsbüro der Deutschen Wirtschaft (Eastern Committee and Bureau for East-West Co-operation)

The eastern committee of the German economy is one of the institutions founded by the top German economic associations, with the aim of sponsoring German companies' economic relationships with Eastern European partners. It co-ordinates the German economy's interests in terms of forming economic relationships with Eastern Europe; it informs and advises Germany's business community about a variety of subjects; it maintains contacts in Eastern Europe for the German economy and organises information events in Germany and abroad on this subject.

The Bureau for East-West Co-operation was founded in 1991 by the Bundesverband der Deutschen Industrie (Federal Association of German Industry), the Deutscher Industrie- und Handelstag (Umbrella Organisation for German Chambers of Industry & Commerce) and the ost-Ausschuß der Deutschen Wirtschaft (Eastern committee of the German economy) with the aim of assisting, in particular, companies of the new federal states in re-establishing and developing their economic relationships with Eastern Europe. In the meantime, the co-operation office has established itself as a contact point across Germany for German businesses which wish to find co-operation partners, initiate trade relationships or want to invest in the former Soviet Union or the Central and Eastern European states.

Foreign chambers of commerce and delegate offices of the German economy

Germany maintains a system of bilateral foreign chambers of commerce worldwide. This makes it easier for German businesses but also for companies in the partner countries to find their feet in the respective sale and purchase markets. So far in Eastern Europe there are German-Hungarian, German-Czech and German-Polish chambers of industry and commerce. In other Eastern European countries there are either delegate offices or representatives of the German economy, as a first step towards foreign chambers of commerce.

Bundesstelle für Außenhandelsinformation (BfAi) (Federal office for foreign trade information)

The BfAi is the central federal institution for foreign trade information in Germany. It maintains a worldwide network of correspondents and provides a multitude of publications relating to sector or regional subjects. For Eastern Europe there is a specific magazine called *BfAi-Osteuropa*. A current publication list may be obtained from the BfAi.

Enquiries or offers from foreign companies will be published free of charge in the BfAi magazine *Märkte der Welt* (markets of the world).

The most important German financing and promotion programmes for Central and Eastern Europe

The federal government and various German financial institutions have devised a series of promotions and financing programmes, in addition to their advice-only initiatives. The major ones can be found in Table 17.1.

Table 17.1 The most important German financing and promotion programmes for Central and Eastern Europe

Institution/ programme	Financing/key aspect of promotion	Financing/promotion mode	Address/contact partner
Federal government/ TRANSFORM-programme/ Responsibility and co-ordination through Federal Ministry for Economy and Foreign Office, KfW (see below)	Advice programme for all Central and Eastern European and former Soviet states for the introduction of democracy and a social economy	Full financing of advice only, no export or economic financing	BMWi, Villemombler Str. 76, D-53123 Bonn Tel: +49 (0)228 6152760 Fax: +49 (0)228 6152662 Total co-ordination: State Secretary (ex office) Walter Kittel
Deutsche Investitions- u. Entwicklungs-gesellschaft (DEG) (German investment and development society)	Investment financing and advice for German businesses in Central and Eastern European and former Soviet states	Loans and assistance for subsidiaries of German businesses in Eastern Europe and joint ventures between German and Eastern European businesses, subsidies for the preparation of studies	DEG, Belvederestr. 14, D-50933 Köln, Hans Joachim Hebgen Tel: +49 (0)228 4986402 Fax: +49 (0)228 4986105

Table 17.1 *The most important German financing and promotion programmes for Central and Eastern Europe* (cont)

Institution/ programme	Financing/key aspect of promotion	Financing/promotion mode	Address/contact partner
Kreditanstalt für Wiederaufbau (KfW) (Bank for reconstruction)	Export and investment financing, advice service for German businesses in Central and Eastern European and former Soviet states	Financing of investments of medium-sized German businesses in Eastern Europe, financing of investment goods exports on the basis of Hermes cover, various advice services in conjunction with TRANSFORM	KfW, Palmengartenstr. 5–9, D-60325 Frankfurt Dr. Günter Zenk Tel: +49 (0)69 74312578 Fax: +49 (0)69 74312944 Advice centre Berlin: Tel: +49 (0)30 20264316 Fax: +49(0)30 20264192
Deutsche Ausgleichsbank (German equalisation bank)	Financing of advice services in Central and Eastern Europe, Russia, Ukraine and White Russia. Start-up assistance	Long-term, low-interest loans for business start-ups in Hungary, Albania, Croatia, Macedonia, Slovenia and Novosibirsk, advice services in conjunction with TRANSFORM	Deutsche Ausgleichsbank, Ludwig-Erhard-Platz 3, D-53170 Bonn Herr Schlegel, Frau Berg Tel: +49 (0)228 8312670 Fax: +49 (0)228 8312919
Ausfuhrgewährleistungen des Bundes (Hermes)	Export credit insurance for German exports to Central and Eastern European and former Soviet states, project financing and countertrade	Stipulation of covering limits for various countries while sponsoring East German businesses; C&EE: mainly bank guarantee required; former Soviet: mainly state guarantee required	Hermes-Kreditversicherungs AG, Friedensallee 254, D-22763 Hamburg Dr Eckhardt Moltrecht Tel: +49 (0)40 88341057 Fax: +49 (0)40 88347744

18

The Icing on the Cake – Investment Incentives in Germany

*John M. Zindar, Foreign Investor Information Center, Federal Ministry of Economics, Berlin**

GENERAL BACKGROUND AND POLICY

When speaking of financial incentives for investors in the Federal Republic of Germany, there is an important distinction as well as a non-distinction to be made up front.

The non-distinction is that German and non-German investors alike are eligible for the same financial incentives. Although the foreign investor may have to overcome the native's comparative advantages in market, business culture and linguistic knowledge, he/she can expect equal treatment playing field in the passing out of incentive packages.

However, foreign investors do need to navigate through the process of securing the maximum possible amount of state financial support. This chapter intends to give a brief practical introduction to doing just that. Further detailed information and guidance can be obtained from the offices in Appendix 1.

---

*Opinions expressed are those of Mr. Zindar, not of the Federal Ministry of Economics. Furthermore, the ministry takes no responsibility for the information in this chapter.

The distinction is between the programmes and money available for eastern Germany (the new federal states) and western Germany (the old federal states). Ever since reunification in 1990, the new federal states have been eligible to award the highest financial packages allowable under EU regulations. The western states, on the other hand, comprising one of the most developed and well-off regions in the world, are limited to offering significantly smaller and more restrictive incentives.

There is good reason for the differences in financial assistance programmes. It is fair to say that what was once the German Democratic Republic (GDR) is experiencing the biggest 'Bang' in the history of economic transition. No other former East Bloc economy has gone through the thorough and wrenching changes, so quickly, as have the new federal states. Overnight, currency union and rapid privatisation set the economy on its head; GDP shrunk by a third in 1991; industrial production dropped even further; trade links with Eastern Europe were severely disrupted and a third of all workers were suddenly idle. Attracting investment is an essential ingredient of the rebuilding process.

Across Germany many of the loan programmes are similar, as are the grant programmes that support research and development, employee training and various consulting services. The big differences are found in tax incentives and investment grants.

In eastern Germany one of the most lucrative incentives is the investment allowance (*Investitionszulage*). These tax credits account for fully half of the value of disbursed incentives in the new states. Small firms can deduct 10 per cent and large firms deduct 5 per cent of their investment from the tax debt. This allowance does not exist in western Germany.

Investors in the East are also eligible for exemptions from capital asset taxes (*Vermögensteuer* and *Gewerbekapitalsteuer*) and capital gains taxes, while in the West they are not. The highest additional (on top of the normal straight-line method) depreciation allowance (*Sonderabschreibung*) rate in the East was 50 per cent until the end of 1996, and will be 40 per cent after that, while in the West the top rate is 20 per cent.

The other significant difference is found in The Improvement of Regional Economic Structures Programme (*Gemeinschaftsaufgabe* or *GA* funds). In the new federal states most small firms can be refunded up to 50 per cent (large firms up to 35 per cent) of their investment. In the old federal states those rates are 28 per cent and 18 per cent respectively. Furthermore, while all of eastern Germany is eligible for GA funding, only areas inhabited by an estimated 22 per cent of the population in western Germany can offer such grants.

An important exception to all of the above is western Berlin, which is now eligible for most of the same programmes and rates as those offered in eastern Berlin. For more details on all of the major programmes, please refer to the overview at the end of this chapter.

At first these discrepancies in incentives were taken for granted by the old federal states of West Germany as just one of the burdens to be borne for the greater good of unification. But by 1993, when the post-unification boom recession set in, the debate over the levels and effectiveness of all of the government's transfers to the states of former East Germany intensified. The imposition of the 7.5 per cent solidarity surcharge on individual income and business profit taxes to help pay for the transfers also underscored to everyone, East and West, the high costs of unification. Revelations of a number of cases of abuse, where subsidies had disappeared or been misallocated or wasted, fuelled the discussion.

However within the larger picture of massive transfers from western to eastern Germany since reunification, subsidies provided to encourage private investment in job-creating undertakings have been relatively small. By the end of the six-year period 1991–96, financial awards for investors will have amounted to less than DM120 billion, or about 13 per cent of the estimated DM902.1 billion in total state handouts to the new federal states. Far larger outlays are provided for such things as keeping loss-making firms afloat, the servicing of debts from the GDR era, injections into state and municipality budgets, unemployment programmes, infrastructure and housing.

Many of the special and generous incentives for eastern Germany were to expire at the end of 1995 or 1996, bringing them more in line with those in western Germany. While in the West complaints were heard about the costs and unfair advantages, defenders of the programmes argued that eastern Germans also paid their fair share in taxes and it was ultimately in the western side's best interest that the eastern side attracted investment and developed into a mature market as rapidly as possible. Besides, the vast majority of financial incentives are awarded to the new federal states' biggest investors by far – investors from the old federal states.

At another level, the discussion over extending the special incentive deadlines for eastern Germany occurred between the economics ministry, headed by Günter Rexrodt, who argued strongly for the need to extend, and the finance ministry, headed by Theo Waigel, who needs to cut government spending so that Germany can meet the Maastricht convergence goals for EMU, set to start in 1999.

In the end, all the major programmes due to expire were extended through the end of 1998, although some of the conditions did change. Additionally, a few new programmes were announced in 1996. This should help ensure that the impressive investment figures in eastern Germany continue. From the beginning of 1991 through the end of 1996 it is estimated that DM953.4 billion will have been invested in the former GDR. The lion's share (84 per cent) is accounted for by private investment, far outdistancing the strong public investments in transportation, communication and other infrastructure projects. Per capita private investment in the East has outpaced that in the West ever since 1993.

Yet the efficacy of financial incentives in attracting investment is difficult to assess. It may be impossible to calculate just how much of the nearly DM800 billion in private investments in the new federal states were drawn to the region by incentives. Rarely do investors make a decision based solely on such packages; incentives are only one of many factors that are considered by business strategists.

Foreign investors are most often attracted to Germany by its reputation for quality and productivity, by its world-class infrastructure, and most importantly, by the largest, richest market in Europe – integrated within the EU and especially well-connected to the emerging markets of Central and Eastern Europe. The incentive programmes are, therefore, often the icing on the cake. Many investors do, however, cite that financial support can be decisive when establishing the physical presence needed to best take advantage of the market opportunities.

It is probably safe to project that special programmes to attract investment to the new federal states will remain in place well into the next century, albeit with progressively less favourable conditions, smaller areas of eligibility and lower funding levels. The biggest cloud on the horizon for the future life of these programmes is now not domestic dissent but an increasingly critical view from Brussels, which itself will have transferred DM34.0 billion in development funds to the new states during 1991–96.

The EU must approve any incentives granted by a member state, always measuring each country's programmes against standards of fair competition. The EU's oversight of eastern Germany, where one can find some of the most generous packages on offer in Europe, was already beginning to sharpen in 1996 when a couple of much-celebrated cases went awry.

The first transpired in February 1996 when the *Bremer Vulkan*, a large ship-building concern in western German, filed for bankruptcy. Vulkan may have misapproriated up to DM800 million in subsidies which were to be used to modernise two eastern German shipyards it had earlier acquired.

Later in the year the EU Commission did something it had never done before – it rejected a proposed investment grant in eastern Germany. Rather than approving the DM779.6 million the state of Saxony wanted to give *Volkswagen AG*, it only allowed DM539.1 million. VW threatened to freeze its investments and Saxony reacted by defying the EU and granting the original amount. As the controversy grew, the EU announced it would begin reviewing its guidelines for all state subsidies to eastern German companies.

Large incentive packages to large firms will, of course, continue to be available. It should be noted that most incentive programmes are tailored specifically for small- and medium-sized businesses – reinforcing Germany's famed *Mittelstand*. But one can assume that in the wake of the above-mentioned events, EU scrutiny over compliance with its guidelines for state investment support will continue to grow.

Knowing that offered incentive packages must meet certain EU criteria is just one of a number of important practical considerations for the prospective investor. Others are reviewed below.

PRACTICAL TIPS ON SECURING FINANCIAL INCENTIVES

The process of applying for and receiving investment incentives in Germany is remarkably straightforward. Hopefully, the following tips will make it even easier. The list is intended to provide a summary of detailed and practical information to foreign investors seeking financial support from the government. It does not pretend to be all-inclusive nor guarantee success, but it does address many of the most often asked questions and concerns of prospective investors.

1. **Do not make any investment expenditures until you have completed the application process for incentives.** In most cases, other than for tax credits, money spent beforehand will be ineligible for consideration.
2. **Keep asking questions and never make assumptions.** This is an important concept in avoiding last minute surprises and bottlenecks. The details and conditions for incentive programmes

can often change. Keeping abreast of the most up-to-date developments is an important task.

3. **Gather as much initial information as possible from** (i) a German chamber of commerce; (ii) a German embassy, consulate or other representation, or (iii) the Foreign Investor Information Centre in the federal economics ministry in Berlin. If you already know for certain which state (*Land*) or states (*Länder*) you are interested in investing in, you can contact directly the appropriate economic development agency. However, it doesn't hurt to touch base with the above-mentioned offices as well.

4. **Ask someone at the federal or state level to print out a computer analysis** of eligible programmes in your case. There are a variety of computer programmes, some only in German, some in English, which can supply detailed descriptions of all the major incentive programmes applicable to the situation. There is also plenty of printed material obtainable in English.

5. **Identify all your necessary points of contact in the different government agencies.** Your company needs to maintain a high profile during the application and decision processes. Important contacts would include the economic ministries at the federal and state levels (other ministries, depending on the project, may also be important, such as those in agriculture, science and technology), the economic development agencies in each of the states, the development banks at the federal and state levels, universities, technical schools and research foundations.

6. **The primary contacts for grant programmes are the economic development agencies** (*Wirtschaftsförderungsgesellschaften*), found in one form or another in each of the 16 states. **The primary contacts for low-interest loans are the federal development banks:** the bank for reconstruction (*Kreditanstalt für Wiederaufbau – KfW*) and the bank for equalisation (*Deutsche Ausgleichsbank – DtA*). All of these organisations have English-speaking experts who provide advice and assistance at no cost.

7. **At the municipality level** the mayor and his/her development agency are important players and should be enlisted as active supporters of your project and application for incentives. A good relationship with the local chamber of commerce (*Industrie- und Handelskammer – IHK*) is also useful. The local employment office (*Arbeitsamt*) needs to be contacted concerning wage, training and other support programmes.

8. **Regional grants.** Germany's strong form of federalism is seen in the investment incentive process for regional grants. Although federal and EU budgets provide much of the money for these programmes, it is the individual states that make the decisions, under legal guidelines, on who gets what.

9. **Take a close look at more than one potential location.** There is healthy competition among, and within, the states for acquiring investment and one needs to carefully compare the advantages, conditions and terms offered by each possible candidate. During negotiations it is to the investor's advantage to have at least one fallback choice of a state and/or region.

10. **Each of the 16 states is different.** Each one has numerous variations in the available incentive programmes. Depending on which industries and areas it wants to support, a state will tailor supplementary programmes to be added to the basic mix of incentives available throughout either eastern or western Germany. Also the decision makers are often located in different agencies in the different states.

11. **Usually the highest decision-maker in each state is the economics minister.** Accordingly, if your project is significant enough, every effort should be made to obtain an introductory appointment with the minister and identify the key people on his/her staff. The minister's office then needs to be kept abreast of your progress.

12. **Company visits.** Although a local representative can shepherd along the day-to-day activities of the application process, a few high-level company team visits are also very important. The money and time spent on foreign travel are always impressive signs of commitment. Good personal relationships need to be established and fostered. The firm should indicate, early on, its eagerness to be a good corporate citizen.

13. All those involved in the process should **attempt to learn rudimentary German and basic cross-cultural etiquette**. Negotiation style, for example, can be very different in Germany than elsewhere. Basic company brochures and introductory letters should be translated into German.

14. **Enlist good local professional assistance.** One must find an accountant and a lawyer familiar with international trans-actions and the incentives system. During negotiations over the levels of financial support both can offer invaluable assistance. The emphasis on local is also important. It usually doesn't make sense to use a law firm in Munich when you are trying to get established in Rostock, and vice versa. A good tax adviser will also be helpful when it comes time to claim credits and exemptions.

15. **Find a commercial house bank**. Identifying a bank legally operating within Germany which will fully support your efforts to obtain grants and loans is key. Most applications need to be submitted through a house bank. Some banks are more interested in servicing this type of clientele than others.

16. **A legal German business entity must be established** in order to receive any financial support. This can be a subsidiary or a registered branch office. The most typical entity is the *GmbH* (company with limited liability), for which the shareholder capital must amount to at least DM50,000. With a good lawyer the establishment of a GmbH can be accomplished within a few days.

17. **A new company must be entered in the commercial register** *(Handelsregister)* where the firm will be located. This could take two weeks or more, varying with local efficiencies.

18. **Grant applications normally need to be accompanied by documentation** such as a description of the firm and its investment intentions, thorough business and financial plans, about two years' worth of financial records, proof of entry in the *Handelsregister*, property titles, construction permits, leasing contracts and tax returns. Depending on the situation, this list could be longer or shorter. The business plan, as one would expect, needs to be the best product possible.

19. **Job creation.** The number of jobs to be created or saved directly and indirectly will often, but not always, be a key consideration in grant levels. Other considerations which can be decisive include such things as technologies transferred, innovative research and development planned, the level of development in the chosen location and industries targeted by individual states/regions for promotion.

20. **There is always an important distinction between small and large firms** when it comes to programme eligibility. The basic definition: a small firm has up to 250 employees and a maximum annual turnover of ECU 40 million or a balance sheet sum of ECU 20 million. If other firms own more than a 25 per cent share of the German company in question then the size criteria are applied to the largest of them.

21. **The EU ceiling for the total percentage of incentive awards** is 35 per cent of the investment for large firms and 50 per cent for small firms. These highest ceilings are only allowed in eastern Germany. The entire amount can be in grant money. However, the benefits derived from the tax and below-market credit programmes are also calculated into the maximum percentage allowed.

22. Most often, **final decisions on incentive packages** are made within two months. Approved grants and loans are usually disbursed within two months of making an investment expenditure.

Part Three

Financial and Accounting Framework

19

The Changing Role of Banks in Corporate Development

Kaevan Gazdar, Publications Department, Bayerische Vereinsbank

THE OVERSEERS OF ORGANISED CAPITALISM

It was a Marxist who coined the term that most fittingly describes the German economy. Rudolf Hilferding, a prominent Social Democrat politician, who was Minister of Finance for a brief spell during the Republic of Weimar, characterised the modern economy as a form of 'organised capitalism'. Indeed, Germany was – and still is – a highly organised economy with an intricate set of checks and balances and a constant process of discussion and consensus on the need for these controls.

Banks played a central role in Hilferding's scenario: he saw banks as pulling the strings from the background in their function as capital providers to industry. According to Hilferding, monopolies and cartels were the result of this dominance of industrial capital.

Hilferding's ideas are echoed in the viewpoints of other critical theorists such as Thorstein Veblen. However, his portrayal of banking preponderance within a highly organised context applies particularly to Germany. Ever since, the *Macht der Banken*, the power of the banks, has been a recurrent *leitmotif* in public debate.

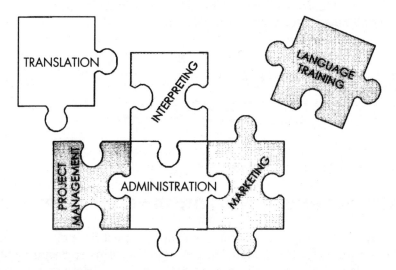

The power and influence of the banking community is historically derived. Germany was late in industrialising and did so at a dizzy speed; the big chemical corporations, BASF, Bayer and Hoechst for instance, were founded as small laboratories in the 1860s and became global players in the space of 15 years. The private banks at the time lacked the financial clout to back industrial dynamism. Deutsche Bank, founded in 1870, the year before Germany unified, plugged the gap with such success that it remains not only the largest but also the most influential bank in Germany to the present day.

Germany's *Großbanken* – Dresdner Bank and Commerzbank rapidly established themselves as major players, though they have never achieved the size and stature of Deutsche Bank – quickly became the 'permanent accompaniers' of German industry, through the loans they provided, their seats on supervisory boards and their corporate shareholdings. They have remained the three largest banks in Germany for almost a hundred years. Their continuing preeminence reflects an implicit continuity in Germany's economic progress.

In the shadow of the three *Großbanken*, all situated in the north, Vereinsbank and Hypobank achieved regional importance in southern Germany. Both held major stakes in real estate loans and later modernised their services. In contemporary Germany, Vereinsbank and Hypobank are counted among the major players.

PIONEERS OF RELATIONSHIP MANAGEMENT

The German banks were pioneers in what was later called relationship management. They have always been closely involved in the entrepreneurial activities of their clients and supervise these activities as members of the supervisory board. This has made them fairly invulnerable to price-based competition and allowed them to take a long-term view of achieving steady profitablity as 'house banks' of major industrial corporations.

The expansion of German banking in the late nineteenth century can also be viewed as a form of economic nationalism. Until 1870, German companies were forced to finance their exports through British banks. Deutsche Bank and the others offered the same services at a lower price and could assure their clients that the money would stay in the country. This made the German companies feel more independent – and gave the banks a steady source of business.

What remains of this power and prestige in the present day? Opinions tend to differ violently: non-bankers contend that banks are far too influential. Foreign investors in particular take a dim view of the cosy German set-up. Joseph Lufsky, for instance, managing director of the investment fund Global Proxy Services in Lincoln Center, Massachusetts, contends that German banks are excessively powerful. Beyond this, Lufsky criticises the conflicts of interest that arise from the multiple roles that German banks play as loan providers, supervisory board members and major shareholders.

German bankers tend to counter by pointing out that their shareholdings are smaller than they seem at first sight and that they do not dominate the companies in which they hold large stakes. Alfred Herrhausen, CEO of Deutsche Bank until he was assassinated in 1989, once pointed out that the country's banks are relatively small in international terms and that their major holdings in around 100 German companies do not give them a stranglehold on the private sector.

Leading banks still hold large chunks of leading corporations, but have reduced their holdings in recent years, reacting to the crisis in prominent 'rust bowl' industries such as machine-building and factory-installations. The best example of this downscaling of corporate holdings is provided by Deutsche Bank, which has reduced its share in Daimler Benz, Germany's largest corporation, by 4 per cent recently.

OPAQUE CORPORATE STRUCTURES

The real obstacles faced by foreigners interested in M&A (merger and acquisition) transactions or out to obtain a commanding equity share in German companies are structural rather than power oriented:

- Germany has a restricted number of public limited corporations: only approximately 800 are quoted on the stock exchange. The vast majority of enterprises are held in private hands.
- Germany's Share Law, the *Aktiengesetz*, favours secrecy of ownership. For instance, it allows German institutional investors to obtain large chunks of companies by proxy holdings. Foreigners are rarely in a position to grasp the true ownership structures of most companies. Beyond this, only a restricted percentage of shares are traded on Germany's sleepy stock exchanges, so that outsiders have virtually no chance of acquiring sizeable share packets.
- In most public limited companies, the Board of Directors (*Vorstand*) and the Supervisory Board (*Aufsichtsrat*) are closely

linked. Supervisory Board members are generally recruited from the 'house bank' and from corporations with which the company co-operates. Germany's Share Law prescribes that a foreign investor needs a 75 per cent corporate share in order to change the membership of the supervisory board. Failing this, he or she cannot dictate terms to top management.

- Germany's system of codetermination (*Mitbestimmung*) makes it difficult for M&A operators to lay off staff or fundamentally restructure the companies they take over. Basically, the German corporate world constitutes a fairly harmonious 'alliance of interest', very different to the adversarial atmosphere in Britain and the United States.

The most important difference between German and Anglo-Saxon banks is also structural: German banks are universal, not specialised. There is no separation of investment and commercial banking or of conventional and real estate loans, no Glass-Steagall Act or other restrictions.

The admirable stability of the country's banks – 13 of the world's 25 best-rated banks are based in Germany – derives from the diversity of their activities. Private savings accounts and loans, real estate financing, corporate credits and project financing, export credits and public sector lending, asset management, trading in shares, foreign exchange and derivatives: the list of business activities is massive.

Germany's five big banks are less important than they seem at first sight. Savings banks (*Sparkassen*) are the heart of the financial community. The overall market share of the 700 savings banks, often called 'local universal banks', together with the clearing banks, amounts to 40%. These banks are particularly strong in the conventional retail banking business.

In a business climate that values stability rather than volatility, *Sparkassen* triumph by offering ultimate security: their liabilities are guaranteed by the regional authorities that own them. Their semi-official status has recently been criticised by private-sector competitors, but structural change is unlikely. The savings banks face more competition from the equally decentralised 'cooperative banks' (*Raiffeisenbanken*), 3000 of which are dotted all over Germany, than from the private banks. The *Raiffeisenbanken* generally consist of agricultural credit co-operatives and credit unions. They also provide grass-roots facilities in retail banking.

THE ALL-IMPORTANT *MITTELSTAND*

Savings and co-operative banks constitute the bedrock of banking. Similarly, the heart of German business is not the large corporation but the *Mittelstand*, the medium-sized, mostly family-owned enterprises, which employ more than half of all working Germans and are to a great extent responsible for Germany's excellent export performance.

The *Mittelstand* is also the banks' major target group in the corporate sector. Many large corporations do not in fact need bank support: Siemens, for instance, is known to have DM24 billion in ready money and is – by Anglo-Saxon standards – hopelessly overcapitalised. The awesome financial reserves held by Siemens has led to it being satirised as a 'bank with a production unit added on'. Companies such as Siemens and VW run their own banking operations and have acquired an expertise in investment management comparable to that offered by leading German banks.

The *Mittelstand*, on the other hand, is chronically undercapitalised and dependent on financial support from outside. This has led to a schizophrenic situation. On the one hand, large banks have a major stake in the *Mittelstand*: 95 per cent of Deutsche Bank's customers and 75 per cent of its corporate loans, for instance, go to medium-sized enterprises. On the other hand, *Mittelstand* companies habitually complain about the excessive security orientation of the banks and about their lack of entrepreneurial orientation. They specifically criticise the favouritism shown to large corporations by major players such as Deutsche Bank.

The banks have indeed tightened up their credit-granting procedures in recent years. New rating criteria for corporate lending, such as potential ecological liabilities and global outsourcing capabilities, tend to disadvantage many *Mittelstand* companies that are slow to adapt to new business trends.

However, the complaints of the *Mittelstand* entrepreneurs need to be viewed in perspective. The typical *Mittelstand* family entrepreneur tends to be both conservative in managerial terms and wary of opening the books to outside perusal. Even the *Mittelstand*'s 'house banks' have problems obtaining complete financial data. This cult of financial secrecy is also a prime reason for the dearth of medium-sized companies going public.

HALF-HEARTED ATTEMPTS AT GOING PUBLIC

Private limited companies in Germany (the so-called GmbHs) are freed from most of the disclosure requirements – balance sheets, profit and loss accounts, information on holdings – that apply to public limited companies (the so-called AGs). Many *Mittelstand* GmbHs take advantage of this legal laxity and avoid publishing any concrete information on their financial performance. Of the 500,000 GmbHs, it has been estimated that fewer than 10 per cent adhere to the rudimentary disclosure provisions prescribed by law. Thus, going public generally forces the *Mittelstand* entrepreneur to disclose a vast amount of core information hitherto kept secret.

Though corporate debt can amount to 75 per cent of the balance sheet total and capital ratios have shrunk from 20 per cent in the 1970s to 17 per cent in the 1990s, medium-sized companies are still wary of seeking capital on the stock market. Some 2000 companies could potentially go public according to statistics provided by Deutsche Bank, which, in company with other large banks, is eager to replace the *Mittelstand* debts held by them with commissions gained from equity issues. But as the last ten years have shown, hardly a dozen companies go public each year. It has been estimated that in Germany, the average company goes public 55 years after being founded. This contrasts with an average of 14 years in the USA and 8 years in Britain.

Share capital traded on Germany's stock exchanges increased sizeably during the 1980s, reaching approximately a hundred billion Marks, as much as had been traded during the entire post-war period to 1980. The percentage of traded capital to total capital rose correspondingly from 16.9 in 1980 to 26.1 in 1990. However, share trading was limited to established companies rather than being extended to start-ups.

Despite several highly successful examples of companies that went public in the 1980s, such as Wella and SAP, new issues still play a minor role in quantitative terms. For instance, the privatisation of Germany's telecommunication authority Deutsche Telekom in 1996 involved a share volume of DM15 billion – as much as all the 130 new share issues between 1986 and 1996 added together.

After some spectacular flops in the early 1990s such as the electronics dealer HAKO and the Sachsenmilch dairy farm, German investors are wary of non-blue-chip stock issues, while foreign investors have yet to discover the new issues market. Banks have also become wary after getting stuck with quantities of unsold shares in their trading portfolios.

In 1996, Vereinsbank led a consortium of banks that issued the shares of an engineering consulting company called Bertrandt. Bertrandt will be one of the pioneer participants in a 'new market' trading segment at the Frankfurt stock exchange, designed to favour corporate newcomers. It remains to be seen whether such initiatives will radically change the highly conservative trading mentality in Germany.

VENTURE CAPITAL: THE 'VENTURE NOTHING' FINANCIERS

An overwhelming majority of young entrepreneurs depend on bank loans to start their businesses. A number of private-sector banks established venture capital funds to encourage start-ups as far back as the mid-1980s. However, the venture capital subsidiaries have proved as averse to risk taking as their parents and start-up business-people continue stridently to complain about the venture capitalists' bureaucratic procedures. One major operator, the Deutsche Wagnis-finanzierungsfonds, has fittingly been satirised as the 'venture nothing' financier.

State funds for start-ups are also available: capital-participation authorities (so-called *Kapitalbeteiligungsgesellschaften*) provide seed money at the regional level. Here again, however, young entrepreneurs are confronted with a series of bureaucratic restrictions.

Lack of ready capital is one of the major reasons for the entrepreneurial spirit in Germany having waned recently: 26% of the total working population was independently employed in 1960, while in the 1990s only around 13% is entrepreneurially active. The situation in Germany's capital city Berlin is particularly dismal. Far from spurring entre-preneurial flair in the reunited heart of Germany, reunification and the elimination of most of the subsidies received by companies sited in West Berlin have led to an entrepreneurial exodus. At the same time, the insolvency rate in Germany, though it has risen in the 1990s in the context of reunification and unsteady entrepreneurial activity in East Germany, is still only 25% of the British rate.

The Germans are slower and steadier businesspeople than their Anglo-Saxon counterparts and their overall financial culture reflects risk aversion rather than profit maximisation in various ways:

- Private investors continue to favour savings accounts, insurance policies and fixed interest rate securities rather than mutual funds or other 'new-fangled' financial instruments. One survey shows that 58 per cent of those who put money aside are simply interested in risk-free bank deposits. As the newsletter *Retail Banker International* points out: 'A traditional aversion to risk has meant that certain pooled investment funds have not been as popular in Germany as investment instruments which offer a guaranteed return.'

- Though 2.5 million German households have an average annual income of over DM200,000, even this upper segment opts for conservative savings outlets, including pooled funds offered by long-standing investment companies such as ADIG. Founded in 1949 by Commerzbank and Vereinsbank, which hold equal shares, ADIG runs over 30 pooled funds featuring blue-chip investments.

- The German system of capital deposits made by all banks into a mutual fund run by the banking association is unique and has ensured that no major German bank has gone bankrupt in the last 20 years.

TRENDS IN PRIVATE AND INVESTMENT BANKING

Despite the risk-aversion attitudes of Germany's consumers, competition in the banking sector has hotted up to a greater extent in retail banking than in corporate development. As Andrew Fisher points out in the *Financial Times*: 'Customers are calling the tune'.

Discount broking and direct banking have made inroads into the traditionally high charges levied on banking transactions. Consumers are comparing prices and consumer associations are pressurising the banks to be more consumer friendly. Competition is fierce because Germany is already one of the world's most over-banked countries: it averages around 1500 inhabitants per branch. On a per capita basis, there are twice as many branches in Germany as the USA or Britain.

Telephone banking is now offered by the subsidiaries of several leading German banks including Deutsche Bank, Commerzbank, Hypobank and Vereinsbank. The use of the telephone for carrying out simple transactions –Advance Bank, the Vereinsbank subsidiary, is the only direct bank that also offers counselling services by phone – has improved customer service while reducing operating costs for the banks.

Vereinsbank CEO Albrecht Schmidt sees the rate of change in private banking as being 'rather like the shift from a fast train to a magnetic levitation railway'. Customers increasingly refuse to accept opening hours, demand more transparent pricing and a more acceptable price-to-value ratio.

In investment banking, only Deutsche Bank shows the potential to become an international major player. Through the acquisition of Morgan Grenfell, it entered the 'big league' and is now rapidly expanding through similar acquisitions in other major markets such as Japan.

Fittingly, Deutsche Bank has adopted Anglo-Saxon methods of remuneration for its investment banking unit that run contrary to the German system of moderate salaries combined with high job security. Germany's leading bank still has a Triple-A rating – and still offers a low return on equity by international standards. But given the fact that 46 per cent of share capital is held abroad, Deutsche Bank will be increasingly exposed to the winds of change and could soon face a downrating, in company with other first-class investment banks like JP Morgan.

Most German banks lack Deutsche Bank's high degree of international exposure. They have reacted to inroads made in their home market by leading investment banks such as Goldman Sachs by seeking areas of specialisation in which they can excel. Vereinsbank, for instance, has floated bonds in exotic currencies: it has issued the largest bond in Greek drachmas to date and the first Eurobond in Czech crowns. It has also successfully introduced jumbo asset-based bonds (*Jumbopfandbriefe*), which are aimed at institutional investors in Germany and abroad.

Asset-based bonds (*Öffentliche Pfandbriefe*), guaranteed by local authorities and mortgage-based bonds issued by banks (*Hypothekenpfandbriefe*), account for approximately a third of all fixed income securities issued in Germany, but have so far been overlooked internationally. As *Institutional Investor* points out: 'Foreigners . . . still tend to dismiss them as illiquid, non-transparent and parochial'. The *Jumbopfandbriefe,* however, are issued with a minimum volume of DM1 billion and thus represent viable risk-free investments for international investors.

The *Jumbopfandbriefe* are a good example of the German approach to financial innovations: they represent a consolidation of the status quo rather than a radical break with past practice.

The German government is increasingly conscious of the need actively to encourage the development of financial markets in Germany. Prominent spokesmen like the Minister of the Economy, Günter Rexrodt, and Bundesbank President, Hans Tietmeyer, agree on basic isses such as the reduction of public-sector capital holdings and the liberalisation of capital transactions. Beyond this, the federal government has already passed legislation accordingly: by eliminating the former turnover taxes for stock exchange transactions, abolishing the restrictions on mutual funds and encouraging a market for commercial papers in DM.

Financial liberalisation is, however, often curbed by a very German zest for perfectionism. The 'Financial Market Encouragement Laws' (*Finanzmarktförderungsgesetze*), for instance, have turned out to be so complicated that international investors partly felt dissuaded rather than persuaded to expand their activities in Germany. In international terms, Frankfurt remains a provincial financial centre.

What chances do Germany's banks have in this context? As we have seen, the country's banking culture is averse to financial trading and more attuned to financial investment, just as its economic credo is stakeholder value and not shareholder value. Its broad-based activities have so far ensured stability in an unstable world financial environment, while limiting profitability.

RELATIONSHIP CULTURE OR DEALER CULTURE?

German critics of the Anglo-Saxon 'dealing culture' contend that both investment and commercial banks in Britain and the United States lack a systematic approach – they simply practise pragmatism. This remains an unpalatable role model in the German context.

Kevan V Watts, who spent seven years at the British Treasury before joining Merrill Lynch in New York as an investment banker, maintains: 'There is room for both – the German and the Anglo-Saxon model'.

It seems unlikely that Germany's banks will ever emulate the dynamism of their competitors in Britain and the USA. However, the move from relationship banking to price banking has started with private customers and will soon extend to corporate clients. If German banks follow the example of Deutsche Bank and are at the same time able to avoid the kind of heedless risk taking that characterised the Barings disaster and that potentially threatens many other investment banks, they should continue to survive and prosper.

20

Significance and Future of the Savings Banks within the German Banking Industry

Dr Stefan Mütze, Economist, Landesbank Hessen-Thüringen Girozentrale (Helaba)

THE GERMAN BANKING INDUSTRY

The banking industry in Germany is composed of the private and public commercial banks, the credit associations sector and the savings bank sector. Each of these three 'pillars' has had its own historical development. The specific conditions surrounding their formation have led to particular tasks and characteristics, some of which have survived to this day. In addition, there are special-purpose banks and other institutions, such as the investment companies or Kreditanstalt für Wiederaufbau (Reconstruction Loan Corporation). The responsibility for national monetary policy lies with the Deutsche Bundesbank.

Commercial banks and credit associations

The commercial banking sector is organised under private law. This group comprises the big banks, the regional banks and other commercial banks, the branches of foreign banks as well as private bankers. The business policy of these institutions has been one of long-term maximisation of profits for the benefit of the owners, typical of a market economy.

Table 20.1 *The German banking industry*

Commercial banks	Credit association sector	Savings bank sector	Specialised banks and other institutions
• The big banks	• Universal banks	• Savings banks	• Mortgage banks
• Regional banks and other banks	• Credit associations	• Central giro institutions	• Banks with special functions
• Private banks	• Central institutions		• Postbank
• Branches of foreign banks			• Building and loan associations
			• Guarantee banks
			• Investment companies

Source: Kloter and Stein (1993), p. 218.

The credit association sector is also organised under private law. However, the objectives of the credit associations differ from the commercial banks since they are not purely profit oriented. In accordance with Section 1 of the Act on Credit Associations (*Genossenschaftsgesetz* – GenG), their primary aim is the 'furtherance of purchases or of the business of their members by means of co-operatives'. This means that the principle of providing assistance for self-help applies to the credit associations. This does not, however, preclude the earning of profits. These objectives began to emerge on the creation of the co-operative movement around the middle of the nineteenth century. During this period, the commercial banks concentrated on the financing of industrial companies. At the same time, however, there was a lack of credit institutions which would provide financing for smaller and less well-capitalised industrial and agricultural businesses. The activities of Franz Hermann Schulze from the town of Delitzsch in the small crafts and trading sector and Friedrich Wilhelm Raiffeisen in the agricultural sector led to the creation of the first co-operatives in Germany. They tried to fill this gap in the market. The separation between the industrial and agricultural credit co-operatives, which lasted for more than 100 years, ended only in 1972 with the formation of the Federal Association of German Volksbanken and Raiffeisenbanken.

The credit associations were founded on the principle of 'help through self-help'. They are 'associations with an open-ended number of members' (Section 1 GenG), with membership based on the purchase of at least one share in the association. The credit association sector has a three-tier structure. The bottom level is formed by the individual credit associations. The medium level consists of their regional institutions. The central institution of the co-operative sector is DG Bank in Frankfurt.

The savings bank sector

In contrast to the two other groups, the savings bank sector is organised under public law. The savings bank sector in the Federal Republic of Germany has a three-tier structure, similar to the credit association sector. The bottom tier is formed by the 624 savings banks. The medium tier is formed by the 13 *Landesbanks* and central giro institutions active at *Länder* level, as well as the 13 *Landesbausparkassen* (building and loan associations). The central institution of the sector is Deutsche Girozentrale – Deutsche Kommunalbank (DGZ), also located in Frankfurt. The S-Finanzgruppe, moreover, comprises other member institutions, such as investment companies and finance companies, leasing and factoring companies, insurance companies and Deutscher Sparkassenverlag (the organisation's publishing house).

A public-sector guarantor is responsible for all liabilities of the savings banks. The guarantors of the *Landesbanks*/central giro institutions are mostly the regional savings banks and giro associations together with the respective *Land*. In some cases, either the *Land* or the regional association has assumed sole guarantorship. The public-law building and loan associations, which are named LBS – Landesbausparkassen, are part of the savings banks group and therefore enjoy the same level of confidence. In addition to the guarantor's statutory liability (*Gewähr-trägerhaftung*), the so-called institutional liability (*Anstaltslast*) applies to both the savings banks and the *Landesbanks*/central giro institutions. According to this, the guarantors are responsible for meeting the institutions' liabilities during the term of their existence, eg by procuring funds, if such liabilities cannot be met out of the institutions' own assets.

The public-benefit objectives of the savings bank sector are associated with its legal form. However, these objectives require that these banks assume tasks which do not cover their costs only to the extent that such tasks are in line with the overall objectives of the savings bank sector. The persistent achievement of profits does not contradict the public-benefit principle. The objectives of this group of institutions have crystallised during their more than 200-year history and can therefore only be understood against this backdrop.

The creation of the savings banks dates back to the second half of the eighteenth century. The guiding principle of the savings banks movement was to provide self-help to the poorer social groups. The philosophical background was the newly awakened feeling of responsibility for all people, which was rooted in the Age of Enlightenment. Over time, the public mandate has changed. The objective is still to promote saving and capital formation for broad sections of the population, as well as to guarantee the nationwide provision of banking services for all social groups. The public mandate includes the function of the 'house bank' for the guarantor. In addition, the activities of the savings banks are characterised by strong commitment in the public area, social and cultural life. Another important task has become the promotion of a regionally better balanced economic structure. Due to their strong presence in the regions, the savings banks are particularly well situated to service local business. With 19,504 domestic branches, a share of 44 per cent, they have the largest branch network among all banking groups in Germany.

The savings bank sector is the largest banking group in Germany, in terms of balance sheet ratios. The balance sheet volume of the sector in 1995 amounted to DM2.867 trillion, 38 per cent of the overall balance sheet volume of all credit institutions. The share of the commercial banks was roughly 24 per cent, and the credit associations sector reached a share of approximately 15 per cent. The share of the savings bank sector in loans to non-banks amounted to 37.4 per cent in 1995. The commercial banks and credit associations reached 25.1 and 14.9 per cent respectively. A special field of activity of the *Landesbanks*/central giro institutions is the granting of loans to public authorities. Together with the savings banks, their market share in this field amounted to 39.7 per cent in overall lendings to central, regional and local authorities in 1995. The commercial banks attained 8.5 per cent in this segment and the credit associations had a market share of 1.9 per cent. With

Table 20.2 *German Banking Groups in 1995*

Group	Number of credit institutions	Number of domestic branches	Number of domestic bank offices[1]
Commercial bank sector	331	7,305	7,636
Credit association sector	2,595	17,248	19,843
Savings bank sector	637	19,504	20,141
inc. Savings banks	624	19,071	19,695
incl. *Landesbanks*/central giro institutions	13	433	446

[1] Total of the number of credit institutions and the number of domestic branches.
Source: Deutsche Bundesbank (1996) p. 104.

375,000 staff, the S-Finanzgruppe is the largest employer in the financial services sector in Germany.

FUTURE TASKS OF THE SAVINGS BANKS

The public mandate of the savings banks has been questioned repeatedly, both by competitors and the Monopolies Commission. The savings bank sector reacts to this challenge with a 'dual strategy'. On the one hand, the benefit for the public sector is stressed, for example through the promotion of cultural activities by the savings banks. On the other hand, the entire savings bank sector is continuously improving its earnings situation and the quality of its services. It is true that this is a necessity not only faced by the savings banks and common to all credit institutions. Nevertheless, the latter still have to bear the costs for their public mandate, which have an adverse effect on the earnings situation. This strategy may also help to earn the funds for a potential expansion of the public mandate in the future.

Stronger focus on commission-earning business

The profitability of the savings banks is good. They achieve a traditionally high operating profit as a percentage of their average business volume. In 1995, for instance, they reached a ratio of 0.85 per cent after evaluation, the highest among all banking groups (see Table 20.3).

Nevertheless, earnings are threatened by increased competition, as they are in the entire banking industry. Thus, net interest received by the

Table 20.3 *Operating result after evaluation by per cent of business volume 1993–5 by banking groups*

	1993	1994	1995
All banking groups	0.55	0.47	0.54
Big banks	0.63	0.49	0.53
Regional banks and other commercial banks	0.58	0.57	0.65
Branches of foreign banks	0.47	0.32	0.32
Private banks	0.61	0.22	0.25
Central giro institutions	0.23	0.25	0.26
Savings banks	0.87	0.77	0.85
Regional co-operative banks	0.27	0.20	0.45
Credit associations	0.91	0.73	0.83
Mortgage banks	0.33	0.26	0.34
Banks with special functions	0.29	0.19	0.27

Source: Deutsche Bundesbank (1996) p. 49.

banks is expected to decline in future, even though it has increased over the last few years. The percentage of higher-yielding deposits in overall savings has increased in parts of the banking industry from roughly a quarter to more than two-thirds over the last 10 years. Both of these developments caused an increase in funding costs for the credit institutions. The savings banks have been particularly hard hit, as the deposit business is of particular significance for them. The savings banks alone account for 51 per cent of overall German savings deposits. Their share in net interest received of the entire banking industry amounted to roughly a third in 1995, whereas their share in net revenue from commissions and service charges received by all banks amounted to only roughly a quarter. From the point of view of the savings banks, it therefore makes sense to offset the trend towards lower net interest received by generating new commission-earning business as well as by cutting costs for administration and risk.

Commission income is mainly derived from payment transactions and the brokerage of *Allfinanz* products, as well as from the international, securities and real estate businesses. The earnings potential of these fields of activity can be assessed positively. In payment transactions, competition has intensified most recently by the addition of charge-free current accounts. This development towards declining margins can only be countered by further automation in this field. In connection with the brokerage of *Allfinanz* products such as insurance policies or building savings contracts, limited increases should also be possible in future. The securities business should have favourable opportunities for growth in Germany, given the trend towards rising financial assets in the personal sector. At the same time, it must be remembered that the discount banks which have sprung up in the recent past have created additional pressure on commission earnings. The savings banks could open up new sources for earnings by offering information services, eg in the fields of consulting, information on the economy or stock-market research. In addition, they should consider offering qualified consulting services against commission payments on a wider scale. A prerequisite for offering such services is greater co-operation between the members of the savings banks organisation.

FUTURE TASKS OF THE *LANDESBANKS*

The savings banks are rooted in their regions. They conduct business with small and medium-sized companies as well as retail business with private customers. The *Landesbanks*, by contrast, have to face international competition. They focus on wholesale business with large corporations, institutional investors and central, regional and local authorities. This results in a dual strategy. On the one hand, the *Landesbanks* offer the savings banks services which these cannot or do not want to offer themselves due to their regional roots. On the other hand, the *Landesbanks* compete with other large credit institutions at an international level.

The services provided to the savings banks include primarily acting as a central bank. These include tasks such as the allocation of joint loans, co-operation in securities, securities deposit and international transactions, as well as the establishment of centralised data-processing systems, such as the Securities Information System (WIS) offered by Helaba, which can be used for investment advisory services and portfolio management. In their capacity as central giro institutions, the *Landesbanks* are the central clearing banks for non-cash payments (giro transactions) and ensure the balancing of liquidity requirements among the savings banks. In addition, they provide services which are of significance for the international business of the savings banks. In future, the further expansion of co-operation between *Landesbanks* and savings banks should be of decisive importance. Only in this way will the organisation as a whole be stronger than the sum of its members. The aim must be to offer new products and services to customers without delay.

However, the *Landesbanks* are not only service providers for the savings banks. They must increasingly adapt to the changing needs of their customers. Companies are increasingly acting globally in a growing European market. New export markets are being opened up; production is in part being shifted to more cost-efficient countries. In order to assist companies in this regard, the *Landesbanks* are becoming ever more international. The establishment of individual branches and representative offices is, however, handled with some restraint due to the high costs involved, which often makes a corresponding contribution to earnings less probable. Co-operation with other institutions, including the *Landesbanks*, in specialised areas is more successful. Some *Landesbanks* may still be too small, so that more mergers may be expected in this sector over the next few years.

It is also the aim of the *Landesbanks* to broaden their range of products. In commission-earning business, new earnings opportunities, for instance in investment banking, may be opened up. In corporate customer business, the traditional loan business is being expanded in the direction of tailor-made project-oriented financing concepts. With rising currency and interest risks, risk management is also increasing in importance for corporate customers. In this field, a broad range of highly specialised products is already on offer.

Over the next few years, particular challenges, both for the *Landesbanks* and for the savings banks, are expected to result from their function as 'house banks' to the central, regional and local authorities. The extreme deterioration of the budget situation of municipalities and *Länder* is increasingly threatening their investment opportunities. In this connection, the task of the public banks is to provide innovative solutions with regard to cost-efficient reorganisation of administration, the transfer of activities to private-sector partners, as well as the sale and transfer of assets. Here, the savings banks can offer a range of new services, such as commission factoring or the realisation of build-operate-transfer (BOT) models and co-operation models by including private-sector companies in the provision of public services. Additional financing possibilities are offered by the various forms of leasing or the silent partnership which does not infringe on the independence of the municipal authority. The cost-efficient financing of public-sector tasks is facilitated by this offer of new instruments.

FUTURE TASKS OF THE *LANDESBAUSPARKASSEN* (BUILDING AND LOAN ASSOCIATIONS)

One of the major cornerstones of the savings banks service organisation are the *Landesbausparkassen*. Building saving has become widespread in Germany. The idea has its origin in the Württemberg town of Wüstenrot, where the first building and loan association was founded in 1924. The aim of the movement was to alleviate the severe shortage of housing. Through regular savings deposits under a savings scheme sponsored by the government, building saving leads to the creation of capital before the commencement of building activities. Therefore, this form is to be more positively assessed in terms of its socio-economic value than other forms of promotion through the tax-deductibility of mortgage interest, which tends to favour borrowing and thus makes the house-financing transaction much more vulnerable. The new measures of 1 January 1996 to promote building saving, which among other factors increased the income limits from DM27,000/DM54,000 to DM50,000 and DM100,000 for single persons and married couples respectively, gave new impetus to the idea of building saving in Germany. The *Landesbausparkassen* also benefit from this momentum.

In order to gain a larger market share, the *Landesbausparkassen* are striving to set their services apart from those offered by competing institutions and to make this clear to their customers. In principle, each innovation of the building saving product can easily be imitated by competitors. Nevertheless, the product as such must be continually adapted to retain its interest for the customer. The major approach for distinguishing a building and loan association in the market is the addition of further services, such as customer friendliness, competent consulting services and prompt handling using improved data-processing systems. The *Landesbausparkassen* are also in a position to offer quick accessibility and the cross-selling of products such as life assurance policies via the savings banks. Moreover, they strive to increase efficiency and productivity continuously in order to be able to hold their ground regarding pricing.

In future, a major issue for the *Landesbausparkassen* will be the opening up of the European markets. Since the beginning of the 1990s, changes in European and German law have made it possible for German building and loan associations to become active in Europe. Nevertheless, a large number of legal problems remain unsolved which impede the opening up of the European market. Thus, no decision has yet been taken on the procedure to be followed if the General Conditions for Building Saving in Germany are incompatible with the legal system of the other EU countries. In these areas, clear rules and regulations and a harmon-isation of the legal situation should be created as soon as possible in order to form a genuine single market for building saving products. Apart from the legal discrepancies, building saving in Europe is also hampered by the fact that it is promoted at different levels. For instance, extensive tax deduction of interest payments may induce savers not to build up capital through regular savings and to borrow funds instead, thereby reducing private consumption. The convergence of the different legal and promotional situations is, however, likely to be a slow process so that the European market for building saving will only be built up gradually.

OUTLOOK

With the introduction of a single European currency and the further harmonisation of markets, competition between the individual banking institutions is likely to increase further. Banking products will change; costs must be cut. Due to its comparatively favourable earnings situation and its flexibility, the S-Finanzgruppe is definitely in a position to make the necessary investments to strengthen its competitive position. The savings banks, with their regional roots and the resulting special relationship with their customers, stand a good chance of achieving high market shares, as they do with new products. In co-operation with the *Landesbanks*, they are able to offer customers a high degree of inter-nationalisation. On the basis of these favourable prerequisites, the S-Finanzverbund is expected to retain its prominent position in the German banking market in the future.

REFERENCES

Deutsche Bundesbank (1996) *Monthly Report, Banking Statistics*, August.

Kloten, Norbert and Stein, Johann Heinrich von (1993) *Geld-, Bank- und Börsenwessen: ein Handbuch* Stuttgart: Obst/Hintner.

21

Corporate Banking in Germany

Laura Covill,
International Financial Journalist

Germany is home to more than three thousand banks and almost all of them are competing to win corporate customers. Some of them at least offer the most sophisticated financial products available anywhere. All are battling to prevent non-banks from copying their products and services and thus breaking up their market. They are prepared to reduce their earnings in order to hang on to those customers.

Described that way, Germany sounds like a paradise for corporate customers. But where German banks are involved, it would be wrong to draw the conclusion that the client is king.

Even in this highly competitive environment, the corporate client does not have many options available, and the consensus among German banks is still so strong that few clients truly succeed in turning the competitive situation to their own advantage.

In addressing some of the paradoxes of the German banking system for international companies, it is worth explaining why German corporate clients appear to make little use of their banks.

By tradition, Germany's largest corporations, such as Siemens, Daimler-Benz or Mannesmann, are highly liquid organisations which tend to finance themselves out of cash flow. For instance Veba AG, the energy, engineering and chemicals group, is currently using cash flow funds to finance most of a DM8 billion capital investment programme over five years.

Natural prudence may have played a role here, but the Germans' hang-ups about getting into debt were in fact created decades ago by the German tax and accounting systems. These regulations encourage firms to retain their earnings after good years and then to draw on those hidden reserves when they need windfall capital or money for invest-ment.

The Bundesbank's annual report on the financial position of German corporations paints a revealing picture. Published in November 1996, the survey of 17,500 corporate balance sheets concludes that German companies benefit from an average cash flow of 12½ per cent. Only 10 per cent of these companies' short-term liabilities were not covered by cash flow or short-term claims. That is a remarkably high average for an economy which is growing by little more than 1 per cent and also facing serious structural problems bred by an inflexible labour market, high wage costs and excessive reliance on manufacturing industry.

Furthermore, the Bundesbank expects corporate earnings in 1996 to improve over 1995 because the domestic economy is gathering pace and wages are increasing only slowly. That will increase companies' ability to rely on their own resources or even to act like banks by lending spare cash to other companies.

Even when multinational companies were much more fragmented, banks found it difficult to win traditional lending business from German-based subsidiaries of foreign companies. Because German banks usually insist on a parent guarantee or local collateral before granting financing terms, foreign firms tend instead to rely on their parent companies at home for financing and treasury needs. Now foreign corporations are investing less and less every year in Germany, citing high taxes, substantial wage costs and bureaucratic difficulties. Those companies that do invest are establishing relatively small offshoots, typically sales and marketing offices rather than factories.

THE HAUSBANK SYSTEM

If these were the only peculiarities of German corporate banking, the banks' position would be critical indeed. But over decades, the German banks have managed to retain the initiative by fostering and perpetu-ating what is known as the Hausbank system. This is still the first rule of corporate banking in Germany.

Standard practice under the Hausbank system dictates that a company will typically choose one bank to handle all its business, allowing a long-term relationship to grow up between bank and company. Some recent corporate collapses have revealed that even very large companies with annual turnover in excess of DM100 million still rely on one major lender. In 1996 Deutsche Bank was forced to carry out a financial rescue of the engineering firm KHD for the third time in a decade. Although the bank had its fingers burned twice in the space of a few years, the third fiasco revealed that Deutsche had remained the largest lender to this company.

From the company's point of view, this loyalty is perhaps the positive aspect of the Hausbank system. A German bank tends to show more patience to a corporate client that finds itself in financial difficulties if it understands that company and has lent to that company over a number of years. That was certainly true in the past. It remains true for clients that are large enough – KHD is the best example here too.

However, the banks have become candid about a change of policy here. Under pressure from competitors and shareholders alike, German banks are calling time on persistent defaulters. If German banks ever had a paternalistic view of their clients, that view has certainly been relinquished. Hermes, the credit insurer, expects German corporate bankruptcies to increase by 13 per cent in 1996 as more Hausbanks pull the rug from under their clients' feet. And when the Hausbank forecloses on a loan, other banks tend to follow automatically.

Another difficult aspect of the Hausbank tradition from the client's point of view is the time it takes to build up a worthwhile Hausbank relationship. The onus is still on the corporate client to gradually build the confidence of the bankers.

In the past, a fledgling entrepreneur had almost no hope of getting a loan from bankers unless he had a track record of at least three years. Bankers were less interested in the entrepreneur's business acumen and management skills than the astuteness of the products and services offered.

That attitude is gradually changing. A survey of 88 German banks carried out in 1995 found that the increasing instability of the markets and shorter product lifetimes were causing German banks to rely less on traditional balance-sheet analysis and collateral checks. Instead, lenders are now guided by indications of management quality, EDP systems and technological standards.

The OECD report on Germany published in 1995 repeated an often-heard gripe that German banks are unwilling to entertain risk in their lending practices, especially when granting loans to business start-ups. In the view of the OECD, this attitude is still hampering the growth of young German companies. In summary, getting a loan from a German company still means revealing every detail of the company's financial situation and that of its proprietors or limited partners.

On balance, companies remain well advised to maintain a Hausbank relationship with one institution, even though they may have accounts at several other banks for cash management purposes. The Hausbank relationship is still the best means of acquiring individual attention from senior bank officials at a time when banks are trying to turn certain forms of advice into a product with a price tag.

CORPORATE BANK SERVICES AND PRODUCTS

Despite the Germans' preference for cash-flow financing, loans remain the core product in corporate banking business. Germany's highly developed economy has a sophisticated banking system to match, and the full range of lending and overdraft facilities is available. Particularly popular are short-term domestic bank loans, promissary notes and banker's acceptances.

Because German banks do not quote a base rate, the Frankfurt inter-bank offered rate (FIBOR) has become the benchmark for lending negotiations. That rate on one-month money averaged 3.1 per cent in October 1996, a full percentage point less than a year before. In that month, banks were charging a premium of between 3 and 7 per cent on overdrafts between DM1 million and DM5 million. Interest rates on agreed loans were lower, but also attracted credit-facility fees of 25 to 50 basis points on the sum committed (not the sum actually used).

There is a single important legal restriction for banks which lend: they are not permitted to lend more than half of their capital funds to a single borrower and the limit may soon be lowered to 30 per cent. However, the rule is unlikely to concern any but the smallest banks.

The relatively high interest rates on longer-term loans are evidence that German firms have traditionally been unwilling to borrow for long-term investment. At present, with long-term interest rates so much higher than short-term rates, corporate customers are restricting themselves as much as possible to borrowing for periods of less than one year. That trend was confirmed by the Bundesbank report in November 1996.

Corporate lending is also carried out by the numerous German mortgage banks and by insurance companies. Thanks to the close network of links and contacts between all the different types of banks and the insurers, firms can rely on their Hausbanks to introduce these opportunistic lenders.

Unlike their counterparts in other countries, small businesses in Germany appear not to suffer discrimination from banks which prefer to lend to larger firms. The Bundesbank study found that, during periods of high interest rates such as 1992 to 1993, loans to medium-sized and large companies in Germany stagnated or even fell, while smaller companies with annual turnovers of up to DM5 million continued to increase their borrowing from banks.

The demands of their major corporate clients and their own ambitions to become international or even global players have ensured that German banks provide a full range of corporate, institutional and banking services. Alongside traditional branch-based services, German banks are fast developing electronic cash management products and improved international payments systems, among many other examples.

A number of banks have recognised the need to provide expert advice and information for companies, and have answered that need by setting up databases and creating publications. Deutsche Bank, for instance, has a database of all the economic development grants and loans available to German companies. Furthermore, banks are creating programmes and publications to explain the implications of the single European currency to their corporate customers.

In all areas the banks are attempting to generate new business – and thus fee-earning opportunities – out of standard transactions. In the large-volume custody and depository business, for instance, German banks are no longer content to receive a simple fee for administering securities portfolios. They are now proposing to clients all kinds of add-on services, such as the possibility of making available the stocks and bonds in their portfolios for securities lending transactions and thus generating an additional fee for client and bank alike.

There is evidence, however, that the further development of corporate banking is hampered, not by a lack of expertise or initiative at German banks, but by meagre demand for certain products. Factoring, for instance, would undoubtedly assist a company whose cash flow is affected by customers settling invoices late. Almost all the major banking groups have operated factoring subsidiaries for some years, but business volumes remain modest. Most of the companies that refuse factoring services express concern that their business partners will interpret their use of factoring as a sign that the firm is in financial difficulties.

At some banks, corporate customers are surprised to find a lack of awareness about the opportunities to cross-sell or even explain a range of different products. That is often because cross-selling is actually discouraged by the banks' own internal structures.

Some banks are still organised in such a way that customer liaison staff take sole responsibility for the earnings booked from a particular client. They were afraid to offer the client a new product which yielded better returns for the customer, but worse for the bank. Nevertheless the banking market was pushing in that direction. Some banks have now solved that problem by restructuring.

In 1992, Deutsche Genossenschaftsbank (DG Bank) created a matrix structure inspired by the idea that responsibility for earnings by any one transaction or customer is split between product divisions, which create products, and customer divisions, which are engaged in relationship management. WestLB is now planning to introduce a similar structure early in 1997.

Expert advice is no longer available at every branch, following reorganisations encouraged by the need to cut costs and the wish to offer more expert advice. Dresdner Bank, for instance, now handles corporate business at only 700 of its 1200 branches nationwide, although the remainder can handle payment transactions. The new strategy of all German banks is to concentrate qualified advisory staff in a smaller number of branches in the hope of cross-selling more products.

Deutsche Bank, the country's largest financial institution, has divided itself into two parts: a corporate and institutional bank and an investment bank. That bare division reflects the expertise available in the bank, but also means that many German corporate customers are in danger of falling between two stools.

To tackle this problem, Deutsche Bank has set up liaison teams in all its main branches who are charged with introducing investment banking services to medium-sized corporate clients who otherwise deal only with the corporate bank. It would be an impossible task to acquaint all corporate customer liaison staff with the fast-changing products available from the investment bank, so Deutsche's board has decided to create these liaison teams instead.

Selling investment banking products and services is the main goal for all corporate banks in Germany, who for too long have seen their clients in terms of lending business.

Large German banks such as Deutsche Bank and Dresdner Bank have invested heavily in international investment banking over the past few years – Dresdner Bank has bought Kleinwort-Benson and Deutsche has expanded Deutsche Morgan Grenfell, its investment bank. It is self-evident that they will try to market their newly purchased expertise to domestic clients.

That coincides with another trend: German corporations are gradually discovering the attractions of raising funds on the capital markets. Deutsche Telekom, the state-owned utility, is the supreme example here. The company relied on public-sector bonds for its financing until a few years ago. Now Deutsche Telekom has become the largest issuer ever in Europe; a consortium of banks earned nearly DM500 million by underwriting Telekom's initial public offering in November 1996.

Companies such as Telekom are also discovering modern financing instruments based on the capital markets, for example asset-backed securities. These financing instruments are bonds issued by the corporate client and backed by assets such as leasing contracts or outstanding invoices for goods and services already delivered.

CHOOSING A CORPORATE BANKER

In this environment, choosing a Hausbank is a complex task in a country with one of the most fragmented banking systems in the world. Germany has more banks than any other European country. What is more, almost all of the 3600 institutions registered with the Bundesbank are engaged in traditional German universal banking, which combines retail, corporate and institutional banking.

In a few industries, the choice may be more straightforward. Some banks have evolved to specialise in certain industries, hence the Deutsche Schiffsbank finances the shipping trade and the shipbuilding industry, while the specialist bankers for the agriculture and food industries are found at the credit cooperatives (*Volksbanken* and *Raiffeisenbanken*).

But companies would be ill advised to be guided by name alone. It often comes as a surprise to non-German companies to discover that the best-known German banks – such as Deutsche Bank, Dresdner Bank and Commerzbank – actually have modest market shares in corporate banking. Market share estimates for each of these banks are in single figures, usually below 5 per cent.

Nevertheless the big banks' influence extends well beyond their market share. It is often said that the German private-sector banks keep tabs on their customers in three ways: by lending, by participations and by their representation on the companies' supervisory boards.

Another group of private-sector banks – headed by Bayerische Hypotheken- und Wechsel-Bank and Bayerische Vereinsbank – offer full-service banking only in their home regions, although specialist products, particularly in the capital markets, are offered to companies nationwide.

Only a few national names – Deutsche, Dresdner, Commerzbank, BHF-Bank and so on – plus a number of very small private banks – Trinkaus & Burkhardt, Bankhaus Metzler, Sal. Oppenheim and Merck, Finck – do not set themselves any geographical boundaries.

Outsiders often jump to the conclusion that the local credit cooperatives (*Volksbanken* and *Raiffeisenbanken*) or the local savings banks (*Sparkassen*) are unable to handle any but the most straightforward services for corporate customers. That is not necessarily the case. It is true that many of the local banks, some of which cover an area no larger than several villages and have assets of less than DM1 billion, define their corporate clients as the local shopkeepers. But a number of larger firms – which have expanded from small beginnings – have remained loyal to their local *Sparkasse* or *Volksbank*.

That is possible because each local bank is affiliated to a regional wholesale bank – a *Landesbank* for the *Sparkassen* and a *Genossenschaftliche Zentralbank* for the *Volksbanken* and *Raiffeisenbanken*. All these regional banks now strive to offer a complete range of corporate banking services, including foreign business, treasury, capital markets trading, underwriting of equity and bond issues, corporate finance, leasing and factoring. Thus even tiny banks are capable of granting large loans with the help of programme credits arranged jointly with their regional affiliates.

In the savings bank sector, these regional banks include Westdeutsche Landesbank (WestLB), Norddeutsche Landesbank and Bayerische Landesbank. Altogether 13 *Landesbanks* support around 600 savings banks located throughout Germany. In the much more fragmented cooperative sector, each of the 2500 local banks derives corporate banking and capital markets know-how from one of three regional banks: WGZ-Bank, SGZ-Bank and GZB-Bank. Frankfurt-based DG

Bank regards itself as the head bank of the entire cooperative system, although this is disputed by the three regional banks.

Prompted by the banks themselves – the foreign investment banks like to claim particular credit here – many corporate clients in Germany are now dividing their business among a number of banks. So, while day-to-day payments and lending business should be handled by a local bank, company directors are keen to gain the best services and prices possible by inviting a number of institutions, including those from other regions, to bid for specific work, such as cash management or underwriting a bond issue. Eventually, competitive tendering may break the still strong consensus between the various groups in German corporate banking.

22

Financial Products in Germany

Klaus Holschuh, Head of Marketing & Research Global Bonds and Barbara Hain, Trading Research Analyst, Commerzbank

THE GERMAN STOCK MARKET

Only shares of public limited companies listed on a stock exchange are interesting as investments. These shares are traded on Germany's eight stock exchanges. This is where spot and floor trading in German shares takes place.

Spot trading in Germany is divided into three market segments: official trading, the regulated market and unofficial trading are distinguished according to the legal requirements for minimum capital amounts, distribution of shares and information provision by the companies.

The most stringent demands are made on those companies whose shares are admitted to official trading. (In 1995 these amounted to over 500.) These requirements are detailed in the *Stock Exchange Act*, the regulation governing admission to the stock exchange and the individual stock exchange rules. Orders can be completed at the official spot price or the variable price. The variable price is fixed continually during the trading hours. The minimum nominal value for orders in variable trade is 50 shares or multiples thereof. A variable price makes sense only for those shares which are traded actively, especially shares admitted to official trading.

All other shares listed which are not traded at a variable price are settled at the spot price, irrespective of the size of the order. The spot price is fixed once a day by the official broker; it is that price at which the highest turnover can be obtained according to the buy and sell orders received on that day.

The requirements concerning minimum capital, distribution of shares and information provision which companies listed in the regulated market must fulfil are less strict. Last year this market segment comprised 173 German companies. Smaller companies and those which are new on the stock exchange often choose the regulated market for a start. They can then change market segment. The price of many shares in the regulated market is fixed only once a day.

Those companies which have their shares listed in unofficial bourse trading must comply with the lowest requirements. Over 100 German shares and large numbers of shares of foreign companies are traded unofficially. As trading volumes are often small, the price at which orders are completed is fixed only once a day. An unofficial listing is a comparatively inexpensive way of being traded on a stock exchange.

Following the model of the *nouveau marché* in France, another market segment is planned for April 1997. It will be subject to less stringent information requirements, and smaller companies will be given access to the stock exchange.

In addition, there is also off-floor trading. The so-called IBIS trading takes place in high-turnover securities. IBIS is the computerised trading system between individual banks and brokers. As minimum volumes for IBIS orders are quite high (500 actively traded shares, otherwise 1000 shares, bonds with a nominal value of DM1 billion), this system is an alternative to floor trading only for large investors. Considerable advantages are the extended trading hours (8.30 am–5.00 pm), which allow trading to take place before and after stock-exchange trading. IBIS is responsible for up to 30 per cent of the daily turnover in German securities.

Off-floor unofficial trading also exists, but its role is insignificant. This unregulated market segment focuses mainly on trading very small enterprises which have at most regional significance. Very little demands are made as to information. Trading takes place over the telephone and is generally carried out by free (private) brokers, brokers and banks.

In 1995, there were nearly 3000 public limited companies and commercial partnerships limited by shares in Germany as well as 500,000 private limited liability companies. That year the share capital of public limited companies and commercial partnerships limited by shares amounted to almost DM 150 billion. The number of public limited companies listed on a stock exchange came to only 527. New issues of German enterprises in 1995 had a total market value of DM 6.975 billion, with their percentage of market capitalisation coming to 0.84. They accounted for 2.08 per cent of share issues in Germany.

The German shareholder profile is also interesting. From 1981 to 1996, the number of shareholders increased by some 40 per cent. Broken down into holders of employee shares and other shares, another important trend becomes evident. While until 1994 the segment of employee shares was still growing strongly, a notable change has been taking place over the last two years from employee shares towards other shares. Shareholders can be detailed as follows:

- Enterprises   42.1 per cent
- Households   14.6 per cent
- Insurance companies   12.4 per cent
- Banks   10.3 per cent
- Foreign investors   8.7 per cent
- Investment funds   7.6 per cent
- Public households   4.3 per cent

The majority of shareholders have had higher education and are either executives or employed in public service. Their age ranges from 30 to 50 years.

TYPES OF SHARES

Shares are securities which give evidence of the economic and legal ownership of part of a public limited company. The terms of shares are not always standardised. Although company law in most countries stipulates the company terms in detail, the rights arising from ownership of shares, and the provisions for assignment of shares, may differ.

At a stock exchange, ordinary and preference shares are traded. Ordinary shares carry the right to participate in the annual meeting of the company, voting rights and the right to receive dividend payments. Preference shares have advantages over ordinary shares, but these are usually accompanied by a disadvantage. In most cases, preference shares pay a higher dividend than ordinary shares, while they usually carry no voting rights. If, however, no dividend is paid on preference shares for one or two years, the voting rights are revived. Only when the outstanding dividend payments have been made will the voting right cease to exist. For this reason, preference shares are interesting to small shareholders, who, due to their small interest in a company, are usually not very interested in voting rights. Also, preference shares are usually less expensive than ordinary shares, thus less capital is required for an investment.

Regarding the assignment of shares in Germany, we distinguish between bearer and registered shares. Bearer shares are most common, as they can be easily assigned simply by delivery. By contrast, registered shares are assigned by endorsement, ie a written declaration of assignment is required. The transferability of registered shares may also be limited; in this case assignment requires company approval. This is a way of keeping unwanted investors from becoming shareholders.

DEBT INSTRUMENTS AND DERIVATIVES

The German bond market is divided into two segments: public-sector bonds and *Pfandbriefe* on the one hand and other bank bonds on the other. German companies' bond market exposure is very small, as traditional financing instruments, such as the bank loan, prevail. There are only half a dozen issues in the German domestic market. Large German companies are somewhat more active in the foreign DM bond market via their foreign finance subsidiaries. Currently, 24 German debtors are represented with over a hundred issues. CP (Commercial Paper) and MTN (Medium-term Notes) programmes are utilised more actively.

Public-sector borrowers

In order to finance their activities, the federal government and other public-sector bodies all issue various types of fixed-income securities:

Federal government bonds

Federal government bonds (*Bunds*) are government bonds issued to finance public-sector outlays. They are evidence of claims on the part of their holders (Section 793, German Civil Code – BGB).

Bunds are obtainable as registered bonds. The claims are, however, no longer documented as physical securities but rather as loan share rights that are entered in the Federal Debt Register. (The Federal Railways, the Federal Post Office and some states similarly maintain a debt register for their issues, one being kept for each bond offering.)

The government's assets, together with present and future tax revenues, provide collateral for the *Bunds*.

Since July 1990, *Bunds* have been issued via a combined syndicate and tendering procedure and placed through public subscription. In addition, market-regulation quotas are placed by the Bundesbank via the stock exchanges. As *Bunds* are issued at irregular intervals, they are referred to as one-off issues.

Bunds, together with other public-sector bond issues, are introduced to official trading on the stock exchange without any admission procedure. On each official trading day, a single price is established. From 3 October, 1988, federal government bonds and post office and railway bonds have been gradually integrated into variable-price trading. The minimum turnover for this purpose is a nominal DM1 million.

Before and after official stock exchange sessions, a brisk trade is carried on in *Bunds* by the banks, the so-called free (private) brokers and domestic and foreign institutional investors, parallel to official business, in unregulated trading activities.

The Bundesbank regularly intervenes to support or regulate *Bund* prices. It reserves a share of every issue for such market regulation purposes.

Bunds normally have a life of 10 years, but there have been offerings with maturities of 12 and 30 years. *Bunds* fall due *en bloc,* ie they are redeemed in a lump sum at maturity. Redemption is made at face value. Neither the lender nor the borrower has the right to call in the bonds prematurely.

Interest is paid annually. Until 1990, all the bonds issued by the federal government and the other public-sector authorities came with a fixed coupon. Since February 1990, floating-rate issues have also been launched. The broken-period interest is calculated and shown separately.

Treasury financing paper

Treasury financing paper *(Finanzierungsschätze),* issued since 1975, are discounted treasury notes, issued by the government, that cannot be redeemed before maturity; they serve to fund government spending. Like treasury discount paper, they are for the most part money-market instruments.

Federal treasury notes (Bundesschatzanweisungen)

Since July 1996 two-year federal treasury notes *(Bundesschatzanweisungen)* are issued. Treasury discount paper *(U-Schätze)* are bonds of the federal government, its subsidiary budgets or the federal states. The term 'discount' means that no interest payment is made, the interest is deducted from the selling price. Treasury discount paper with a life of one or two years count as money-market paper.

Treasury discount notes (BuBills)

BuBills are short-dated money-market paper in the form of treasury discount notes of the Federal Republic of Germany.

Five-year special federal bonds (Bundesobligationen)

Five-year special federal bonds *(Bundesobligationen)* are instruments used by the federal government to finance public-sector spending. These medium-dated papers have been issued in successive series since December 1979.

Loans against borrowers' notes (Schuldscheindarlehen)

Schuldscheindarlehen are short, medium or long-term, large-scale credits for which a written loan agreement or a written acknowledgement of debt is provided. *Schuldscheindarlehen* can be transferred by way of assignment and, unlike normal credits, may therefore become fungible (exchangeable).

By signing the note, the borrower acknowledges an obligation to make interest payments and redeem the principal. The note is handed over to the lender so that – in the case of conflict – he or she is able to prove the claim arising from the credit and have it enforced in a court of law.

Schuldscheindarlehen are loans, not securities. The popularity of this funding instrument is attributable to the lower costs, smoother adjustment of its terms to the individual needs of the borrower, a simple issuing procedure, rapid settlement and greater discretion than in the case of a bond issue.

For the institutional investor, *Schuldscheindarlehen* are attractive since they are not securities and so, if the prices of the latter fall, they are not obliged to make write-downs on their securities portfolio with regard to such borrowers' notes.

What is more, the lender and the borrower can work out directly conditions such as the life of the loan and the amount raised; this makes it easier to place *Schuldscheindarlehen* with investors.

MORTGAGE BANKS

Mortgage banks specialise in providing generally longer-term credits secured by real-estate liens and ship mortgages. Their second main field of business is lending to local governments. Private and public-law mortgage banks exist alongside one another.

The private mortgage-lending banks include private-sector mortgage banks of both the 'pure' and combined types, and ship-mortgage banks. At present, there are 23 pure and three combined private-sector mortgage banks in Germany, specialising in real estate and communal loans. They grant long-term credits to finance residential construction as well as business and agricultural investments secured by mortgages on the property. In order to fund this lending, the private-sector mortgage banks issue mortgage bonds. The funding of credits to German public-law bodies and institutions is covered by the issue of communal bonds.

Alongside the private-sector banks, public-sector credit institutions play a considerable role in the Federal Republic. In recent years, the significance of the savings banks and their central institutions has increased greatly. Originally, the savings banks were only involved in savings and mortgage lending business. Now they have taken on the character of the universally active commercial banks, even though their traditional functions may still represent the focal point of their business operations.

Mortgage bonds

Mortgage bonds *(Pfandbriefe)* are fixed-income securities which serve to fund loans that are secured by senior mortgages or land charges. Securities may only be issued under the name of mortgage bonds by private mortgage banks, ship-mortgage banks and public-sector credit institutions if these meet the provisions of the legislation relating to either mortgage banks, ship-mortgage banks or those of the legislation pertaining to mortgage bonds and related bonds issued by public-sector banks.

Mortgage bonds come in the form of both bearer and registered paper. While they could be issued as order paper, this does not in fact occur. Most mortgage bonds take the form of bearer securities.

In the case of bearer paper, possession entitles the holder to the right evidenced by the bond. Any bearer is therefore recognised as the recipient of the payment by the borrower. Bearer bonds may be transferred by simple delivery.

Registered bonds are made out in the name of the first or second purchaser. The borrower is obliged to pay only the last-named person. For their transfer, registered bonds require assignment or a direct registration in the name of the second purchaser. Registered bonds are sold only in large denominations of DM1 million and upwards, since they are primarily designed to be placed with institutional investors. At the time of issue, registered bonds may be tailored to the needs of the creditor. For institutional investors, registered mortgage bonds have the advantage that they can be shown in the balance sheet at their cost price, which removes the need to make write-downs

Mortgage bonds have to be covered by matching funds. Covering claims (eg mortgages) equal to the nominal value of the mortgage bonds are needed in order to cover the mortgage bonds outstanding.

Usually, mortgage bonds are covered by senior mortgages on German real estate and buildings which are used either privately, commercially or for agricultural purposes. Such cases are known as ordinary coverage.

Communal bonds

Communal bonds *(Kommunalobligationen or Kommunalschuldverschreibungen)* – recently also referred to as 'public-sector mortgage bonds' – are fixed-income securities issued by private-sector mortgage banks and public-sector credit institutions to fund loans to local governments. As a rule, they bear a fixed coupon; floating interest rates are rare.

Communal loans comprise credits to domestic bodies and public-law institutions, as well as loans to the business sector which are wholly guaranteed by such an entity or institution. These bodies also include the European Union, the European Coal and Steel Community, the European Atomic Community and the European Investment Bank.

Communal bonds may only be issued under that name if they comply with the provisions of the German *Mortgage Bank Act* or the legislation on mortgage bonds and the related bonds of public-sector credit institutions. This is intended to guarantee that anyone purchasing a communal bond acquires a paper with a special degree of security.

Communal bonds are issued in the form of bearer and registered paper, known as registered public-sector mortgage bonds. The issue of order bonds, while possible, is not usual.

The fact that a public-law institution has guaranteed the repayment of the principal and the payment of interest provides security for the communal bonds issued by the mortgage banks.

The upper limit for the amount of mortgage and communal bonds which a pure mortgage bank may have outstanding is 60 times its equity capital; for institutions engaged in other kinds of banking business as well, the ceiling is set at 48 times their equity capital.

Jumbo issues

In order to attract international institutions into the *Pfandbrief* sector, radical changes have been made this year to both the issuing mechanism and trading practice, resulting in the so-called '*Jumbo Pfandbriefe*'.

The term 'jumbo' is applied to issues which have a minimum initial size of DM1 billion and are issued through a syndicate whose members undertake to maintain a secondary market on a bid–offer spread of 5–10 pfennigs. This combination of large volume, widespread distribution and a number of competing dealers provides the transparency and liquidity demanded by international institutions.

The first issue to offer a liquid secondary market was the AAA-rated Frankfurter Hypobank 5.7/8% June 1999, issued by Frankfurter Hypobank themselves in May 1995, although this was not a true 'jumbo' in that there was no syndicate for primary distribution. The first true 'jumbo' was the Bayerische Vereinsbank 6.1/2% 6 June 2005, with an initial issue size of DM1 billion (since increased to DM1.5 billion) and distribution through a syndicate of German banks. Meanwhile, the market has a total volume of over DM 100 billion. It is already fair to say that the domestic market now has a new segment, that trading is carried out on the basis of a considerable discount to smaller tap issues, and that even larger discounts in the future will result in a definite split on the mortgage bond market.

It will be difficult for small and medium-sized issuers of *Pfandbriefe* to keep pace with these developments. Greater concentration is expected to occur within this sector. For some time, the mortgage bank sector has been preparing for hanging market and growing European competition by undertaking mergers and founding new companies. Only the big mortgage banks are in a position to launch jumbo issues.

Profit-sharing certificates

Profit-sharing certificates *(Genußscheine)* are profit-sharing rights issued in the form of securities. They are tradeable paper, occupying an intermediate position between equities and bonds. As a result, they represent both creditor claims and property rights; they do not, however, confer voting rights. As far as terms are concerned, this instrument offers a great deal of scope as no special legal provisions were established for profit-sharing certificates. Profit-sharing rights primarily represent creditor claims, entitling the holder to claims under contract. At the same time, such rights are also property rights, if, for example, the payout is linked to the company's profits or it is agreed that the investor will participate in liquidation proceeds. Profit-sharing certificates have become popular as financing instruments, as they may be recognised, under certain conditions, as part of a company's equity capital; as a result, they offer companies a further means of improving their equity capital base, alongside capital increases through the issue of shares.

Profit-sharing certificates are financing instruments that have been used by companies for many years, but which have only been issued on an extensive scale again since the mid-1980s. As the right to issue profit-sharing certificates is not dependent on the specific legal form of a company, those which otherwise lack access to the stock exchange (eg a private limited company) can also raise equity capital via the stock exchange in this way.

Derivatives

Deutsche Börse AG is the carrier of DTB (the German Options and Futures Exchange). On DTB are traded:

- DAX futures (German share index of Deutsche Börse AG – 30 shares);
- M-DAX futures (another 70 shares);
- Options on the DAX futures;
- DAX-Index options;
- Options on 35 shares (since 23 September 1996, previously only 16 shares).

And on the interest derivatives side:

- *Bund* futures (notional 10 years);
- *Bobl* futures (notional 5 years);
- Options on these futures;
- FIBOR futures;
- LIBOR futures (starting November 1996);
- Options on money-market futures are planned
- There is an over-the-counter market for further share options and forward rate agreements, caps, floors, collars, swaptions, interest rate swaps etc.

DEVELOPMENTS AND CHANGES IN LEGISLATION

The legal framework of the capital market in Germany has been improved considerably with the Amendments to the *Stock Exchange Act* of 1986 and 1989, the *First Capital Market Promotion Act* of 1990, the *Act on Small Public Limited Companies and the Deregulation of Company Law*, and the *Second Capital Market Promotion Act* of 1994. This development is furthered by the *Third Capital Market Promotion Act*, which will focus on three areas: stock exchanges and securities, investments and equity participation.

In the stock exchange and securities area, the new law envisages not only deregulation measures to widen market participants' room for manoeuvre, but also a modernisation of the stock exchange and securities laws. Another major objective is the promotion of Germany as an investment location. New spheres of activity are to be opened up for the investment business, while its existing room for manoeuvre will be widened. Investment trusts shall receive permission to issue holding funds and equity funds with limited maturities. The use of OTC options and the admission of securities repurchase agreements are also planned. Funds' liquidity shall become more flexible with the admission of money-market fund certificates as liquidity investments. Finally, it is planned to create the legal framework for investment companies having the legal form of a public limited company.

The third major objective of the new Act is an amendment to the *Equity Investment Company Act*. In the future, misusing equity investment companies as holdings will be prohibited, whereas it will be permissible to add venture capital for companies not listed on a stock exchange.

The federal ministry of finance is also planning measures designed to 'further enhance the standing of the federal government as issuer of benchmark securities and to strengthen the competitiveness of Germany as a financial center with a view to EMU'. In this connection, 30-year bonds and strips (separation of coupon and nominal to obtain zero bonds) were mentioned.

OUTLOOK

An important impulse for the German market in the long term is the fact that as from 1 August 1994 the *Second Capital Market Promotion Act* reduced the minimum nominal value of a share from DM50 to DM5. This change was devised after surveys conducted in international stock exchange centres showed a positive correlation between low average share prices and turnover. Over the last two years, the opportunity to reduce the minimum nominal value of shares has been taken many times. The results of the first part of this study also indicate that small investors are increasingly inclined to accept shares as a means of investment.

Another factor supporting the increasing stock market exposure is the government's privatisation plans. A current example is the Deutsche Telekom issue, which was launched in November 1996. This enterprise is the largest telecommunications company in the world. The Federal Republic of Germany is still the sole owner. For this issue the bookbuilding method will be used; the nominal volume resulting from the capital increase will be DM2.5 billion. The share capital thus comes to a nominal DM12.5 billion, of which DM2.5 billion shares will be issued at a nominal amount of DM5 per share. According to the latest information, the share will be priced from DM25 to DM30. As an incentive for private investors, Deutsche Telekom will grant a discount of DM0.50 per share, which can be obtained for up to 300 shares.

The German bond market has registered two-digit growth rates over the last few years. A major reason is surely to be found in German unification, but future growth forecasts will be much less enthusiastic.

THE PRINCIPLE

that takes

partners

to the top

Photographed by Eric Valli

◀ In today's increasingly difficult business envi-ronment, one inevitably runs up against obstacles that are best surmounted with the help of an experienced partner. ◀ You're at the right address with DG BANK. Partnership based on the natural self-interest of both parties is the core of our business policy. Here customer-oriented counselling leads to tailor-made concepts. Backed by the bank's expertise, international dimension, and a principle that makes every customer a partner in a singular way. ◼ It is called the WIR PRINZIP, to which DG BANK and its staff are wholeheartedly committed. The WIR PRINZIP is rooted in the classic tradition of the cooperative system linking equal business partners. And it has a great future. Because it exemplifies the central idea of partnership: that mutual cooperation leads to mutual success.

THE **WIR** PRINZIP

Head Office: DG BANK, ✉ D-60265 Frankfurt am Main, Germany. Office London: 10 Aldersgate Street, London EC1A 4XX, tel. 01 71-7 76 60 00, fax 01 71-7 76 61 00. Offices in: Amsterdam, Atlanta, Bombay, Hong Kong, Luxembourg, Madrid, Milan, Moscow, New York, Paris, Rio de Janeiro, Shanghai, Tokyo, Warsaw, Zurich.

DG BANK ◕

23

Business Formation: Taxation and Fiscal Implications

Christoph Schreiber, C&L Deutsche Revision AG and Adrian Yeeles, Coopers & Lybrand

A variety of business forms is available in Germany. The choice of which form to use in a particular situation will depend on commercial and tax needs.

SOLE PROPRIETOR

An individual operating a business on his or her own, ie not through a separate legal entity and without any partners, is automatically considered a sole proprietor. Income derived from the business is taxed together with earnings from other income categories, although a reduced top marginal rate of 47 per cent applies to the business income. Subject to a number of restrictions, losses may be offset against income from other categories. In addition, trade taxes on income and business capital are imposed, as described in more detail in the chapter on Business Taxation. A sole proprietorship is easy to establish and normally provides the appropriate organisational form for craftspeople and small businesses. There are limited accounting requirements and little administrative work, but personal liability for all debts and legal obligations incurred in connection with the business is unlimited.

PARTNERSHIP

A general partnership is an association for business purposes formed by two or more general partners. These general partners can be either individuals or corporations, but the former is more common. A general partnership is easy to establish as no written partnership agreement is required (although advisable). A general partnership, however, must be registered in the local commercial register. Even though the general partnership does not qualify as a separate legal entity, it can act in a legally binding manner under its own name, can incur liabilities and can sue or be sued. As in the case of a sole proprietorship, each general partner can be held personally liable with the entire business and private property for the debts of the partnership.

A general partnership is a tax subject as far as VAT and trade taxes are concerned, but for income taxation purposes the business income is allocated to the single partners and taxed at the individual's level, considering the personal circumstances of each single partner. Property tax falls due at the partner's level only. The general partnership is a popular vehicle again for craftspeople and small businesses which are run by more than one individual.

The limited partnership represents a special form of a partnership in that, in addition to at least one general partner, there are one or more limited partners who promise to contribute a fixed amount of money. As is the case with the general partnership, the agreement on a limited partnership need not be in writing, but registration in the commercial register is mandatory. Whilst the general partner is fully liable in person for all debts and obligations relating to the business, the limited partner's liability is limited to the amount of capital contribution.

The tax treatment is the same as that applying to the general partnership, ie trade taxes and VAT are imposed on the partnership itself whereas the business income is attributed to the partners, usually in proportion to the share of their capital contributions.

A popular vehicle is the GmbH & Co KG, a partnership with a GmbH as general partner and one or more individuals as limited partners. Many family businesses favour this structure which combines the advantages of limited liability with the opportunity of direct loss offsetting at the level of the individual partners. A GmbH & Co KG has fewer accounting requirements to fulfil than a corporation, but a number of formalities need to be considered when setting up this type of structure.

COMPANIES

Business corporations, of which the limited liability company (GmbH) and the public stock corporation (AG) are the most important, qualify to the full extent as separate legal entities and are thus in all regards tax subjects. Income derived by such corporations is always regarded as business income so that the levy of trade taxes is mandatory. A disadvantage of a corporation is that property tax is actually imposed twice: first on the assets of the corporation and second on the value of the shares at shareholder level, even though the economic substance is identical.

Several formal requirements need to be observed when a business corporation is set up. In the case of a GmbH, the articles of incorporation as well as a number of other transactions must have been executed in front of a notary public, before they are submitted to the authorities for registration. There is a minimum capital requirement of DM50,000, of which at least DM25,000 must have been paid in on registration. The minimum nominal value per share is DM500. If capital in kind is contributed instead of cash, further prerequisites must be observed.

The GmbH is by far the most popular form for doing business, regardless of industry and size of the undertaking. The GmbH is understood as a highly flexible and rather informal type of corporation which simultaneously offers the major benefit of limitation of liability. Although many transactions affecting the GmbH require the involvement of a notary public, an assignment of shares, an increase or decrease of the capital and liquidation can still be performed relatively easily.

ACTING THROUGH A BRANCH OR A SUBSIDIARY

Perhaps the most important decision to be taken by a foreign investor who plans to run a business in Germany is whether to set up a local subsidiary or merely act through a German branch of the foreign headquarters. Even though there are practically no restrictions as to the activities which a branch can carry out, one must consider the fact that a branch does not represent a separate legal entity of its own. Hence, all business operations conducted by the branch are looked on as operations carried out by the head office. Consequently, all claims relating to the branch activities expose the head office to liabilities to the full extent of its assets. Inter-company agreements between head office and branch are legally impossible, although the separation and allocation of branch profits and branch expenses must be performed under analogous consideration of the general transfer pricing rules.

The constitution of a branch normally involves almost as many formal requirements as the set-up of a subsidiary, in particular as a branch office must be recorded in the local commercial register. However, no withholding taxes fall due when the branch profits (after German profit taxes) are transferred to the foreign head office. Further commercial and accounting requirements may be less strict than the corresponding rules for corporations.

A major aspect of starting up a business in the form of a branch is often whether or not start-up losses can be offset against other profits of the company in the head office jurisdiction. Losses incurred by a German corporation can be carried forward indefinitely, but may only be used against future profits of this corporation and do not reduce the tax burden of the head office. Closing down a branch office is generally easier than liquidating a corporation and this is why some foreign investors prefer the constitution of a branch office for the start-up phase and convert it into a GmbH when the business has strengthened. According to the amended transformation laws, the reorganisation of a branch into a subsidiary can in most cases be performed at book value in a tax-neutral way, on the condition that the whole business or at least whole segments of the business are transferred.

Finally, the decision taken by foreign investors may depend on the level of profit taxation. In this regard, a local subsidiary is clearly more beneficial than a branch office since the corporate income tax is 30 per cent (on distributed earnings) versus 42 per cent in the case of a branch. Even in light of the fact that the difference of 12 per cent is, on account of the deductibility of trade income tax, reduced to less than 10 per cent, net profits transferable under a parent/subsidiary structure are still higher than in the case of a branch. Even withholding taxes which may fall due depending on the location of the parent company do not make up for the difference. For this reason, foreign investors tend to set up a GmbH rather than open a branch.

FISCAL REQUIREMENTS ON FORMATION OF A BUSINESS

Irrespective of whether the business is run in the form of a sole proprietorship, partnership, corporation or branch, a permit to conduct a business is required prior to the commencement of any activities. In most cases this permit is granted immediately on application, and the costs of obtaining the permit are not great. Only when a certain type of business is to be conducted – eg activity as an insurance broker, sale of dangerous goods – the entrepreneur needs a special permit which is granted only after examination of his or her character and abilities.

The next step is to notify the local tax authority of the existence of a new business and to ask for a tax identity number (and a special VAT identity number, if necessary). In response to such notification the local tax authority will forward to the company or entrepreneur a question-naire on the type of business carried out, size of business, organisational form, number of staff, expected turnover, expected profits etc. The tax-paying enterprise is required to fill out the form and to return it to the authorities. Depending on the figures presented to the tax office, the authorities may or may not determine prepayments on income/corporate income and trade taxes. If staff are employed, the company will also receive information on the tax office to which payroll tax payments have to be made.

Individuals who carry out independent work and perform their duties in Germany are mandatory members of the German social security system. Thus, when starting up a business the employer must register the employees with the appropriate social security authorities. This is normally the local health insurance authority (AOK) or, if the employee has opted for private health insurance, the local office of the employee's health fund.

Apart from the registration charges payable to the commercial register and expenses for the services rendered by the rotary public – the costs depend on the amount of capital involved – no tax whatsoever will fall due on formation or alteration of a business. Stamp duty and capital transfer tax triggered by the creation and the assignment of shares in a corporation were abolished some years ago.

Investors who have chosen to set up a corporation must keep in mind tax and other potential liability risks connected with business operations carried on prior to the final registration of the company in the com-mercial register. Any business activity carried on before the articles of incorporation have been certified by a notary public is regarded as being performed by a civil partnership. In other words, each of the founders can be held personally liable without any limitation. Furthermore, expenses incurred during that stage cannot be deducted from reven-ues received by the corporation after it has come into existence so all expenses and profits, if any, derived during this period only affect the individual founders. Especially in the case of non-residents this often results in the irrevocable loss of start-up costs. In contrast, expenses incurred by the corporation after certification of the articles but before final registration in the commercial register qualify as those of the corporation. The same applies with regard to income, ie all expenses and revenues derived during this period are then taken into account when determining the corporation's income as both entities are deemed to form a single unit. A corporation already operating its business prior to registration must add to its name 'in formation' (*in Gründung* – i.G.).

Depending on the size of the business and some other factors, there is an obligation to keep accurate accounting records and especially to draw up an opening balance sheet. Since all contributions in kind have to be shown in the balance sheet at the lower of acquisition cost and going concern value, contributions of assets taken from another business may lead to the realisation of taxable profits (losses) at the level of this other business.

24

Financial Reporting and Accounting

Wolfgang Suchanek and Sven Rosorius,
C&L Deutsche Revision AG

In spite of the existence of EU directives, International Accounting Standards and the ever-increasing number of international business transactions, German accounting retains the reputation of being something of a mystery. Considerable attention has been devoted to gaining a better understanding of German accounts and this remains an important task for anyone engaged in or contemplating doing business with Germany. This chapter covers the most important rules regarding financial reporting and accounting in Germany and highlights some of the most frequently encountered differences from UK, US or international practice.

REPORTING

Source of generally accepted accounting principles

German accounting principles are derived predominantly from the German Commercial Code, German generally accepted accounting principles (*Grundsätze ordnungsmäßiger Buchführung* or GoB), tax court rulings, pronouncements of the German Institute of Certified Public Accountants (*Institut der Wirtschaftsprüfer*) and the German Stock Corporation Law and Limited Liability Companies Law.

Contents of financial statements

With regard to the content of financial statements there are certain differences between companies (stock corporations, AG, and limited liability companies, GmbH) and other types of business organisations.

The financial statements of all German companies contain a balance sheet, an income statement and notes to the accounts. A statement of retained earnings and a statement of cash flows or statement of changes in financial position are not required.

Whereas companies must follow the prescribed balance sheet format, they have a choice between two income statement formats. The more common of the two follows the *Gesamtkostenverfahren*, which classifies costs by their nature (eg total wages and salaries, total depreciation) and might be called the 'cost categories format'. With this format, therefore, cost of sales and gross profit cannot be calculated. The other format might be called the 'operations-oriented format' and follows the *Umsatzkostenverfahren*. This classifies items by function, is similar to the most common UK and and US formats and does calculate cost of sales and gross profit.

The Commercial Code requires that financial statements are prepared in a clear, understandable and complete manner; that both the balance sheet and the income statement are presented for the current and preceding years; and that the opening balance sheet agrees with the closing balance sheet of the preceding year (thus ruling out prior year adjustments).

The notes to the financial statements must provide an adequate explanation of the balance sheet items and all additional details necessary for the financial statements to give a true and fair view of the net worth, financial position and results of the reporting entity. All companies are required by the Commercial Code to disclose certain basic information in the notes; large companies (see below) are required to make additional disclosures, while medium-sized and, in particular, small companies may omit some disclosures.

Furthermore, all medium-sized and large companies are required to prepare an annual management report on the company's economic condition and circumstances (*Lagebericht*), which does not, however, constitute part of the financial statements. The management report must give a true and fair view of the company's economic progress and position and must also cover significant events that occurred subsequent to the balance sheet date and expected developments within the company and its markets. The management report is covered by the independent auditors' report.

Statutory reporting and audit requirements

The extent and form of the publication of the financial statements and management report depend on the size of the company.

Two of the three requirements in Table 24.1 must be met for two consecutive years to determine the size of a company.

Table 24.1 *Requirements to determine size of company*

Companies	Total assets in millions (DM)	Total sales in millions (DM)	Total numbers of employees
Small	< 5.31	< 10.62	< 50
Medium-sized	5.31–21.24	10.62–42.48	51–250
Large	> 21.21	> 42.48	> 250

Quoted companies or those traded on a stock exchange are always deemed to be large companies.

Table 24.2 briefly summarises the requirements for each size category.

Table 24.2 *Financial statements required*

	Large companies	Medium-sized companies	Small companies
Balance sheet	Unabbreviated presentation	Unabbreviated presentation	Abbreviated presentation
Income statement	Unabbreviated presentation	Abbreviated presentation	Abbreviated presentation
Notes to the financial statements	Full disclosure	Limited disclosure	Limited disclosure

All companies must file their financial statements and management report with the local Commercial Register within nine months (small companies 12 months) of the year end and notice of their compliance must be published in the Federal Gazette (*Bundesanzeiger*). Small companies do not need to file the income statement. Large companies must in addition publish their full financial statements and management report in the Federal Gazette.

It should be noted that the penalties for non-compliance with the publication requirements are minor and in any case very difficult to enforce. For this reason the great majority of small- and medium-sized companies tend not to file or publish their financial statements.

Audit

All medium-sized and large limited liability companies and stock corporations are required to have their annual financial statements audited.

Partnerships and sole proprietorships

Some partnerships and sole proprietorships, because of their size, are regulated by the Law on Disclosure Requirements for Large Enterprises (*Publizitätsgesetz*). The size thresholds are as follows:

- Total assets (DM millions)   125
- Total sales (DM millions)   250
- Total employees   5000

If these thresholds are exceeded for two consecutive years then these types of businesses also require annual audits and the financial statements must be published in the Federal Gazette and filed with the local Commercial Register. In this case, however, financial statements consist of balance sheet and income statement only – notes to the accounts are not legally required.

ACCOUNTING

General accounting principles

The general accounting principles apply to all types of business organisations. However, in the Commercial Code there are special requirements for companies, so the detailed comments which follow do not in all cases apply to sole proprietorships or partnerships.

Annual financial statements must be prepared using the historical cost basis of measurement and must strictly adhere to the going concern and accrual concepts. The prudence concept also has to observed. This requires the recognition of all anticipated risks and losses arising up to the date of the balance sheet and becoming known up to the time of preparation of the financial statements and prohibits recognition of any unrealised profits.

In any system of accounting there are occasions when the accruals principle conflicts with that of prudence, but it is clear that in Germany prudence takes precedence. This is apparent from professional commentaries but also in its practical application. For example, no particular method of foreign currency translation is specified in the Commercial Code; however, in accordance with the prudence concept, and unlike in the UK or US, unrealised exchange gains may not be recognised as income. The precise method used must be disclosed in the notes.

The principle of individual valuation requires that an item-by-item approach be applied in any measuring process; offsetting assets against liabilities and income against expenses is not allowed.

German accounting also includes one particular concept which is almost unknown in other countries, this being that commercial financial statements are the authoritative basis for the tax accounts, which are not an independent set of accounts. On the other hand, most tax incentives can be claimed only if the treatment of a particular item in the commercial financial statements and in the tax accounts is identical (the 'conformity rule'). This principle results in a strong interaction between tax law and the accounting requirements, and this chapter gives several examples of its practical impact.

The Commercial Code requires that the financial statements give a true and fair view. However, in contrast to the position in the UK, in Germany the true-and-fair-view requirement is not an overriding principle. The Commercial Code assumes that compliance with detailed rules will generally ensure truth and fairness, but if that is not the case then the position is to be explained in the notes to the accounts.

ACCOUNTING PRINCIPLES FOR SPECIFIC ITEMS

Intangible fixed assets

Intangible assets such as franchises, patents, licences and similar rights must be capitalised at cost if they have been acquired. Capitalisation of self-generated intangibles, that is those not acquired from third parties, is not permitted. Perhaps the most important result of this rule is that research and development expenses may not be capitalised but must be commented on in the management report.

The Commercial Code requires amortisation of capitalised intangible fixed assets over their estimated useful life.

If the value of an intangible asset is lower than the carrying amount, the carrying amount must be written down to the current value if the decrease in value is permanent (extraordinary depreciation). A write-down must be reversed under the same conditions as for tangible fixed assets (see the chapter '*Specific Accounting Techniques*').

Expenses incurred in starting up or expanding a business

Under a special concession, expenses incurred in starting up or expanding a business may be capitalised. This amount must be amortised in each following year by at least 25 per cent. Profits may be distributed only to the extent that distributable revenue reserves and retained earnings exceed the amount capitalised.

Goodwill

Capitalisation of purchased goodwill is optional. If goodwill has been capitalised, it is amortised over four years or systematically over the years that the company is likely to benefit from it. For income tax purposes, the amortisation period is fixed at 15 years starting with the year of initial capitalisation, and many companies will also adopt the 15-year amortisation period for their commercial financial statements.

Tangible fixed assets

Fixed assets are carried at their historical acquisition or construction cost, net of accumulated systematic depreciation. Carrying fixed assets at revalued amounts is not permitted.

Fixed assets costing DM800 or less may be fully written off immediately (effectively taken straight to expenses).

Expenditure for improvements and replacement is capitalised, whereas expenditure for maintenance and repairs is expensed immediately.

Depreciation

A variety of different depreciation methods is acceptable in Germany and these are discussed in greater detail in *Specific Accounting Techniques*, Chapter 27. The key points to note are that:

- depreciation in German accounts frequently exceeds that which would be charged in UK or US accounts;
- German depreciation is often influenced by tax regulations.

Government grants

There is no codified accounting standard covering government grants. In practice, the accounting treatment of grants related to capital expenditure is different from financial assistance towards current expenses.

To the extent that grants related to capital expenditure are subject to income tax, they are usually netted against the cost of the related fixed assets. If they are income tax free, they are usually included directly in other operating income. Financial assistance received towards current expenses is generally included directly in other operating income in the same period in which the corresponding expense is recorded.

Leases

Accounting for leases is not dealt with in the Commercial Code. Whether the leased asset is to be capitalised by the lessor or the lessee depends on a number of different criteria, but in most cases the accounting treatment of a lease follows its treatment for income tax reporting purposes. The tax rules allow capitalisation only in rare circumstances, so in practice in Germany leases are generally treated as operating leases.

The decision as to whether the lease is a finance lease depends on a number of criteria including:

- whether there is full payout during the non-cancellable period;
- whether the non-cancellable lease period covers less than 40 per cent or more than 90 per cent of the leased asset's normal useful life; and
- whether the lease agreement includes a purchase or lease renewal option at the end of the non-cancellable period; if it does, the accounting treatment depends on the terms of the option.

Whether capitalisation is by lessor or lessee is further dependent on the nature of the leased asset; that is, whether it is land, a building or a moveable asset.

For operating leases, the rental payments are expensed by the lessee and recorded as income by the lessor in the periods to which they relate. Lease commitments that do not appear on the balance sheet are required by the Commercial Code to be disclosed in the notes.

Investments

The valuation of investments depends on their classification as current or fixed asset investments:

- *current asset investments:* these are investments which are not intended as permanent investments of capital, are marketable and are carried at the lower of acquisition cost or market value;
- *fixed asset investments:* these are carried at acquisition cost. Equity accounting is not used in single-entity financial statements. If an investment has declined in value, it may be written down to current value and must be if the decline is considered permanent.

Should the reasons for the write-down cease to apply in subsequent years, commercial law requires that the write-down be reversed unless a reversal would have tax consequences. Since currently all write-backs of fixed asset investments do have a tax effect, such reversals are, in effect, optional. This is another example of the 'conformity rule' in operation.

Current assets

Inventories

The cost of inventory consists of the purchase or manufacturing cost. Purchase cost is calculated net of discounts and allowances. Manufacturing cost includes the cost of direct material and labour and any specific production costs such as special moulds and tools and manufacturing licence expenses; it may, and generally does, include manufacturing and material overheads. Certain general administrative expenses may also be included, but selling expenses are not allowed.

Inventory cost should in principle be determined on an item-by-item basis. In practice, however, the moving average method, FIFO and, unlike in the UK, LIFO methods are also permitted.

The Commercial Code requires inventories to be carried at the lower of cost or market value. Market value is generally represented by:

- replacement cost for raw materials and supplies;
- net realisable value (sales value less costs of completion and disposal and, at the company's option, profit margin) for work in progress and finished goods;
- for goods purchased for resale, the lower of replacement cost and net realisable value.

Provision may be made for fluctuations in value in the near future. Furthermore, a lower value can be optionally used if permitted by tax law.

Long-term contract work in progress is valued at cost (completed contract method), less any provisions necessary, and not by the percentage of completion method. This is an example of prudence in German accounting since it means no profits are taken on unfinished contracts.

Debtors

The key points relating to accounting for debtors in Germany are as follows:

- Receivables due after more than one year that are non interest bearing or bear interest at a rate lower than the prevailing commercial rate should be written down to their present value.
- Foreign currency debtors are translated at the lower of the transaction rate and the year-end rate, so no gains arise.
- In addition to specific bad debt provisions, flat rate provisions may be established for general credit risks; since these are also tax deductible they are more common (and perhaps larger) than in the UK or US.

Liabilities and accruals

General accounting treatment

There is no authoritative distinction between current and non-current liabilities. The Commercial Code subdivides liabilities into accruals (with separate items for pension, tax and other accrued liabilities) and accounts payable (with separate items for debenture loans, amounts owed to credit institutions, trade payables, notes payables, amounts owed to affiliates and other payables).

If there is certainty as to the existence and amount of an obligation, the item must be included in accounts payable; if there is any uncertainty about either existence or amount, the item must be included in other accruals. If only the due date of an obligation is uncertain, it is presented as a payable.

While the concept of matching expenditure with related income is fundamental in Germany, the concept of prudence has priority. Accordingly, accruals must be set up for uncertain liabilities and impending losses. Uncertain liabilities are estimated liabilities for which it is either known or probable that an asset has been impaired or a liability incurred as at the balance sheet date.

Accruals

In general, accruals must be set up for foreseeable losses. The following specific accruals are mandatory:

- uncertain liabilities and impending losses from uncompleted business transactions;
- deferred maintenance or waste removal costs incurred within 3 months (maintenance) or 12 months (waste removal) after the end of the business year;

- guarantee costs not incurred under a legal obligation; and
- pension commitments entered into from 1 January 1987 (see also below).

In addition, the following accruals are optional:

- maintenance deferred from the current year, to be carried out more than three months after the year end;
- future major repairs, limited to specific conditions.

In many countries, including the UK, accruals for items such as deferred maintenance would not be established.

Dividends paid or payable

Proposed dividends are not accrued for at the balance sheet date, but shown as a transfer from retained profits in the following year's accounts.

Pension accruals

It is widespread practice in Germany to accrue future pension obligations; external funding of pension obligations is the exception rather than the rule. The value of the accrual may be based either on an actuarial calculation or, as is generally the case, on the German tax regulations. The tax regulations use an actuarial method with a number of standard assumptions and rules which tend to reduce the accrual compared to what would be considered necessary under UK or US rules.

The impact of these limitations and assumptions is discussed in more detail in the chapter *Specific Accounting Techniques*.

Deferred taxes

There are many areas in the German income tax regulations where an accounting method chosen for income tax purposes is also required to be used for financial reporting purposes. Accordingly, there are relatively few differences in Germany between taxable income for financial reporting purposes and that for tax reporting purposes.

The Commercial Code requires a net deferred tax liability to be recorded using the full liability method when taxable income under tax regulations is lower than pre-tax accounting income due to timing differences. The recording of a deferred tax asset is optional, but if it is done, profits may be distributed only if, after such distribution, the freely available revenue reserves plus retained profits less any accumulated losses brought forward are at least equal to the recorded tax asset.

Contingencies

Practice regarding contingencies is relatively straightforward:

- contingent gains are normally not recorded or disclosed;
- for contingent losses the accounting treatment (accrual or disclosure only) is governed by the concept of prudence. Accordingly, all contingent losses that are likely to occur must be accrued on an estimated basis. A contingent liability that has not been accrued must be disclosed on the face of the balance sheet or in the notes.

Extraordinary and exceptional items

Extraordinary items are items which are material in size, not regularly recurring and of unusual character. Items such as gains and losses on the sale of major assets or investments or of part of a business could be disclosed as extraordinary items under German rules, as could items related to mergers, acquisitions or restructuring.

All extraordinary items must be explained in the annual report.

Unlike in certain other countries, including the UK, no distinction is made between extraordinary and exceptional items.

Consolidation requirements

German parent companies meeting certain size criteria are required to publish consolidated statements comprising all group companies under common control, both domestic and foreign. The uniform German accounting principles, which may well differ from the ones used for local statutory accounts, must be applied for all companies included in the consolidation and all intra-group profits and losses must be eliminated.

It is currently being discussed whether, under certain conditions, consolidated financial statements may also be prepared using international rules (eg US or International Accounting Standards).

For investments in companies in which 20 per cent or more is held, but not the majority of the voting rights, the equity method must be used. However, it should be noted that the equity method is allowed only in consolidated statements, not in single-entity financial statements.

Table 24.3 *Summary of significant differences in basic accounting principles*

	Germany	UK	IAS
Intangible fixed assets Capitalisation	Only purchased intangible fixed assets can be capitalised. Own research and development expenditure should not be capitalised, but expensed.	It is permissible to capitalise concessions, patents, licences, trade marks and similar rights and assets, if they are created by the company as intangible fixed assets and the historical cost can be determined. Expenditure on pure and applied research and development cost should be written off. Development costs may be capitalised, provided that specific conditions are met.	Generally in conformity with UK GAAP. However, capitalisation of development expenses is <u>required</u> when specific conditions are met.
Valuation	Intangible assets may not be revalued above cost.	Intangible fixed assets may also be stated at current cost.	No special IAS rules.
Expenses incurred in starting up or expanding a business	Start up expenses and business expansion may be capitalised and must be amortised in each following year by at least 25 per cent.	Expenses incurred in starting up or expanding a business may not be capitalised.	Generally in conformity with UK GAAP.
Goodwill	Goodwill in individual entity accounts may not be deducted from reserves.	Normally immediately written off against reserves but, if capitalised, goodwill should be amortised systematically through the profit and loss account, over its useful economic life.	Generally in conformity with German GAAP.
Tangible fixed assets Cost	Strict historical cost concept	Revaluation possible (particularly for land and buildings).	Historical cost concept, but alternatively revaluation permitted.
Depreciation	All depreciation claimed for tax purposes (including reducing balance and accelerated depreciation) must be reflected in the commercial financial statements.	Reducing balance method permitted but not widely used. Accelerated depreciation for tax purposes not permitted in the financial statements.	Depreciation for tax purposes not permitted.

Table 24.3 *Summary of significant differences in basic accounting principles (continued)*

	Germany	UK	IAS
(Finance) leases	Capitalisation by the economic owner based on a series of tests, but definition is related to tax rules.	Same, but test criteria differ significantly.	Same, but test criteria differ significantly from German GAAP and in details from UK GAAP.
Investments	Strict historical cost concept. It is not permitted to revalue fixed asset investments above cost – they should be carried at cost less provision for permanent diminution in value.	Alternatively investment may be stated at revalued amounts (market value/current cost).	Alternatively investment may be stated at revalued amounts; for investments in associates equity accounting should be used.
Current assets Inventories: Purchase or manufacturing cost	Average cost is the most usual method for determining cost; however, FIFO and LIFO are allowed.	LIFO not usually acceptable (SSAP9).	LIFO method is permitted, but average method and FIFO are preferred.
Revaluation	Stocks may not be valued above cost (alternative accounting rules not permitted).	Where a company adopts alternative accounting rules, stocks may be included at current cost.	Historical cost concept.
Lower of cost or market value	Not always based on sales market. For all purchased goods (raw materials, maintenance materials, supplies and merchandise) the relevant market value is the replacement cost in the procurement market.	Net realisable value test only uses the selling market price as the basis for market value.	Generally in conformity with UK GAAP.
Long-term construction type contracts	Use of the completed contract method with rare exceptions.	Use of the percentage of completion method unless information as to cost or progress is unreliable, in which case the completed contract method may be used.	Percentage of completion method is used. Where the outcome cannot be estimated reliably, revenue should be recognised equal to the contract costs expended.
Current asset investments	Strict historical cost concept.	Readily marketable securities should normally be stated at market value.	Generally in conformity with UK GAAP.

Table 24.3 *Summary of significant differences in basic accounting principles (continued)*

	Germany	UK	IAS
Liabilities Accruals for future repairs and maintenance	Certain accruals must be set up and others can be set up depending on various conditions.	Generally not permitted.	Generally not permitted.
Pension accruals	Unfunded system: actuarial method, generally with a number of fixed assumptions according to the tax regulations. Pension accruals in respect of benefits granted before 31 December 1986 are optional.	Funded system: actuarial expertise is required to determine an appropriate level of contributions to fund the obligations; however, the assumptions differ from the German fixed assumptions.	Generally similar to UK GAAP.
Deferred taxes	Recording of a deferred tax asset optional. Full liability method.	A deferred tax asset should be recognised unless recovery is not assured. Partial liability method (it must be probable that a tax asset or liability will materialise in the foreseeable future).	Option between full or partial liability methods.

25

Business Taxation

Christoph Schreiber, C&L Deutsche Revision AG and Adrian Yeeles, Coopers & Lybrand

INTRODUCTION

The taxation of business activities in Germany is an important factor in determining the scope and form of investment. The tax system is relatively complex and often difficult for foreign investors to deal with, which can place them at a competitive disadvantage to German businesses. On the other hand, with appropriate planning investors can turn their foreign status to advantage. The key aspects of the tax system are highlighted in the following paragraphs.

MEANING OF 'BUSINESS'

Any person or entity who is engaged in any kind of ongoing trade or other commercial activity with the intention of making profits and who is not self-employed (such as solicitors, tax advisers, architects, doctors etc) is carrying on a business within the meaning of German civil and tax laws and is termed an 'entrepreneur' (*Unternehmer*).

A business operation can be run in the form of a sole proprietorship, a partnership or a corporation. The entrepreneur or enterprise may have a registered seat or place of central management either in or outside Germany. In the former case it qualifies as a resident taxpayer, in the latter as non-resident. While the characterisation of a business depends solely on the nature of the activities performed, the actual tax consequences, such as the scope of taxation and level of tax burden, depend on the legal form of the business, the status as resident or non-resident and a variety of other factors.

TAXES ON BUSINESS

The following taxes apply to business activities:

- income tax or corporate income tax (*Einkommensteuer, Körperschaftsteuer*); imposed on the taxable earnings of individual entrepreneurs and corporations respectively;
- trade taxes (*Gewerbesteuern*) levied on income from the trade and on business capital;
- net worth tax (*Vermögensteuer*) payable by individuals and corporations on the basis of a specially assessed total net asset value (not levied from 1997 onwards);
- value added tax (*Umsatzsteuer*);
- real estate transfer tax (*Grunderwerbsteuer*) payable when real property (or, in certain situations, shares in a company owning real property) is transferred.

DETERMINATION OF TAXABLE INCOME

Entrepreneurs are required by law to keep books and records and to prepare statutory annual financial statements, irrespective of whether the business is organised in the form of a sole proprietorship, partnership or corporation. These form the basis for determining taxable profits or losses.

As a general rule all business-related expenses are deductible in computing taxable profits, provided they have actually been incurred and are not on capital account. As a result, deductions are given for costs which are often not allowable in other countries, such as the cost of business entertaining, provision of company cars and even, in some circumstances, bribes. By way of exception to the general rule, certain costs are not allowed:

- *taxes on business profits and capital,* including corporate and income tax, solidarity surcharge and net worth tax;
- *certain entertainment costs* – no deduction is given for excessive costs, and only 80 per cent of reasonable costs is allowed;
- *business gifts to non-employees* if the net value per person per year exceeds DM75;
- *charitable contributions* above prescribed legal limits;

- *50 per cent of compensation payments* made to supervisory board members.

In addition, the tax laws allow for non-taxable reserves in limited circumstances. The most important provisions are those dealing with pension reserves and clearly defined uncertain liabilities. Provisions can be made in respect of these items which are deductible for tax purposes. Other than these, general accruals and provisions recorded in the commercial books are not allowed for tax purposes.

DEPRECIATION

Depreciation is the major non-cash cost which reduces taxable profit in Germany. In line with general principles, depreciation on fixed assets used in the business is regarded as a business expense and hence is deductible. The main exceptions to this are land and financial assets.

The amount of depreciation depends on both the expected useful life and the depreciation method chosen by the taxpayer. The federal fiscal authorities have published a list setting out the standard periods of useful life for most depreciable assets and it is common practice to adopt these for both book and tax purposes.

Under income tax law there are two different depreciation methods available, the use of which depends on whether the asset in question is movable, immovable, tangible or intangible. For tangible movable assets the taxpayer may choose between:

- the *straight-line method* under which a fixed percentage is applied annually to the asset's acquisition cost; and
- the *reducing-balance method* under which a fixed percentage is applied to the opening book value each year.

The percentage rate used under the reducing-balance method may not exceed three times the percentage under the straight-line method or a maximum percentage rate of 30 per cent, whichever is the lower. A change from the reducing-balance method to the straight-line method is allowed but not vice versa. The federal government has been considering reducing the maximum percentage rate under the reducing-balance method to 25 per cent but has not yet taken a decision to change this law.

In contrast to the depreciation rules for movable assets, the useful life doctrine does not apply to immovable tangible assets such as buildings. Rather, standard straight-line percentage rates must be used according to the Income Tax Act, whereby the applicable rates depend on the date of acquisition or construction of the building. Buildings completed before 1 January 1925 may be depreciated at 2.5 per cent per annum, whereas the rate for those completed after 31 December 1924 is 2 per cent per annum.

Where a building is used exclusively for business purposes and a construction permit was applied for after 31 March 1985, a rate of 4 per cent per annum is given.

As an incentive for small and medium-sized businesses with a net worth of not more than DM240,000 and a trade capital not exceeding DM500,000, a total 20 per cent additional write-off on the acquisition or construction cost of certain fixed assets has been introduced recently and is granted in the year of acquisition/construction and the following four years. For 1995 these businesses may also build up a tax-free investment reserve up to a maximum 50 per cent of the anticipated costs of planned expenditure on certain types of fixed assets. This allows a tax deduction for a provision for future costs. The release of the reserve must take place within the following two years when depreciation on the actual expenditure can be claimed.

Depreciable movable assets costing not more than DM800 each (exclusive of VAT) can be fully depreciated in the year of acquisition or construction.

A higher depreciation rate or even complete write-offs for movable as well as for immovable assets may be available in cases of exceptional wear and tear, although a number of legal restrictions apply. Intangible assets may in principle be depreciated under the straight-line method provided that the asset has been purchased and has a finite useful life. A special rule covers acquired goodwill which must be depreciated over 15 years. Intangibles originally created within the business are excluded from depreciation.

Investments in new assets located in the five Eastern states are encouraged by special depreciation allowances of up to 50 per cent. A number of requirements must be fulfilled, most importantly that the investment has to be made before 1 January 1997. Investments made after that date will benefit from a maximum special depreciation allowance of only 40 per cent.

TAXATION OF COMPANIES

Resident companies

Resident companies are subject to tax on their worldwide income. This includes business undertakings organised as separate legal entities under German law, such as the limited liability company (GmbH) and the public stock corporation (AG), and potentially also some foreign legal entities with a presence in Germany. Tax residence is established where a company has either its registered seat or place of central management in Germany.

The corporate income tax rate for residents is 45 per cent. This is reduced to 30 per cent on distribution of the profits by way of dividend to shareholders. Where a company retains profits and pays tax at the higher rate, a refund of tax down to the lower rate is given on a subsequent dividend distribution.

A 7.5 per cent solidarity surtax relating to the financial burden resulting from German unification was introduced on 1 January 1995. The surtax is levied on the assessed corporate income tax *after* deducting any imputed tax credit received by the corporation from its German subsidiaries. The federal government had announced its intention to cut the surtax by 1 per cent with effect from 1 January 1997, although this reduction was withdrawn during the passage of the 1997 Tax Bill. The earliest rate increase is now expeced to be in 1998.

Imputation system

A rather complex full imputation system (*körperschaftsteuerliches Anrechnungsverfahren*) forms the backbone of the German corporate income tax law. In a nutshell, it means that a resident shareholder receiving a dividend from a German corporation is taxed on the gross dividend (including withholding tax) *and* the corporate income tax paid by the distributing entity. In return, the shareholder is entitled to a tax credit for the corporate income tax and solidarity surcharge paid by the company and tax withheld on the gross dividend.

The dividend withholding tax amounts to 25 per cent of the distributable profits after corporate income tax and is also subject to solidarity surtax. A liability to withhold falls on the company on the date the distribution is due.

In many cases the tax credit available on a distribution may exceed the shareholder's own tax liability, in which case a refund of the excess tax is given. The effect of the full imputation system is therefore to tax corporate profits at the shareholder's marginal tax rate.

Distributable reserves

In order to determine the actual corporate income tax burden underlying profits which are paid out as a dividend distribution, all income derived by a corporation is categorised under one of the following six headings:

- *EK 45* retained earnings which have been taxed at a rate of 45 per cent. Accordingly, if a dividend is paid out of EK 45, corporate income tax at 15 per cent of the gross amount is refunded (and forms part of the dividend).
- *EK 30* income tax at 30 per cent, the normal rate for distributed earnings.
- *EK 01* tax-free income from foreign sources such as profits derived from a foreign branch (net profit after tax in the foreign jurisdiction) and dividends received from non-German subsidiaries under the affiliation privilege. Notably, dividends paid out of the EK 01 reserve can be paid to the shareholders free of any German corporate income tax but without entitlement to a credit.
- *EK 02* tax-free German income. Losses are deducted from this basket and may lead to negative EK 02. Dividends paid out of this basket trigger German corporate income tax at a rate of 30 per cent of the grossed-up amount (ie dividend × 3/7).
- *EK 03* reserves accumulated prior to 1 January 1977 (when the imputation system was introduced) and not distributed until now. The treatment of dividends taken from EK 03 is the same as that for payments made out of EK 02. However, a foreign shareholder is entitled to a refund upon application.
- *EK 04* capital contributions made by direct or indirect shareholders after 31 December 1976. Consequently, dividends paid out of this basket are in fact regarded as repayment of capital and not as profit distributions and therefore do not trigger any corporate income or dividend withholding tax.

The *Corporate Income Tax Act* requires dividends to be sourced from the equity basket with the highest tax burden (ie EK 45) until this basket is empty. If this is not sufficient to fund the dividend, reserves must be taken from the basket with the second highest burden, and so on. Repayments of capital contributions qualifying as EK 04 are therefore often blocked until the liquidation of the company.

Foreign source income

Resident companies are subject to tax on foreign source branch and dividend income, but most of the German double tax treaties provide for an exemption (participation exemption). As far as branch profits are concerned, the exemption is given to avoid double taxation, as international treaty practice is to give taxing rights to the country in which the branch is established. In the case of dividends, the tax exemption at treaty level normally requires a stake of at least 25 per cent in the subsidiary, although this is reduced under domestic law to 10 per cent. Where an exemption is given there is no credit for foreign taxes paid. However, dividend withholding taxes paid in a foreign jurisdiction on dividends which do not fall within the scope of the affiliation privilege qualify for a tax credit, irrespective of the percentage of the shareholding. In addition, a few treaties grant a tax credit rather than an exemption, and some contain the proviso that treaty benefit depends on the activity of the foreign company.

In addition to treaty benefits, unilateral relief for foreign tax, including underlying tax, is provided for in the Corporate Income Tax Act. Broadly, the requirements are that the German corporation holds at least 10 per cent of the subsidiary for an unbroken period of not less than 12 months prior to the end of the fiscal year. Depending on individual circumstances, this credit opportunity is also available for foreign profit taxes incurred by a second-tier subsidiary.

Alternatively, the German corporation may opt to deduct foreign taxes in computing taxable profit, for example where it has losses and is not tax-paying. These unilateral relief rules are only relevant in practice if the foreign earnings stem from a non-treaty country.

Taxation of non-resident companies

A foreign corporation which has neither its seat nor its place of central management in Germany is not resident for tax purposes and is therefore subject to tax on its German source income only. The scope of the tax liability, the applicable tax rate and the taxation method all depend on the type of income and the availability of treaty benefits.

Foreign companies operating through a branch in Germany are taxable on branch profits at a flat corporate tax rate of 42 per cent. Although this is lower than the tax rate on retained earnings for resident companies, it is significantly higher than the 30 per cent rate on distributed earnings. On the other hand, there is no withholding tax on branch profits, so the decision as to whether a branch or company is cheaper from a tax point of view comes down to the dividend withholding tax rate applicable to the foreign investor.

As noted above, the domestic dividend withholding tax rate is 25 per cent. This is reduced under most treaties to 15, 10 or even 5 per cent. Since 1 July 1996 dividends paid by a German corporation to a qualifying EU parent company are not subject to withholding tax at all. In most cases it is normally more tax efficient to operate through a company in Germany if profits are expected.

Tax is also withheld on royalties at a standard rate of 25 per cent. Again, this is often reduced under a treaty provision, in many cases down to nil. Surprisingly, there is no withholding tax on payments of interest to non-residents.

An assessment of taxes payable takes place on filing of a non-resident corporate income tax return. Normally, this only applies to branches (or permanent establishments) of non-residents or to receipts of rental income. The tax due is also subject to solidarity surtax.

Taxation of partnerships

Partnerships are a common feature of business life in Germany, and have also provided flexibility in cross-border tax planning structures. The most important partnership vehicles for a business activity are the general partnership (oHG) and the limited partnership (KG). The latter is often managed by a GmbH as the general partner, thus forming a so-called GmbH & Co KG.

Since a partnership is not a separate legal entity, federal taxes on income are imposed at the level of the partners, who can be either individuals or corporations. As the partners generally qualify as business entre-preneurs, any salaries and other benefits in kind granted to them as consideration for the performance of management duties are not respected as tax-deductible business expenses. The same is true for pension reserves referring to a pension commitment made by the partnership *vis-à-vis* its partners. There are several other specific regulations and principles which also need to be taken into account in calculating the taxable income.

The partners are taxed on their share of the partnership's adjusted taxable profits in proportion to their share in the partnership capital (unless provided otherwise in the partnership agreement). Accordingly, if a partner is a corporate entity, corporate income tax at a rate of 45 or 30 per cent falls due. For individuals the regular straight-line pro-gressive income tax tariff applies. However, while the maximum marginal income tax rate is currently 53 per cent, the maximum rate for income from business has recently been reduced to 47 per cent. This rate applies to any taxable business income in excess of DM100,224 (single status) and DM200,448 (married status and filing jointly with spouse). Solidarity surtax is added on top of the aforementioned rates. Tax credit entitlements, for instance relating to dividends received from a corporation of which the partnership holds the shares, originate at the partner's level only and thus can be utilized against the partner's personal income tax (or corporate income tax).

If a foreign investor holds an interest in a German partnership, ie he or she is either a general or a limited partner in an oHG or KG, the foreign corporation (or individual) is deemed to have a German permanent establishment for tax purposes. Consequently, profits derived by non-resident partners of a German partnership are subject to German taxes. Expenses incurred by that partner and relating to profit share can be claimed as a deduction and reduce the partner's taxation basis. This can include interest on loans taken out to fund the share in the partnerships. Again, the legal status of the non-resident partner (either a corporation or an individual) determines whether the authorities assess corporate income tax at 42 per cent or personal income tax at a maximum of 47 per cent.

For the purposes of trade tax, partnerships are treated as if they were separate legal entities, ie the partnership and not the single partner is the taxation subject.

Taxation of a sole proprietorship

An individual who carries on a business activity in Germany on his or her own forms a sole proprietorship. Income taxes are finally assessed on filing of a separate return. The tax rate again ranges up to 47 per cent plus solidarity surtax. Income from business realised by an individual will be taken into account from one out of several income categories for the determination of the overall tax liability. A special formula applies in order to make sure that the maximum tax rate covering business income does in fact not exceed 47 per cent where the taxpayer also derives earnings from other income categories.

TRADE TAX

Trade tax is by far the most important municipal tax levied in Germany and is imposed on all forms of business enterprise, both incorporated and unincorporated. It comprises two elements: trade tax on income (*Gewerbeertragsteuer*) and trade tax on capital (*Gewerbekapitalsteuer*).

Trade income tax is in principle based on profits subject to corporate income tax. However, a number of adjustments are required under tax law. The most important of these are as follows:

- *Interest on long-term debts is deductible at 50 per cent only.* A liability qualifies as long-term debt if it has been incurred either in connection with the setting up, the acquisition and the expansion of the business or if the term of the liability exceeds 12 months.
- *Payments to a typical silent partner* are excluded from deduction unless the partner is subject to trade tax.
- *Profits and losses derived from foreign permanent establishments* as well as dividends received from both domestic and foreign subsidiaries (restrictions apply) are not taken into consideration when the basis for trade income tax is calculated.
- *1.2 per cent of the assessed unit value of real property* owned by the business undertaking shall be deducted from the sum of taxable earnings.

Business income so ascertained forms the basis for the trade tax levy. Trade tax on income is calculated by multiplying the federal rate of 5 per cent (lower percentage brackets apply to unincorporated businesses) by a percentage factor set by the municipality (local multiplier). These multipliers currently range from 300 to 515 per cent, leading to trade income tax rates between 15 and 25.75 per cent. Confusingly, the trade tax is itself deductible from the trade tax basis, so that the effective trade income tax rate might vary between 13 and 20.5 per cent depending on the municipality in which the business is run. The final burden is further reduced by the fact that trade tax is also a deductible expense for income and corporate income tax purposes. Hence, the income tax rates as described apply to the taxable profits of a business after trade tax. Trade tax losses may be carried forward for an indefinite period whereby the computation of the loss carry forward varies from that for income and corporate income tax purposes. A loss carry back is not possible.

Trade tax on capital is assessed at 0.2 per cent times the local multiplier which has been determined by the municipality. The taxation basis is the assessed value of the net assets of the business undertaking as determined for net worth tax purposes. Adjustments apply of which the most important ones are the following:

- *50 per cent of the long-term debts* as defined for trade income tax purposes must be added back to the assessed value provided they exceed an exemption amount of DM50,000.
- *The value of investments in foreign and domestic corporations* and partnerships and in foreign branches shall be deducted from the assessed value.

- *The assessed value of the business must be reduced by the assessed unit value of real estate* in order to avoid double taxation (the ownership of real estate triggers real property tax which is another municipal levy).

Trade tax on capital is imposed on the net value of the business after consideration of a tax-free threshold amounting to DM120,000.

NET WORTH TAX

Net worth tax will not be levied from 1 January 1997 onwards, although the tax has not been repealed.

Net worth tax is levied on the assessed value of the net assets of corporations and permanent establishments maintained by a non-resident investor. The first DM500,000 of the assessed value is tax-free, and only 75 per cent of the remainder is subject to tax. The tax rate is 0.6 per cent. Individuals operating a business are subject to net worth taxation as well, whereby the business's net value represents only one element of the total sum of assets owned by the tax payer. The same principle applies to partners in a partnership, ie the value of their partnership's interest is considered for purposes of the individual's net worth tax liability but not at the level of the partnership itself. The tax rate for individuals is basically 1 per cent but only 0.5 per cent on assets within an operating business and on shares.

VALUE ADDED TAX

As a member of the EU, Germany's VAT regime is very similar to that of the other member states. In principle, all transactions – both the supply of goods and the supply of services – performed by an entrepreneur are subject to VAT. Depending on the individual circumstances of the transaction and the legal criteria, ie terms of delivery, type of service, residence of recipient, etc, the transaction may be either taxable, tax exempt or even outside the scope of German taxation. Exports are often tax free as the transaction is considered to be performed outside Germany, while a number of other specified transactions are explicitly declared tax exempt although the supply takes place in Germany.

The standard tax rate is 15 per cent. A reduced rate of 7 per cent applies in certain cases. Specific rules may apply to transactions within the EU according to EU directives.

Goods which have been imported from countries outisde the EU are subject to import VAT at the same rates as the regular turnover tax. Entrepreneurs may deduct import VAT paid from their output tax liability if they utilise the imported items within their business or resell them.

One of the most important features of the VAT system is the entitlement of an entrepreneur to a deduction of any input VAT incurred on supplies of goods or services by other businesses. Entrepreneurs in Germany arc in general obliged to prepare monthly preliminary VAT returns in which they offset input VAT against output VAT. Where the balance results in excess input VAT, a cash refund is obtained from the authorities. The entitlement to input VAT deduction is subject to limitations and whether the resident entrepreneur carries out tax-exempt transactions. The performance of exports from Germany does not affect the right to deduct input VAT. Foreign entrepreneurs who do not realise taxable trans-actions in Germany but have, for whatever reasons, incurred business-related input VAT are eligible to a recovery of input VAT. An application must be submitted to the federal VAT office not later than six months after the year end. With effect from January 1996, the refund option is linked to reciprocity from the foreigner's own tax administration.

REAL ESTATE TRANSFER TAX

On transfer of real property, a real property transfer tax at a rate of 3.5 per cent is levied. This rate is generally applied to the consideration as determined in the purchase agreement. Where no such consideration has been agreed upon, i.e., in the case of mergers and spin-offs, when only shares are transferred, the relevant value shall be determined on the basis of the actual or estimated gross rent to be derived from the actual or an assumed lease of the real property. If an appropriate rent cannot even be estimated such as in the case of industrial properties, the taxation basis is the sum of half of the land's value and the book value.

Although according to the law both parties are liable to real property transfer tax as joint debtors, it is common practice in Germany that pursuant to the individual purchase agreement the buyer bears the entire burden.

26

Special Issues in Fiscal Strategies for Foreign Companies Operating in Germany

Christoph Schreiber, C&L Deutsche Revision AG and Adrian Yeeles, Coopers & Lybrand

INTRODUCTION

Foreign investors have traditionally regarded Germany as a high tax country with a sophisticated tax system which has driven fiscal strategy towards minimising taxable income through a variety of mechanisms. The prime focus of this is usually to take profit out through dividend or interest stripping and through appropriate transfer pricing policies. In many cases these techniques interact with the local tax consolidation system. The German legislative bodies have committed themselves to changing this perception through a wide range of measures which include reductions in tax rates, abolition of certain taxes and specific reforms designed to encourage foreign investment. In this chapter we look at the traditional planning tools and the government's counter-measures as well as the current status of Germany as a holding location.

DIVIDENDS PAID TO FOREIGN INVESTORS

When profits derived by a German subsidiary are repatriated to the foreign shareholder, domestic law provides for a 25 per cent dividend withholding tax which can be reduced by a tax treaty and/or by the EU Parent/Subsidiary Directive. In most German treaties the dividend withholding tax withheld at source from dividends paid to qualifying corporate shareholders is reduced to either 5 or 10 per cent of the gross dividend.

After 30 June 1996 the EU directive took full effect in Germany. This means that dividends paid by German subsidiaries to qualifying European parent companies will no longer suffer the 5 per cent withholding tax. Specifically, dividends paid to such qualifying EU parents who own at least 25 per cent of the share capital in the distributing German subsidiary for not less than 12 months will be fully exempt from German dividend withholding tax. The exemption is granted through advance application to the federal tax office in Bonn. Where a dividend is paid within the first 12 months, withholding tax is provisionally levied but can be reclaimed. The minimum shareholding requirement of 25 per cent is reduced under national law to 10 per cent provided that the parent company's country of residence also permits such lower percentage for dividends to be paid to German parent companies without triggering withholding tax (requirement of reciprocity; examples are the UK, Ireland and the Netherlands).

The dividend payment date is generally taken to be the date stipulated for payment in the dividend resolution. In the absence of a specified date, the day after the resolution is deemed to be the payment date.

TREATY SHOPPING

With effect from 1 January 1994 Germany introduced an anti-treaty shopping provision. This provision effectively overrides both tax treaties and EU tax directives and is aimed at tax planning strategies that use treaty provisions or EU directives to mitigate or eliminate taxes.

Under the new provision a foreign company such as a holding company is not entitled to treaty benefits under a German tax treaty or benefits under the EU parent/subsidiary directive to the extent that:

- the shareholders of the foreign company would not be entitled to such treaty benefits had they received the income directly;

- there are no business or other valid reasons for interposing the foreign company;
- the foreign company does not carry on its own business.

Where the indirect shareholder is carrying on an active business and would be entitled to the same treaty benefits as the direct shareholder, the latter will normally qualify for benefits. However, where the anti-treaty shopping provisions apply, a foreign shareholder loses the tax advantages granted in Germany on the basis of a tax treaty or an EU directive. This includes reduced or nil withholding tax rates on dividends and royalties.

For example, a US company, which would normally suffer at least 5 per cent withholding tax on a dividend from Germany, sets up a UK company and transfers its German GmbH to it. The GmbH then pays the dividend to the UK company instead. Under UK law, it can pass the dividend on to the US parent without withholding tax. It is also entitled to the benefit of the EU directive and so should suffer 0 per cent withholding tax in Germany. If the anti-treaty shopping clause applies to the UK company, it would suffer a 5 per cent dividend withholding tax on a dividend distribution according to the US-German tax treaty rather than obtaining the zero rate for dividend payments within the EU.

At the moment it is contentious whether the provisions apply to capital gains as well, although this seems to be the view of the tax authorities. According to most German tax treaties the country of residence is entitled to impose capital gains tax on profits derived from the disposal of shares in a German subsidiary. If this protection is not applicable, Germany will make use of its domestic law which does provide for such a capital gains taxation.

INTEREST STRIPPING AND THIN CAPITALISATION

A typical inward investment strategy for corporates is to acquire a German target through a newly formed debt-financed German subsidiary. The interest expense is then used to shelter the target's profits under fiscal unity (if possible) or to obtain a federal tax refund on dividends from the target. This structure also reduces withholding taxes on outbound dividends and offers potential savings in trade and net worth taxes and has been extremely popular with investors from countries with low tax rates compared to Germany. Naturally this structure is unpopular with the federal tax authorities, but in the past the courts have been reluctant to disturb the principle that investors are free to finance their subsidiaries with debt and equity as they see fit. Similarly, attempts to legislate against it have consistently met with failure. However, in 1993 the government proposed legislation to increase the attractiveness of Germany to foreign businesses, including clear statutory rules on excessive debt financing (widely known as 'thin capitalisation'). These became law on 1 January 1994.

The new thin capitalisation rules work on the principle that there is a relationship between debt and equity which in cases involving third-party lenders has a limit. In cases where the lender is connected to the borrower this limit may be overlooked and so the rules lay down clear guidance on the maximum permissible ratios ('safe harbours') of debt to equity in a range of circumstances involving loans from shareholders and others to German resident companies. These make a broad distinction between loans on which interest depends on profit or turnover ('participating' loans) and loans on which interest is a fixed percentage of the principal amount borrowed ('fixed interest' loans). The safe harbour for participating loans is 50 per cent of equity (paid in capital and reserves). Interest on debt in excess of the safe harbour is automatically treated as a hidden dividend. The safe harbour for fixed interest loans is 300 per cent of equity for a trading or non-qualifying holding company and 900 per cent for a qualifying holding company. Interest expense on debt in excess of these limits is requalified as a dividend unless the borrower can show that it could have obtained the loan under similar conditions from an unrelated third-party lender.

The consequence of excess interest being treated as a dividend can be costly: no deduction is given for corporate income tax purposes, rather the interest is deemed to be post-tax profit on which a form of distribution tax can arise depending on how the various equity baskets are funded. Further, a constructive dividend is subject to regular dividend withholding tax. Instead of achieving the stated objective of reducing the German tax burden, excessive debt financing often leads to a significant increase in tax.

Although the safe harbours are generous by most standards, the rules are complex and contain many traps for the unwary. For example, safe harbours are not available to German subsidiaries held under a qualifying German holding company. Further, companies which fail the holding company test must, when calculating their safe harbour, reduce their equity by the book values of all their subsidiaries. In order to qualify for the holding company safe harbour, the borrower needs at least two subsidiaries and must pass an activity or balance sheet test. Although more care is now needed, the legislation provides certainty to foreign investors and this is generally regarded as very positive.

Despite the new rules, the traditional inbound planning model is alive and well.

GERMAN TRANSFER PRICING RULES

Germany has been a leading proponent of the arm's length principle in transactions between related parties. Section 1 of the *Foreign Tax Act* requires that arm's length prices be used for all inter-company transactions. The provisions are similar to transfer pricing rules in most of the industrialised countries. It is the intention of Section 1 of the *Foreign Tax Act* to place the controlled taxpayer on a par with an unrelated taxpayer and to determine the appropriate taxable income, should the controlled taxpayer have agreed terms and conditions which deviate from those which an unrelated taxpayer would have agreed.

The 'Administration Principles on Income Allocation' were published by the Federal Minister of Finance in 1983 as an interpretation of Section 1 of the *Foreign Tax Act* and have been a standard bearer for the development of transfer pricing as an international tax issue. They include general guidelines on the determination of an appropriate transfer price and also contain detailed comments on various inter-company transactions such as the delivery of goods, granting of loans, rendering of services, transfer of intangibles etc. Technically, the guidelines merely serve as directives for the evaluation of transfer prices at a tax audit in that the tax authorities are required to apply the principles when they audit a controlled tax-payer and review his or her transfer pricing policy. Accordingly, the guidelines are not legally binding for the tax-payer. However, due to the scarcity of existing case law on transfer pricing issues and considering the strict enforcement of the principles by the tax authorities, related companies in Germany and their tax consultants also use the administration principles as the yardstick for measuring the appropriateness of transfer prices.

In general, the administration principles stipulate that inter-company transactions will only be approved for tax purposes if the parties have acted as though they were unrelated (dealing at arm's length principle). In this respect, the tax authorities are obliged to refer to the specific transaction in question and to take into account the economic substance of the actual facts. The yardstick for the arm's length character of a transaction among related entities is the standard of customary care employed by an orderly and prudent manager when dealing with unrelated persons.

The administration principles provide three specific methods for determining an arm's length consideration which a prudent manager would also have agreed. These three methods are:

- *Comparable uncontrolled price method*   adopting with any necessary modification the uncontrolled market price for the same or similar transaction, or adopting the internal price for the same or similar transaction to independent third parties.
- *Resale price method*   taking the price at which the goods or services are sold by the related purchaser (reseller) to independent customers and subtracting an arm's length mark-up equivalent to the functions performed and risks borne by the reseller.
- *Cost-plus method*   determining the supplier's or vendor's cost by using the cost accounting concepts of the supplier or vendor applied towards independent parties or, if no uncontrolled transactions occur, another acknowledged accounting method and adding a mark-up which is customary in this industry or trade.

The German administration principles do not provide for either a comparable profit or profit split method as used in some countries, most noticeably the US, of which Germany has been a consistent critic. They stress, however, that due to individual market conditions it may be necessary to apply more than one method. Therefore, it is acceptable to make the standard methods more specific, use them in combination and to take other factors into account when determining the appropriate price. Although the administration principles do not establish a priority to use in applying the three standard methods, they outline in further sections which method normally appears to be the appropriate method to determine an arm's length consideration in a range of circumstances. For the sale of tangible property, especially finished products, the principles state that generally the resale price method would be used for the determination of an appropriate transfer price provided that no comparable uncontrolled price is available. The gross profit margin to be received by the reseller must fairly reflect the scope of its responsibilities and the level of assumed risks.

As can be seen from the tax administration's approach during tax audits and from recent statements of German fiscal courts, the relevant criteria for the evaluation of inter-company business relationships have been continually broadened during the past decade. In particular, the Supreme Fiscal Court holds – and the tax authorities have apparently adopted this doctrine – that, irrespective of the appropriateness of the applied pricing method pursuant to the administration principles, a controlled distributor of intra-group manufactured products must always be left with a reasonable pre-tax profit. The philosophy behind this additional arm's length requirement is that, according to the federal judges, an unrelated reseller would not continue its distribution activities if it could market a certain product only at minimal or no profit.

Germany is a signatory to the OECD Transfer Pricing Guidelines for multinational enterprises and tax administrations. These do not contain binding rules but represent merely an international consensus on the application of the arm's length standard to test the appropriateness of inter-company prices. Yet, even though the guidelines are not law, they encourage member countries to follow them; in fact, prior OECD guidelines were traditionally well received (as they enhance the level of consistency) and partly even transferred into national legislation of single member countries. The revised OECD guidelines as issued in July 1995 take into account practical experience as well as interim developments in the member countries. Even though they still express a strong preference for the use of one of the three standard methods for testing the arm's length character of a transfer price for the transfer of tangible property, the new guidelines emphasise the importance of comparability as to functions performed, risks assumed and assets employed. Further, they introduce a so-called transactional net margin method which compares the operating profit of the controlled enterprise to a similar measure of operating profit realised by comparable uncontrolled parties. To a certain extent matching up with the approach described in the above paragraph, the (new) net margin approach makes clear that an accurate review of inter-company prices amounts to more than the determination of the right pricing method.

FISCAL UNITY

German corporate tax law allows the consolidation of profits and losses among related business entities for income/corporate income tax, trade tax and VAT purposes provided that a fiscal unity (*Organschaft*) exists. Fiscal unity means that a resident corporation is integrated into another domestic business enterprise by reference to three criteria: financial, economic and organisational. While only incorporated businesses can act as the controlled company, the controlling entity must not necessarily be a corporation but may also have the organisational form of a sole proprietorship, a partnership or the German branch of a foreign company.

The main feature of a fiscal unity arrangement is that profits and losses of the controlled subsidiary corporations (*Organgesellschaften*) are immediately attributed to the controlling company (*Organträger*). Thus, taxation occurs with few exceptions at the level of the controlling entity only. Depending on its legal nature, either income tax or corporate income tax is imposed on the consolidated result. Losses incurred by the controlled company prior to the installation of the fiscal unity are excluded from a transfer to the controlling entity and thus cannot be utilised against profits distributed up the chain from other subsidiaries.

Financial integration is assumed if the dominant company holds more than half of the voting rights of the controlled corporation. Economic integration is a less precise concept. It refers to the business activities run by both the controlling and the controlled entity and is usually given if the dependent enterprise through its own activity supports and supplements the business of the dominant company similar to the division of an enterprise. Economic integration is therefore a sensitive criterion when a managing holding company operates as the controlling entity. In order to achieve organisational integration, the controlling enterprise must be in a position to enforce its directions and instructions *vis-à-vis* the management of the dependent company. Organisational integration can, for instance, be safeguarded by appointing the managers of the controlling entity simultaneously as the managers of the controlled corporation, or by conclusion of a domination agreement. Most importantly, in order to benefit from the tax advantages of a fiscal unity for corporate income tax purposes, the conclusion of a profit and loss pooling agreement between the controlling and the controlled entity is mandatory. A number of requirements apply, eg the agreement must have been entered into and actually performed for a period of at least five years.

GERMAN HOLDING COMPANIES

In the light of substantial tax disadvantages compared to more favourable tax regimes in neighbouring countries, many foreign investors have in the past refrained from setting up a German holding company. However, many of these have been removed, partly as a result of EU integration and partly with the clear intention of improving Germany's reputation as a business location, and the country has become an attractive territory for the establishment of a holding company. In particular, the recent amendments relating to dividend and capital gains taxation now mean that Germany offers the standard tax features expected of a holding location, without requiring any special type of holding company or imposing limits on the class of transactions allowed.

The most significant tax advantages, all of them under generally applicable law, are as follows:

- *capital gains* realised on the disposition of qualifying investments in foreign corporations are entirely exempt from taxation;

- *dividends* received from qualifying investments in foreign corporations residing either in a tax treaty or in a less developed country are also tax-exempt;
- *low German dividend withholding tax at source* on dividends paid by a resident corporation to shareholders in many non-EU countries, and even zero rate withholding tax on dividends paid to qualifying EU-parent companies;
- *no withholding tax on dividend income received from qualifying EU-subsidiaries*, and often low dividend withholding tax on dividends coming from other countries;
- *no additional German corporate income tax on dividend payments sourced from tax-exempt foreign EK 01 earnings,* regardless of the residency of the receiving corporation (withholding tax may be charged);
- *an extensive exemption system* due to close-meshed German treaty network;
- *favourable 9:1 debt-equity safe harbour rule* for certain types of holding companies.

DEDUCTIONS FOR FINANCING COSTS

Expenses (including interest) incurred in connection with earning tax-free income are generally not deductible. As dividends from foreign subsidiaries are normally exempt from tax in Germany, in principle no deduction is given for interest on loans to finance the acquisition of these subsidiaries. However, the fiscal courts have held that this restriction is valid *only* for tax years in which a dividend has actually been received. Therefore, tax relief for interest payments economically connected with foreign exempt income may enjoy tax relief, if structured properly. This gives Germany an advantage over other tax-privileged holding locations such as the Netherlands.

REORGANISATIONS

Pursuant to the regulations contained in the amended *Reorganisation and Transformation Act,* many restructurings and company reorganisations such as mergers, share deals, spin-offs etc can be performed in a tax-neutral way. A number of restrictions and a variety of preconditions apply.

INCENTIVES

Both domestic and foreign investors who decide to run a business in less industrialised regions of Germany may be eligible for public subsidies funded either by the federal or state government or by specific EU incentive programmes. The main criterion is in most cases the number of jobs which the investor is expected to create.

27

Specific Accounting Techniques

Peter H Combrink,
C&L Deutsche Revision AG

GERMAN INTERNATIONAL FINANCIAL STATEMENTS

The need for large German companies to avail themselves of the international capital markets led to Daimler Benz AG being the first German corporation to break with tradition and publish consolidated financial statements for the years ended 31 December 1991 and 1992, prepared in accordance with US accounting principles ('US GAAP'). These were prepared in addition to those complying with the provisions of German commercial law, making direct comparisons possible. A subsidiary of Hoechst AG has meanwhile followed suit, and other companies are expected to do the same in the not too distant future.

Other global German corporations such as BASF, Bayer and Deutsche Bank have published consolidated financial statements prepared in accordance with International Accounting Standards ('IAS') as promulgated by the International Accounting Standards Committee ('IASC').

It should be noted, however, that financial reporting using US or international standards has so far been limited exclusively to consolidated financial statements (prepared by just about every quoted company). At present, German commercial law requires parent companies to prepare their individual entity accounts as well as their consolidated financial statements in accordance with the provisions of German law. There is no doubt that with regard to the individual entity accounts this will continue for the foreseeable future, since the commercial financial statements form the authoritative basis for the tax accounts.

In respect of consolidated financial statements, however, since 1995 the German Department of Justice has been pursuing plans to grant corporations, particularly those whose securities are traded on exchanges abroad, permission to replace their conventional group accounts by financial statements prepared on the basis of US GAAP or IAS. A survey by C&L Deutsche Revision in 1995 revealed that a significant majority of German academics and key players in industry advocate the preparation of consolidated financial statements on the basis of US GAAP or IAS; about 75 per cent of the academics believed that the informative value of US GAAP financial statements exceeds that of those prepared in accordance with German commercial law.

There are a number of areas in which the differences between US, IASC and German accounting rules will need reconciliation before 'international' group accounts can replace, rather than merely supplement, the local German consolidated financial statements. For example, capitalisation of self-developed intangible assets is prohibited by German commercial law but accepted under certain circumstances in the USA and compulsory within the framework of IAS. Similarly, recognition of deferred tax assets is optional in Germany but compulsory under US GAAP or IAS.

A number of other differences are referred to in the chapter on *Financial Reporting and Accounting*. In this chapter we focus on several specific issues which frequently give rise to the most significant differences from UK, US or IAS accounting and which are key to an understanding of German accounts. These are the areas of depreciation, pensions, reserves and goodwill and group accounts.

DEPRECIATION

Fixed assets subject to wear and tear must be systematically depreciated. Various depreciation methods are considered acceptable in Germany: straight-line, reducing-balance (limited to three times the straight-line rates), sum-of-the-digits, units-of-production or hours-of-use. Sinking-fund depreciation or any other methods which initially result in a lower annual charge than the amount determined by the straight-line method are not permitted. If the reducing-balance method is used for buildings, the depreciation rates are systematically reduced as times goes on. For movable tangible fixed assets, reducing-balance depreciation rates remain unchanged; in order to maintain the tax deductions at their highest possible level, it is common practice, however, to switch to the straight-line method as soon as this method results in a higher depreciation charge for the year than the reducing-balance method would.

The useful life assigned to a fixed asset should be based on the asset's prudently estimated useful economic life. Guidance on useful lives is provided by tables issued by the tax authorities. Since German commercial law is flexible on the subject of systematic depreciation, companies usually use the tables for general accounting purposes as well. In determining the annual depreciation charges, the cost of the asset is not reduced by its expected residual value at the end of the assigned useful life, unless the residual value is expected to be very material.

In the year in which an asset is placed in service, depreciation is time apportioned; for movable tangible fixed assets tax rules permit companies to take a full year's depreciation charge for items acquired in the first half of the year and half the annual charge on those acquired in the second half. This has now become common practice in Germany.

Stand-by equipment and major spare parts held in reserve for break-downs are accounted for as fixed assets rather than inventories; depreciation is normally charged in accordance with the useful economic life of the corresponding main equipment.

While there is an option to recognise temporary diminutions in the value of a fixed asset to below its carrying amount by charging extraordinary depreciation, this is compulsory where the diminution is anticipated to be permanent. A reversal of the extraordinary depreciation is required if the reasons that gave rise to the charge no longer exist. However, if tax regulations permit the lower value to be retained and its retention in the financial statements is a prerequisite for keeping the tax benefit, the lower value may also be retained on the balance sheet. In such cases the facts would require disclosure in the notes to the financial statements.

Tax regulations permit special accelerated depreciation for various reasons, for instance to encourage investment in former East Germany or for environmental protection. For this accelerated depreciation to be tax deductible, it must be charged against reported annual income.

While depreciation rules for accounting and tax purposes are based on entirely separate systems in the UK and differ significantly for certain assets in the USA, often leading to large amounts of deferred tax, depreciation reflected in the financial statements of German companies, substantially tax driven as it is, must often be considered excessive when measured in accordance with British or American accounting rules. Therefore, when financial statements of German subsidiaries of British or American companies are to be prepared for consolidation purposes abroad, it frequently becomes necessary to adjust the depreciation expense downwards. The tax effect of such adjustments may need to be reflected in the calculation of any deferred tax balances at group level.

PENSIONS

In contrast to the position in the UK and the US where companies provide against their future pension obligations by irrevocably contributing funds to outside, non-controlled pension funds, with few exceptions German companies accrue for all future pension obligations under a related heading in their balance sheet.

Generally, there are no assets specifically designated to cover future pension payments; management use the resources for the operations of the company and in this sense pension schemes are often a major source of funds for German companies. Vested rights are covered by mandatory insurance to provide protection to employees in case of the employer's insolvency. However, under this insurance the employer is not ultimately released from his obligations as the insurer is entitled to claim a refund from the employer or the company's liquidator for pension payments made to the employees. The accrual must cover all pension rights granted to individuals after 31 December 1986 and all subsequent increases. Until that date the recognition of future pension obligations was optional; if a company did make accruals it could choose either to charge all past and prior service costs to expense immediately, or to spread them over three years when adopting a new, or amending an existing, pension plan. While this alternative is not available for new pension rights granted after 31 December 1986, it is still permissible to spread over three years increases in pension benefits which had been granted up to that date.

While the actuarial method of providing pension accruals in Germany in many respects resembles the 'entry age method' used in Anglo-Saxon countries, it is largely influenced by German tax regulations. It measures individually for each pension plan participant the total benefit obligation as the present value of the future benefits, net of the present value of assumed future premiums, that would be payable if a life insurance policy had been purchased.

The difference in the sum of these actuarial calculations for all pension plan participants between the current year and the preceding year constitutes one part of the annual pension expense. The other part consists of the actual benefit payments made during the current year. Actuarial gains and losses are recognised currently as adjustments of pension expense rather than spread over a number of years, as they would be in the UK. This leads to greater fluctuations in pension costs.

There are several significant differences from UK/US practice in the detailed actuarial calculations. These have a direct bearing on the amount accrued and can be summarised as follows:

- The actuarial calculations do not normally take personnel fluctuations into account.
- The entry age into the plan is assumed to be 30 years for all participants.
- The calculations are based on current salaries, ie future increases are not taken into account even though pensions are usually based on final salaries.
- The assumed interest factor used to compute present values is set by the tax authorities at 6 per cent.

From what has been said it is evident that the calculation of pension cost in Germany is significantly different from the Anglo-Saxon approach and, in fact, the pension accruals of German companies are often found to be seriously deficient when they are compared with the sum of future obligations determined on the basis of British or American accounting principles.

Disclosure in the notes to financial statements is required if, in comparison with the grand total value of future pension obligations, the year-end accrual is deficient; this includes benefits granted on or before 31 December 1986, or amendments thereto, that have not been accrued.

In the context of post-retirement benefits in general, it should be noted that benefits other than pension payments are rather uncommon in Germany.

RESERVES

German rules require a larger number of subdivisions of reserves than do UK or US rules. Under the first overall division, as provided for in the Fourth Directive, reserves are classified as either capital or revenue reserves.

Capital reserves include:

- amounts received for the issue of shares or warrants in excess of their nominal value;
- amounts received which are related to conversion rights or options attached to debentures issued;
- amounts paid in by shareholders in consideration of preferences awarded by the company;
- any other capital contributions from shareholders.

Revenue reserves include only such amounts as are created by transfer from the profits of any financial year. They would generally include:

- legal reserve;
- reserve for treasury stock;
- reserves prescribed by the company's articles;
- other revenue reserves.

Legal reserve

German stock corporations must allocate 5 per cent of each year's profit until, together with certain components of the capital reserves, the legal reserve is equal to 10 per cent of the par value of share capital; the articles may prescribe a higher reserve amount. The legal reserve may, substantially, be utilised only to compensate for losses which the company has incurred or to increase the company's share capital.

Treasury stock

It is a requirement that any holding of treasury stock or investment in shares of a controlling company must be offset by a reserve of the same amount. This reserve may only be released in tandem with a reduction of the corresponding asset.

Reserves prescribed by the company's articles

These comprise appropriations of earnings as prescribed by a company's articles and may, but need not, be earmarked for certain purposes.

All activities during the year in the reserve accounts must be disclosed in the balance sheet or the notes to the financial statements.

German accounting and disclosure standards or prevailing practices surrounding reserves substantially comply with International Accounting Standards.

Special items with an equity portion

A peculiar feature of many German balance sheets are 'special items with an equity portion' (*Sonderposten mit Rücklageanteil*). Such items may be recorded only to the extent that tax recognition of certain transactions is dependent on their inclusion in the balance sheet. They have the attributes of both an accrued liability and a reserve: one portion is an accrued liability in that income taxes will have to be paid in the future when the item is dissolved; the other portion is in the nature of a reserve (equity).

For example, German income tax law permits taxpayers under certain circumstances to defer for tax purposes gains on the sale of certain fixed assets until they are applied against qualifying reinvestments within a limited period of time (rollover relief). This is only possible, however, if the gain is posted to 'Special items' rather than to income. On the purchase of eligible new assets, an amount equivalent to the gain realised earlier on the sale of the old asset is deducted from the cost of the new asset as a depreciation charge against current income, while the previously deferred gain is restored to taxable income. Thus the net carrying value of the new asset is reduced by the earlier gain without an effect on income.

Other examples include crediting government grants to 'special items' rather than recording them as a reduction of the carrying value of the related asset, and crediting special depreciation for tax purposes here rather than to provisions for depreciation.

Special items with an equity portion are shown on the liability side of the balance sheet between equity and current liabilities.

Items of this nature are not recognised on balance sheets in the UK or the USA; to the extent that tax-free gains arise from disposals of certain assets these would be recognised as income, but would be taken account of in the determination of any deferred tax balances.

GOODWILL AND GROUP ACCOUNTS

Present German consolidation accounting techniques follow the provisions of the Seventh Directive of the Council of the European Community. In certain areas the directive offered optional accounting treatments and thus the related provisions in German commercial law may vary from those in other EU countries. The general principles of consolidation are that all domestic and foreign subsidiaries must be consolidated; and that all assets and liabilities of the enterprises included must be valued uniformly within the framework of methods available to the parent company.

German commercial law exempts parent companies from preparing consolidated financial statements if total group assets or sales or the total number of employees do not meet certain size tests; also exempted are parent companies which are, in turn, subsidiaries of a parent company that is resident in a member state of the EU and that prepares consolidated financial statements in accordance with EU regulations, provided that minority shareholders of the German parent company do not oppose the exemption.

The difference between the fair value of the identifiable net assets acquired in a business combination and the fair value of the consideration given is recorded as goodwill. Two methods are available to calculate goodwill: the 'book-value' and the 'revaluation' methods.

The book-value method is the more commonly used method in Germany. The fair value of the consideration given is compared with the book value of the net assets acquired and any excess of the consideration given is allocated to the individual items up to their fair value. Any remaining excess would be recorded as goodwill. Negative goodwill cannot arise under this method, as long as the purchase consideration exceeds the acquired book values.

The revaluation method, which is commonly used in the UK and the USA, requires that the net assets acquired be stated at their fair values throughout before they are compared with the fair value of the consideration given and goodwill is calculated.

The two methods can lead to significantly different results when less than 100 per cent of an investee company is acquired.

The calculation of goodwill is performed either at the time of acquisition of the subsidiary company or on first inclusion of the subsidiary in the consolidated financial statements.

Any goodwill that has arisen is capitalised as an intangible fixed asset and amortised either over a period of four years or, systematically, over the financial years which are likely to benefit from the goodwill. For income tax purposes, however, the amortisation period is fixed at 15 years, so many German companies also use the 15-year tax amortisation period for their financial statements. As an alternative to capitalising and amortising goodwill, it is also permissible to charge goodwill arising on consolidation to reserves.

If negative goodwill should arise, this is to be shown on the consolidated balance sheet as a 'difference arising on capital consolidation' and may be released to income at a later date if certain conditions are met. This is substantially different from the approach prescribed by US accounting rules which require a pro rata write-down of certain non-current assets before any negative goodwill can be recorded on the balance sheet.

CONCLUSION

The above commentary highlights the extent of the hurdles which will need to be overcome if German accounting is to be 'internationalised'. It is true that some of these differences can be removed by systematically utilising options currently available under German, US and IAS rules. In other areas, however, further changes, in particular to German practice and law, will be required. This is unlikely to be a quick process.

28

Investing in Germany

Günter Betz and Andreas Kopp,
C&L Deutsche Revision AG

INTRODUCTION

During 1995 the German M&A (mergers and acquisitions) market was able to break away from the declining trend experienced in 1993 and 1994. Market estimates show that the number of deals increased by about 10 per cent. The German M&A market has become more and more international and the interest in German targets is high. Approximately 280 German companies were the subject of a takeover by foreign purchasers in 1995. The most active were buyers from the US, the UK and Switzerland. In turn, German companies were busy acquiring targets abroad, the most sought-after acquisitions being in the US, followed by Switzerland and China.

CULTURAL ISSUES

Despite its size, the German M&A market is not a very sophisticated one, at least not by Anglo-Saxon standards. A considerable number of deals are completed without involving a specialist M&A consultant but with the help of the local tax adviser or accountant.

Historically, selling a company in Germany has been perceived as a sign of failure. Selling was regarded as a soft option, as not being able to manage the business properly. The typical German vendor feels a strong social responsibility for the business and employees and often considers that selling the business represents an abdication of these responsibilities. Many potential vendors have inherited their businesses or started them from scratch and have a strong sense of duty to their workforce and the community. However, this view is slowly changing. Gradually the selling option is considered more socially acceptable. Many private company shareholders simply have no other alternative than to sell the business either to an industrial buyer or by way of a management buy-out or buy-in ('MBO' or 'MBI').

GATHERING INFORMATION

Gathering information on German companies before approaching them can be difficult. German companies, many of them family owned, are very reluctant to disclose financial information. Public companies, as well as most sizeable German limited companies (*Gesellschaft mit beschränkter Haftung* or GmbH), are required to file financial information. However, the majority (according to estimates, up to 90 per cent) simply do not disclose anything. In addition, many partnerships (with the exception of the very large ones) are exempt from disclosing financial information. The partnership corporate structure, especially the so-called limited liability partnership company (GmbH and Co KG), is a common corporate form in Germany.

There is less difficulty in obtaining information on public companies (*Aktiengesellschaft* or AG). However, there are only approximately 500 quoted companies in Germany plus another 2300 unquoted. For all other corporate structures it is often impossible to obtain more than only basic financial information.

For the outsider seeking more information there is a whole host of databases, online datalinks and CD-ROM systems where publicly available information on companies is summarised. The majority of trade associations will also usually distribute information on their industry sector and in some cases on their members. However, the best source of information is often an external consultant who knows the particular industry well and has high-level contacts with senior executives within the sector.

DEAL SOURCES

It is estimated that there are approximately 300,000 medium-sized companies (*Mittelstand*) with succession problems in Germany. Typically these companies are family owned and the need to resolve these succession problems has become more acute as the age profile of shareholder owners who set up businesses in the post-war period has increased. The trend for many corporate groups to restructure their operations in order to focus on core activities will also generate many more transactions. A number of businesses in eastern Germany privatised in the early 1990s are also coming on to the market again, in order either to cash in on short-term success or to give financial investors an exit from their investment.

ANALYSING ACCOUNTS

It is important to recognise that the accounting philosophy in Germany differs from that in Anglo-Saxon countries, in which accounts aim to reflect the commercial substance of the company's performance and financial position. In Germany the preparation of accounts is essentially tax driven. While still subscribing to the principal accounting concepts, ie going concern, consistency, accruals and prudence (which plays a prominent role), German accounts reflect a quite unique concept: the principle of *Maßgeblichkeit*, often called the 'authoritative principle'. This basically means that the commercial accounts; determine the tax accounts; which, on the face of it, seems to make sense. However, in practice, more often than not 'reversed *Maßgeblichkeit*' tends to prevail. The effect of this is that tax law generally has a significant impact on the commercial accounts, which in turn may not fairly reflect the actual performance of the company.

In Germany, certain reported figures in the commercial accounts bear little resemblance to the underlying commercial reality but are drawn from tax regulations and concessions. In fact, certain tax allowances can be claimed only if they are dealt with in exactly the same manner in the financial accounts. The effect of this close correlation between the financial statements and the tax treatment is that certain assets might have been subject to excessive depreciation and are therefore stated at values considerably below their true market worth. This difference between market value and book value is often referred to as hidden reserves (*stille Reserven*).

In addition to differences in accounting philosophies there are other differences in German accounting practice compared with Anglo-Saxon concepts. Some prominent examples include the treatment of long-term construction contracts and pensions and the fact that fixed assets cannot be revalued. In general, it is advisable to seek guidance from a local accounting firm familiar with cross-border and international accounting conventions in order to pick one's way through this minefield. More detailed guidance is given in the chapter on financial reporting and accounting.

One further pitfall in this regard relates to the fact that in Germany there is a greater tendency for company and private items to be mixed in the accounts of owner-managed businesses. It is important therefore to ensure that income and expenditure and assets and liabilities are carefully analysed so that any purely private items can be identified and disregarded in any assessment of net worth or maintainable profitability.

ACQUISITION PROCESS – RISK AND SUCCESS FACTORS

A surprisingly high proportion of acquisitions fail to meet their objectives. Based on international experience and historical research, there are five principal issues which contribute to the success (or otherwise) of an acquisition:

Clear purpose: there must be a clear business purpose for undertaking acquisitions in general and the planned acquisition in particular. A number of acquisitions are often driven by the personal objectives of the decision maker which have little to do with the strategic requirements of the acquiring company.

In-depth knowledge of target: an acquisition requires an in-depth knowledge of the target and its industry. All sources of information must be employed and the most appropriate management resource must devote sufficient time to prepare for the deal.

Management culture: poor management and poor management practices in acquired companies are a frequent reason for failure. Once the decision to make an acquisition is made, the acquirer should demonstrate its interest and commitment to the deal by involving high-ranking officers to negotiate the deal and evaluate the management of the target company. This is particularly true in Germany where senior managers are often reluctant to deal with people who they feel are not as experienced as themselves. It is also necessary to recognise that there may be differing management cultures or attitudes. Some differences might be related specifically to German cultural issues, others might be more to do with the individuals running the business. It is important to check the cultural fit before the deal is completed.

Post-acquisition integration: acquirers should think about post-acquisition integration before the deal is signed. Detailed integration plans will help to ensure effective communication, the reconciliation of operational functions, eg production, research and development, salesforce, the management control and IT functions, as well as the internal management structures. In addition, speed of implementation is of the essence in order to realise synergies quickly and deliver the benefits offered by the target.

Advisers: it is important to choose an adviser for your acquisition who has sufficient appropriate experience, especially when the deal is taking place in a new market or territory.

DUE DILIGENCE

A proper due diligence investigation will also enhance the chances of success of the acquisition by providing more information to the acquirer's management. The process should identify any inherent risks and help to avoid unpleasant surprises. Although vendor confidentiality is one of the most important issues in any German disposal, sellers are becoming more and more used to the due diligence procedure as part of the acquisition process and are more willing to provide relevant information. However, the timing of the exercise is still a matter for negotiation. German sellers seek to have the due diligence investigation take place as late in the process as possible, preferably after the signing of the purchase agreement.

VALUATION ISSUES

Valuation practice is still very much influenced by a procedure recommended by the German institute of accountants in 1983. The procedure recommends that businesses are valued by aggregating the present value of future maintainable earnings with the net present value of the sale proceeds of assets surplus to business requirements.

Valuations based on multiples applied in comparable deals are also used. However, as information on the purchase prices of German deals is scarce, it can be difficult to identify enough comparable transactions both in the German domestic market and abroad in order to draw meaningful comparisons.

As an alternative, the discounted cash-flow method of valuation is becoming more common in Germany as shareholder value concepts are aired more frequently and take on more importance. There are other valuation methods, such as the Stuttgart formula, which are mainly applied by the tax authorities for certain tax computations.

This valuation process will normally include tax-planning measures to maximise the post-tax yield, for example by obtaining tax relief for any premium paid to net assets or gaining effective deductions for tax losses. As most acquisitions take the form of a share purchase, some post-tax restructuring is often necessary in order to achieve these goals.

CONCLUSION

Germany is an interesting market for prospective investors, despite the criticisms voiced about its strict regulatory environment and high cost base. As in other European states, there is a need for some domestic revamping of infrastructure. This is particularly true in the case of the welfare system and the taxation rules. However, there are signs of widespread support for the necessary measures for change.

From the acquirer's perspective, it is interesting to observe that the German M&A market has developed into a buyer's market, with purchase prices going down in many industries. Targets are becoming more and more available due to the restructuring strategies of large corporate groups and succession problems in the German *Mittelstand*. With the proposed advent of monetary union, Germany will be at the hub of a single currency market and will also continue to be seen as an important gateway for overseas companies wishing to exploit the relatively untouched markets lying to the east.

29

Corporate Disposals

Wolfgang Wagner and Andreas Kopp,
C&L Deutsche Revision AG

FOCUSING ON CORE ACTIVITIES

Germany has seen a number of corporate disposals in recent years. Diversification strategies applied in the 1980s created large German conglomerate groups with a wide range of activities which are now being restructured. Focusing on core activities is the most recent corporate trend.

A good example of a diversified company now focusing on core businesses is the Daimler Benz group, a leading German car manufacturer which embarked on an acquisition strategy and acquired companies such as AEG and Fokker. Other new activities such as IT services were also acquired. However, the enlarged group turned out to be difficult to manage and the companies generated large losses. Management finally decided to rethink its strategy and restructure. Daimler's stated focus is now on core activities as the company strives to divest itself of a number of loss-making operations.

Other examples of restructuring have been less dramatic. However, large German corporates such as Veba and Mannesmann have also streamlined their activities. Head office at these companies has communicated its objective to be a top player in clearly defined markets. If this is not achievable in a reasonably short period of time the divisional line managers may risk having their activities disposed of. Many companies are currently scanning their portfolio in order to decide whether to hold or to sell operations.

The fact that a business is being sold does not necessarily mean that the activity is loss making. Often the contrary is true. Small and profitable subsidiaries which can attract a premium purchase price are also being put up for sale. The proceeds of these disposals are used to offset other operational losses in strategically important markets or to invest in other core activities and more promising industries. Mannesmann is a good example. It sold Hartmann & Braun AG, a company involved in process automation and measuring, for almost DM1 billion. The money will probably be invested to strengthen Mannesmann's telecommunication activities in order to achieve a market-leading position in that sector.

POTENTIAL BUYERS

In the early 1990s most German companies could have been sold several times over, mostly to industrial buyers, but were often not available. Although auction processes are not common in Germany even now, sellers could usually choose between a number of interested parties. This golden age of mergers and acquisitions (M&A) for German vendors seems to be over for the short term.

Companies are much more difficult to sell in the current market unless they represent a really first-class opportunity. However, some companies do not find a buyer at all. The trend towards a buyer's market has been driven by the effects on company profitability of the recession in Germany and increasing competition for German products in world markets. Other companies have simply been put on the market too late or have experienced management problems. In some cases, the integration of acquired businesses has also proved difficult due to inefficient planning and these experiences have left a bad taste in the mouths of some acquirers, fuelling their reluctance to consider acquisition opportunities.

Corporates and institutional buyers

The trend for focusing on core activities has generated more disposals in the German market but has also led to the exercise of more caution when considering new acquisitions. German corporates regard acquisitions as an important part of their strategy. However, they are confining themselves to a smaller number of clearly defined activities. Times are getting tougher, even in Germany. Shareholder value concepts are coming to the fore as companies return to core activities and top management is forced to react to inefficient operations.

In some industry sectors institutional buyers backing a management buy-out or buy-in ('MBO' or 'MBI') team have taken a more prominent role. The fact that institutional buyers are considered as a realistic sales option is a relatively new feature of corporate disposals. Venture capitalists have money available and many of them are desperate to do deals in Germany. To the surprise of many German-based M&A professionals, some venture capitalists are able to offer competitive purchase prices. Others wonder how such acquisitions can be successful given the high interest burden and internal returns required on the equity. However, the institutional money is there, the interest rates are low and industrial buyers are sometimes rare – all of which combine to increase investment opportunities for the financial institutions.

MBOs, MBIs and venture capitalists

The number of MBOs and MBIs in Germany is increasing, although this method of disposal is not as common as it is in the UK. It is often pointed out that German managers are spoilt with high salaries, secure pension schemes and big company cars and that there is no wish to take on the entrepreneurial risk of acquiring a company. Similarly, within the *Mittelstand*, there is typically a psychological divide between owner–manager and employee and the two roles are clearly defined. Employees look to their bosses to provide an environment in which to work. The readiness to assume business risk among employees in this environment is less well defined.

Nonetheless, venture capitalists are active in Germany. More than 70 are members of the German Venture Capital Association (BVK). There are many differences between their investment criteria: some buy majorities, others do not; some have a narrow industry focus, others choose a more opportunistic strategy; some invest in turnaround situations, others in start-up situations; some confine themselves to MBOs and MBIs in already well-established businesses; some like to take on management responsibility, others rely on retaining existing management. They also differ in their preferred exit strategies and the desired term of their investment. One thing does unite them, however: they all want to make money and are tough negotiators!

Flotations

Another strategy for corporates and investors in exiting unloved markets is to consider the flotation of a company or business division. However, this option takes more time and often the vendors will prefer to sell to an industrial buyer or to an institutional buyer who might later want to do the flotation themselves. There is, in general, a lack of detailed understanding of the equity/stock exchange culture in Germany, especially within the *Mittelstand*. This may change in the short to medium term if the various German stock exchanges consolidate, and major listings such as Lufthansa and Deutsche Telekom increase the relative size and importance of public shareholder participation in the domestic markets.

Larger companies, such as Daimler Benz, have already looked to overseas stock markets for an international listing and have been forced to adjust their reporting of results to meet US disclosure regulations.

SALE STRATEGY

An important stage in deciding on the appropriate sale strategy is to consider the objective of the sale. If the aim is to avoid a winding up of the company which can result in huge costs, for example laying off personnel, the sale strategy will be different from a situation in which one has an attractive business for sale and can expect interest from several parties. Whatever the situation, proper preparation is key to a successful deal and all options should be assessed before proceeding. There may be situations where the obvious buyer is a major competitor, which could cause confidentiality problems if information were to be disclosed and a sale did not take place. It might also be useful to compare a trade sale with other exit strategies such as a flotation.

Taxation aspects normally have a bearing on the form of sale too. Vendors usually prefer to sell shares rather than the assets of a company. Not only does this avoid potential double taxation on any gain, but it also gives German individuals the possibility of either an exemption from or reduction of tax on the gain. Non-resident vendors are, in principle, subject to tax on the gain, but in many cases an exemption is available under a double tax treaty.

It is necessary to compile all relevant information before starting any marketing of the opportunity. Potential deal-breaking issues need to be anticipated and weaknesses identified to avoid surprises during negotiations. Top management should be involved at an early stage. Skillful and motivated management is an important factor in conducting successful discussions and, if necessary, managers may need to be groomed for presentations.

Another important consideration is to establish a realistic timetable and try to stick to it. Clearly, this will be determined by the quality of the disposal opportunity. However, vendors must take into account the holiday seasons. Germany has a long period of summer holidays and Easter is a preferred time for skiing.

In most industry sectors, buyers currently have the upper hand and it is therefore more difficult to create competitive situations which would normally help to increase the value of the transaction. This makes the organisation of a controlled auction process more difficult. Controlled auction processes are still not very popular in Germany and some buyers will often refuse to take part.

PERSONNEL ISSUES

Workers' representatives cannot usually block the sale of a subsidiary. However, there are some notification obligations within certain deadlines which can give rise to problems and affect the timetable, and these need to be managed during the German disposal process. If possible, the local workers' council (*Betriebsrat*) should be informed of the decision to sell early on, since its support can make the completion of the deal easier. Clearly, however, informing the workers' council risks a breach of confidentiality and this must also be taken into account when determining the sale strategy in any proposed transaction.

SALE PROCESS

Not only the final purchase agreement but also the letter of intent (or memorandum of understanding) needs to be notarised to be legally binding, if shares or land and buildings are being sold. Often the parties will not notarise the letter of intent and live with some uncertainty until the purchase agreement has been notarised. The formal administration of these documents must be carried out by a German notary, which is relatively expensive. In accordance with German regulations, only certain notaries in other, cheaper jurisdictions can be used.

The sale process in Germany (approach, vendor presentations and information disclosure, negotiations, letter of intent, due diligence, completion) is similar to that undertaken in other countries but with some peculiarities. An adviser with experience of such matters and of doing transactions in Germany can assist in effecting a successful and stress-free deal.

Part Four

Legal Aspects

30

Choice of Organisational Form

Clifford Chance

There are basically three forms of business formation under German law: sole proprietorship, partnership and corporation.

In a sole proprietorship an individual owns the business assets and is liable for all business debts. In a partnership at least two persons run the business. German law provides for the following categories:

- general partnership (*offene Handelsgesellschaft* (oHG));
- limited partnership (*Kommanditgesellschaft* (KG));
- silent partnership (*stille Gesellschaft*).

Persons can also form a corporation which is a legal entity distinct from the incorporators. The following forms of corporations are the most common:

- limited liability company (*Gesellschaft mit beschränkter Haftung* (GmbH));
- stock corporation (*Aktiengesellschaft* (AG)).

In addition to these basic organisational forms other variants are used, such as the joint venture which is basically a partnership with a defined and closed-end objective, and also the European Economic Interest Grouping (EEIG), which was introduced by statute in 1989 and is similar in structure to a general partnership. The EEIG provides the only cross-border organisational structure within the European Union countries.

Most of the organisational structures of a business have to be entered in the Trade Register. The Trade Register provides the public documentation for general information which is of greatest legal significance for commercial transactions, such as: the entity name, equity of a corporation, managing directors or 'Prokura' (full power of attorney). The register is maintained by the local court in the area where the company is located. It is open to public inspection. All registrations in the Trade Register prove evidence of an existing legal fact.

All the above-mentioned forms of business have to be registered in the Trade Register, except for the silent partnership. Also, a joint venture will normally not be registered as this is only a limited purpose organisation. Even a sole proprietor must be entered into the register if he or she is deemed to be a 'large scale entrepreneur' (*Vollkaufmann*) who is engaged in:

- the purchase and resale of movable goods;
- processing or fabrication of merchandise for others;
- underwriting insurance contracts in exchange for premiums as well as banking and financial exchange transactions;
- transactions of commission agents.

where the scope or volume of business requires a commercially organised business operation.

Only large-scale entrepreneurs possessing their own businesses have the duty to prepare yearly commercial financial statements and can also grant a 'Prokura'.

SOLE PROPRIETORSHIP AND PARTNERSHIP

A single person can carry out a commercial business without choosing any specific organisation structure for his or her business. If more than one person wants to run a commercial business together they can do so in a commercial partnership. In a commercial partnership the property is held jointly by all partners and not in distinct shares. Each partner has an interest in the undivided business.

Sole proprietorship

If a person runs a business under his or her own name this business is carried out as a sole proprietorship. The sole proprietor has unrestricted personal liability for all business debts and obligations.

Creation of the sole proprietorship

The Commercial Code does not provide any requirements for the creation of a sole proprietorship. If the sole proprietor is a large-scale entrepreneur, his or her business has to be registered in the Trade Register. There are no further requirements for its registration. Notification has to be given to the local trade authority and the local tax authority. However, these notifications are not essential for the creation of the sole proprietorship.

Under certain circumstances the business is also subject to a special permission by the local trade authority, in particular auctioneers, brokers, real estate developers, casinos etc.

Business name ('firm')

A sole proprietor (large-scale entrepreneur) enters into transactions in the course of business under the name of his or her business (firm). The firm of a sole proprietory is his or her family name, with at least one first name reproduced in full.

The firm name may not include any additional remarks that might mislead or indicate a partnership relationship. Only if the sole proprietorship was acquired *inter vivos* or by inheritance may the existing firm name be retained.

General partnership

Under German law two types of commercial partnerships are usually formed for the purpose of running a commercially organised business operation: general partnership (*offene Handelsgesellschaft*, oHG) and limited partnership (*Kommanditgesellschaft*, KG). In a partnership two or more persons associate to carry on a business as co-owners in order to share profits and control. The partners can be natural persons, legal entities or partnerships.

The Commercial Code provides the essential provisions governing commercial partnerships. However, much is left to the discretion of the partners.

Creation and dissolution

A general partnership is created by a partnership agreement among all founding partners. The partnership agreement is the constitution of the partnership which determines the legal relationships between all partners. Usually it sets out for every partner the duties of contributions, the participation in the management and representation, the distribution of profit and loss and the rights and obligations in the event of a dissolution of the partnership. The (non-mandatory) stipulations of the Commercial Code only apply to the extent that partnership agreement does not provide otherwise.

There is no minimum capital required for the formation of a general partnership because all partners bear unlimited liability and their personal assets are at risk.

The existence of a general partnership with respect to third parties begins from the moment at which the partnership starts its commercial business or has been registered in the Trade Register. Unless otherwise provided for in the general partnership agreement, a general partnership dissolves on the death, bankruptcy or withdrawal of any partner.

Management and representation

Under the Commercial Code each partner can bind the partnership towards third parties. However, the partnership agreement can provide that the management is delegated to one or more of the partners. The remaining partners will then be excluded from the management of the business. Also a joint representation may be stipulated in the partnership agreement.

Business name ('firm')

The business name of the general partnership must contain at least the family name of one partner with an addition indicating the existence of a partnership or the family names of all partners. Other names may not be used in the firm. Only if the partnership was acquired *inter vivos* or by inheritance may the existing business name continue with or without additions indicating the succession. Whether or not the business is carried on with an addition revealing the successor relationship, the successor is liable for all obligations of the previous owner arising out of his or her conduct of the business. Any agreement to the contrary is effective against third parties only if it is registered in the Commercial Register, or if the third party has been informed thereof.

Partnership interest and capital share

Each partner holds joint ownership in the partnership's assets from the time when he or she becomes a partner. The ownership is not divided into distinct shares but each partner has an interest in the undivided business.

Except as provided otherwise in the partnership agreement, the partnership interest is not freely transferable. Every transfer of a partnership interest needs the approval of all partners.

The partnership interest does not reflect the extent of each partner's rights and obligations. Instead, the partnership agreement usually details a so-called capital share (*Kapitalanteil*) which gives a basis for the assignment of all rights and obligations to the respective partners. The capital share often also serves as the basis for the participation in the partnership's gains and losses that are distributed to each partner at the close of the business year.

The profit due to each partner will be credited to the partner's account. Likewise, the losses as well as the money that was withdrawn from the account within the business year will be deducted therefrom.

Limited partnerships

The limited partnership is distinguished from the general commercial partnership to the extent that not all partners are liable for partnership obligations without limitation. The liability of the limited partners with respect to partnership creditors is limited to the amount of their respective specific capital contribution (*Kommanditanteil*). At least one partner must be a general partner with unlimited liability. The general partner, like all other partners, does not have to be a natural person. If the general partner is a limited company (GmbH) the personal liability of the general partner is practically limited to its corporate assets, which will normally be equal to the stated capital of the limited company (so called GmbH & Co KG).

The limited partnership enjoys great popularity because of its limitation of liability and freedom to organise a company structure without being subject to the high level of restrictions in the statutes applicable to corporations. This company structure is therefore often used to create a forum in which a large number of limited partners can participate in a business without bearing any risk except losing their invested capital.

Creation and dissolution

Like every other partnership, a limited partnership is also created by a partnership agreement between all partners. The partners must agree on the general and the limited partners. Each limited partner has to agree to a fixed amount of capital that is set out in the partnership agreement which constitutes the amount for which the partner will be held liable (*Hafteinlage*). The amount the partner will have to contribute (*Pflichteinlage*) usually corresponds with, but may be different from the amount for which the partner is liable.

The part of the contributed capital that shall be liable for the partnership's creditors has to be registered in the Trade Register, and the limitation of the liability commences only with the registration.

Management and representation

Unless otherwise agreed, only the general partners have the authority to bind the partnership as to ordinary matters. Limited partners are excluded from managing the company but have the right to inspect the books of the partnership. A limited partner is also not authorised to represent the partnership towards third parties.

Business name ('firm')

The business name of a limited partnership must contain at least the family (or corporate) name of one general partner with an addition indicating the existence of a partnership. If the sole general partner is a corporation this must be made visible in the partnership name. The names of persons other than those of the general partners may not be used in the firm name of a limited partnership.

Silent partnerships

The silent partnership (*stille Gesellschaft*) is a partnership in which a partner participates in a commercial enterprise owned by another person or company by paying a contribution into the business of the owner and shares in the profit and losses (the liability for losses can be excluded) arising from the operation of the business. The contribution becomes the property of the active participant. Therefore, unless otherwise provided, the silent partner does not normally participate in any increase in hidden reserves in the event of dissolution of the silent partnership.

The commercial enterprise is run by the business owner. The silent partner is not revealed to third parties and all dealings are handled exclusively by the owner of the business. The silent partner does not participate in the management of the business.

Formation and significance

Silent partnerships are created by contracts between the owner of the business and the silent partner. The silent partner's contribution to the business entitles him or her to participate in the profits of the business. Since the partnership is silent, the business is carried out under the business name of the proprietor and no registration is required.

Liability

In relation to third parties, the active participant is the sole owner of the commercial enterprise. He or she carries on the business in his or her name and is authorised to conclude transactions within the operation of the business. Consequently, the silent partner cannot be held personally liable for any business debts.

CORPORATIONS

Corporations are usually the principal means of organising businesses with complex organisational structures and large capital needs. However, the corporate form works for any size of business, including a one-person limited company. Under German corporate law the most common types of corporations are the limited company (*Gesellschaft mit beschränkter Haftung* (GmbH) and the stock corporation (*Aktiengesellschaft* (AG)). More specialised forms of organisation exist for insurance companies (VVaG) and for cooperatives (eG).

Limited company (GmbH)

The GmbH is the most popular organisational form for small and medium-sized businesses in Germany. A company may be established for any legitimate purpose by one or more persons. The capital of a GmbH has to amount to at least DM50,000.

Each shareholder is only entitled to subscribe for one share at the time of the corporation's formation. The nominal value of the shares may be different for each shareholder, but the minimum nominal value of each share must amount to DM500 and has to be divisible by 100. The total of the nominal value of all subscribed shares must equal the share capital of the GmbH.

The shareholder's contribution payable to the corporation depends on the nominal value of the share for which he or she has subscribed. Normally the amount of the contribution is equal to the nominal value of the shares. However, the contribution may also have to include a premium.

Where contributions are to be made in kind, the value of the items comprising the contribution in kind must cover at least the nominal value of the share. To confirm this, the shareholders are obliged to set out in a report the major considerations supporting the appropriate valuation of the non-cash contributions. Frequently the registrar will require the shareholders to show evidence for the valuations.

The formation of a corporation

Forming a corporation involves four essential steps:

- preparing the articles of association;
- appointment of the Managing director;
- paying the contributions;
- registration in the Trade Register.

The articles of association must be signed by all shareholders and have to be notarised. Signing by proxy requires a notarised power of attorney.

The articles of association must specify the following:

- the company's name and registered office;
- the purpose of the enterprise;
- the amount of the share capital;
- the amount each shareholder shall contribute to the share capital.

The inclusion of these items in the articles is mandatory. However, usually the articles of association provide internal regulations governing the relationship between shareholders, such as regulations concerning indemnification governing the relationship between the dissolution or withdrawal, the terms and conditions for various classes of shares, management and representation responsibilities and duties, provisions for the installation of and the representation of a supervisory board etc.

On the establishment of a GmbH, the founders must pay at least one-quarter of the subscribed capital, being not less than DM25,000 in aggregate.

Once a quarter of each original contribution – other than contributions in kind – has been paid up, registration in the Trade Register can be requested. Every corporation must file for registration in the register with the court in the district of its domicile.

The application for registration must be supported by the following:

- articles of association and the powers of attorney of each proxy who signed the articles of association;
- list of shareholders signed by the applicant showing name, first name, profession and residence as well as the original share subscribed by each shareholder;
- for contributions in kind, the contracts underlying the title transfer documents in favour of the corporation;
- documents establishing the proper assessment of the assets contributed values to the equivalent of the share value;
- evidence of the appointment of the managing directors.

The application for registration shall further contain details of the managing director's powers of representation to which sample signatures of the directors must be attached. All these declarations have to be made in the presence of a notary.

The application for registration shall be signed by all managing directors of the GmbH.

The existence of the GmbH commences with its registration in the Trade Register. So long as the shareholders have only agreed on the articles of association, the GmbH exists as a pre-corporation. Statutory law (*GmbH Gesetz*) applies to the pre-GmbH only to a certain extent. However, a pre-corporation can commence business, but operates similarly to a general partnership in this condition.

Management and representation

The business is run by one or more managing directors who separately or jointly represent the GmbH towards third parties. Only natural persons unrestricted in their capacity to transact business can serve as managing directors. Shareholders or other persons – even foreign nationals who are not domiciled within Germany – can be appointed managing directors.

Any change in the managing directors, as well as the termination of managing directors' powers of representation, must be filed for registration in the Commercial Register. The company derives title through the actions of its managing directors and is bound by transactions entered into in its name by the managing directors. The managing directors will – generally – not be liable for their activities towards third parties. Exceptions to this principle are in particular the obligations to pay taxes and social security contributions.

However, the managing directors are responsible for their actions to the company. A managing director shall apply the due care of a prudent business person in the affairs of the company. If managing directors should infringe these duties they are liable to the company for any damages that are caused.

The shareholders' meeting is the supreme organ of the corporation. The shareholders acting in the shareholders' meeting have overall power and control regarding the activities of the managing directors. They may give binding instructions to the management but may not manage the corporation.

GmbHs may have a supervisory board, which is mandatory if the GmbH employs more than 500 employees.

Business name

The name of the company must either derive from the purpose of the company, or it must contain the names of the shareholders or at least of one of them, with an addition indicating that it is a limited company.

Stock corporation

Like the GmbH, the stock corporation is a commercial company with its own legal personality. The corporation's capital derives from the contributions of its shareholders and is divided into shares. Every shareholder subscribes for shares in exchange for his or her capital contribution. The stock (*Aktie*) represents an ownership interest in the corporation.

Formation

The procedure and the essential steps for the formation are very similar to those already set out for the limited corporation above, with the addition of the appointment of the supervisory board and the board of directors.

In the articles of association one or more shareholders agree on the formation of a stock corporation. In particular, the shareholders have to agree on the subscription for all shares in the corporation which has to be stipulated in a notarial deed.

The notarial deed must include the name of the founders, the face value and the issuing price of the shares and the types of stock for which the founders will subscribe. The mandatory content for the articles of association of a stock corporation is basically the same as for the articles of a limited corporation. However, the minimum amount of the capital stock must amount to DM100,000. The articles shall also contain statements with regard to the face value of the shares as well as the number and types of shares that are issued, whether they are registered shares and the number of the members of the supervisory board. The minimal face value of a share is DM5.

After the articles of association have been established the corporation has to be capitalised. The shareholders must contribute according to their subscription for shares. Before registration all contributions in kind have to be made in full. A cash contribution has to be made for at least one-quarter of the face value of the stocks.

Subsequently, the founders appoint the members of the supervisory board, which in turn will appoint the board of managing directors.

Thereafter, the founders shall draw up a report confirming the incorporation of the company.

The corporation shall be submitted for registration in the Trade Register. In particular, the application form shall contain:

- articles of association;
- any agreement made concerning special privileges of certain classes of shareholders;
- the documents of appointment of the board of managing directors and the supervisory board;
- the formation report.

If the formation of the corporation and the application for registration are completed, the Trade Register will register the company. From this time on, the stock corporation commences its existence.

Management and representation

Three major representative organs exist in an AG:

- the general meeting of the shareholders;
- the supervisory board (*Aufsichtsrat*);
- the board of managing directors (*Vorstand*).

The board of managing directors manages and represents the corporation towards third parties. The members of the management board are appointed by the supervisory board. Depending on the articles of association, the management board may comprise one or more natural persons. If more than one person is on the board, usually one person is appointed as chairman (*Vorstandsvorsitzender*). Any natural person who is unrestricted in his or her capacity to transact business can serve as managing director of a stock corporation. Shareholders or other persons, even foreigners who are not domiciled in Germany, can be appointed as members of the board.

The supervisory board is appointed at a general meeting of the shareholders and elected for a period of four years. In large stock corporations, with more than 500 employees, one-third of the supervisory board shall consist of employee representatives. There are additional rules for employee participation in management.

The supervisory board supervises the activities of the board of managing directors in large corporations.

The shareholders have a limited role in corporate governance, which they exercise at properly convened meetings. The corollary to the shareholders' limited role is the dominant role of the board of managing directors.

Shareholders have powers to approve corporate transactions only on the specific request of the management. However, shareholders vote on fundamental corporate changes such as amendments to the articles of association or mergers with other corporations. Shareholders also have the power to appoint the members of the supervisory board. Further, votes on the distribution of dividends and the nomination of the auditors lie within the competence of the shareholders.

All decisions at the shareholders' meetings are made by vote. The voting rights of each shareholder depend on the face value of the stock unless the right to vote is excluded for certain types of shares.

It is very common within large stock corporations which trade their stocks publicly for small shareholders to authorise proxies to vote in their names. Usually the shareholders' bank offers its customers the service of voting in the name of the shareholder.

Liability

Every corporation separates the risk and assets of the business from those of its investors and managers. This separation implies the rule of limited liability under which a shareholder (equity investor) is not liable for corporate obligations beyond the shareholder's investment. Creditors may look only to the corporation's assets. However, directors are liable to the corporation for any breach of duty owed to the corporation.

Transfer of shares

Bearer's shares are freely transferable. If the shares are listed, they are usually sold through registered brokers and traders. Registered shares may be transferred by endorsement. Sometimes the articles of association may provide for the requirement of an approval to a transfer by the corporation.

31

Corporate Combinations, Mergers and Acquisitions

Clifford Chance

ACQUISITIONS

In Germany, as in many other jurisdictions, an acquisition can be made by acquiring either shares or assets in the target company. The preferred course will be influenced primarily by tax considerations, but there are also major differences under commercial law.

A share deal consists of the acquisition of the target company. The acquiror, therefore, assumes responsibility not just for the assets, but also for the liabilities of the target company, whether known or unknown, disclosed or undisclosed. Existing contractual relationships usually remain in effect – this may be relevant if the target company is dependent on licence or distribution agreements, which sometimes contain clauses providing for early termination, should there be a change in the shareholder structure of either one of the contracting parties. This, inter alia, makes thorough due diligence highly advisable.

In an asset deal, the purchaser acquires only selected assets. This normally cuts out the possibility of unknown liabilities passing to the acquiror. The target company's existing contractual relations are not automatically transferred – all licence, service, distribution or other contracts which are important for the business can only be transferred with the third party's approval. This can sometimes result in renegotiation of the contractual conditions.

Where the assets acquired constitute the whole, or almost the whole, of the seller's property, a statutory transition of the seller's liabilities may occur, including possible tax liabilities related to the business.

Where the assets transferred constitute the substance of a given business, or a distinct part of that business, German law provides for the automatic transition of all related employment contracts, along with any seniority rights already accrued.

TRANSFORMATIONS

Mergers have always been possible in Germany; company divisions, however, have proved more problematic. But matters were improved by the 1995 Transformation Act (*Umwandlungsgesetz*) which set out various techniques for restructuring and combining the businesses of companies within Germany, although there is no legislation enabling international mergers. The Act embraces corporation/corporation, partnership/corporation and corporation/partnership relationships and covers the following methods of restructuring:

- merger;
- splitting a company into its constituent businesses;
- change of legal form.

In a merger, one company is absorbed by another. The surviving company globally acquires all the assets of the subordinated company and all of its liabilities, taking its place in all pending litigation. Once the merger has taken place the subordinated company disappears. Except where the surviving company already held all the shares in the subordinated company, the surviving company must increase its stated capital. In exchange for the transition of assets and liabilities, shareholders in the subordinated company receive shares in the surviving company in direct proportion to the net asset value of their pre-merger stake.

Three different legal techniques exist for splitting a company into its constituent businesses:

- A company can split up its aggregate assets by a single transfer to two or more surviving entities (*Aufspaltung*). At the end of this transaction, the transferring company ceases to exist.
- A company can, in a single transaction, spin off parts of its assets to one or more new entities (*Abspaltung*). The original company survives this spin-off, and its shareholders become, in addition to their original shareholding, shareholders in the new entities, in direct proportion to the transferred net assets.

- A company can also split off parts of its assets to a new entity, in which it becomes the shareholder (*Ausgliederung*). In this case, both companies survive the transaction.

Common to all these transactions is the fact that all assets and liabilities, along with all contractual relations, pass to the respective new entities in one package. There are no transfers of individual assets and – unless a specific contract provides to the contrary – existing contracts can be transferred without any need for third-party approval.

A business entity can also change its legal form. A partnership can be changed into a limited company, a limited company into a partnership, a stock corporation into a limited company, and vice versa. Other possibilities are also available.

Under the new legislation, any change in legal form does not automatically imply a change in the identity of the transformed entity. Consequently, neither liquidations nor transfers of assets are required. This means that an entity's existing contractual relations all remain in effect, if there is no specific agreement to the contrary with a third party.

Certain formalities attach to all transformations under the new legislation. In most cases, a contract is required between the entities involved, and the respective companies or partnerships must approve this at a general meeting. Both the contract and the resolutions must be recorded by a notary.

Where a workers' council exists, it must be informed of the proposed transformation at least one month before the transaction is submitted to the shareholders for approval.

The transformation must be registered in the trade register. It becomes effective only after registration. For commercial purposes, however, the transformation may be dated back to an earlier accounting date. This removes the need for preparing a new statement of accounts on an odd date, provided that the preferred accounting date for the transformation does not predate the filing of the registration request by more than eight months.

OTHER COMBINATIONS

Companies may be joined in other ways. A common combination is a domination and consolidation of profits agreement (*Beherrschungs- und Gewinnabführungsvertrag*). Under this sort of agreement, a subordinated company places itself under the direction of a dominating company; the management is then directed by the dominating company on all business matters. The subordinated company also agrees to transfer its profits automatically, and not as a dividend, to the dominating company. The dominating company must agree to assume – and pay for – all future losses incurred by the subordinated company. Also, minority shareholders (not themselves parties to the agreement) must be guaranteed a profit share in line with what existed before.

Other similar agreements may involve either profit pooling or contracts to supply management services.

The law requires that these agreements are made in written form and approved at the shareholders' meetings of the companies concerned (there must be a notarial record for the subordinated company). A registration in the trade register is then required. This is a prerequisite for the enforceability of the agreement.

32

Legal Framework

Clifford Chance

German law, in its origins, is based on Roman law. It is part of the civil law system and is widely codified. At the end of the nineteenth century a series of codes were introduced which in essence are still applicable today. These main codes are:

- *Bürgerliches Gesetzbuch* (Civil Code);
- *Handelsgesetzbuch* (Commercial Code);
- *Zivilprozeßordnung* (Code of Civil Procedure);
- *Strafgesetzbuch* (Penal Code).

Other statutes which were enacted around the turn of the century which continue to be of major significance are *Aktiengesetz* (Stock Corporation Act), *Gesetz betreffend die Gesellschaften mit beschränkter Haftung GmbH-Gesetz* (Limited Companies Act), *Scheck-Gesetz* (Cheque Act) and *Wechselgesetz* (Bills of Exchange Act).

All these statutes have been frequently amended and modernised. However, many rules are still in effect which sometimes strangely reflect commercial customs of the year 1900, in particular the rules concerning company and partnership names and the formalities relating to the deposition of authorised signatures.

In a civil law system operating on the basis of statutory law, the answer to any legal question must, in principle, be found by interpretation of the statutes. In practice the four classical Roman rules of interpretation apply: statutes shall be interpreted historically, grammatically, teleologically and by analogy. Precedents are not binding. However, they may be used to support a specific interpretation of a statute, and they are a helpful guideline to anticipate what position a court might take in interpreting certain rules of law in a dispute. It is possible by presenting proper arguments to convince a court to deviate from a precedent even if given by the Federal Court.

In practice, the differences between the German and a common law system should not be overestimated. Even if the approach to the solution of a specific legal question may be entirely different in the two systems, the answer under the German law might well be very close to the one found under common law.

PUBLIC REGISTERS

German law provides for certain public registers which are efficient and helpful in establishing, for example, land titles or the existence and legal representation of companies.

The local courts keep land registers (*Grundbuch*) where all real property is recorded with the name of the present owner. Also previous owners and the reason for the transition of title can be seen from the land register and its supporting files. The land register also shows all encumbrances of the property, including easements, mortgages and land charges.

For the transfer of title to real property or the creation of an easement or a mortgage, registration in the land register is a prerequisite. Therefore it can always be assumed and is guaranteed by the law that the contents of the register reflect the true situation of a certain property.

The land register and the supporting documents are open to inspection by any person who can establish a reasonable interest in the registered data.

The local courts also keep a trade register (*Handelsregister*). All business enterprises (excepting only very small businesses), partnerships and corporations must be registered in the trade register. The trade register shows the name, purpose and the city of the seat of the business. It gives also details on the persons authorised to represent the business, partnership or corporation. For a corporation the stated capital is indicated. The trade register also shows the existence of profit consolidation or domination agreements.

As the trade register is kept on a continuous basis, the history of a company can normally be seen from the entries in the trade register.

The trade register also maintains files containing specimen signatures of the authorised signatories, the articles of association and the names of the shareholders of limited companies. The names of the partners in a general or limited partnership are shown in the register itself. For larger companies the registry files also contain copies of the annual statements.

The trade register and the supporting files are open to inspection by anybody. It is guaranteed by statute that everybody acting in good faith may rely on the entries in the register. Consequently, when a partnership or company is acting in a transaction it will suffice to make reference to the trade register. It is not necessary to establish otherwise by board resolutions or similar documents the authority of a person acting on its behalf.

PUBLIC RECORDING

Specifically in view of registration requirements, many types of transactions require public recording. This applies in particular to real property transactions, the formation of corporations and the transfer of shares in limited companies.

The necessary public recordings will be done by notaries. Civil law notaries are generally trained lawyers. In some German states they form a separate profession, in others they act in combination with their position as attorneys at law.

Unlike the competences of a notary in a common law country, the German notaries are responsible for the viability and enforceability of the deeds they record. They must act impartially in the interest of all parties concerned. It is customary in larger transactions that contract documents will be drafted by the attorneys assisting the parties in negotiating the transaction. However, if the transaction requires notarial recording, the notary by law assumes a responsibility for the transaction document recorded even if he or she was not involved in the drafting.

The substantial responsibility of the notaries is reflected by their fees, which are set out in a federal statute. The notarial fees follow a scheme of a decreasing percentage in the value of the transaction and can be relatively high.

In order to avoid the high fees of German notaries there is a tendency to use notaries in other civil law countries, such as Switzerland or the

Netherlands, for the recording of certain transactions. This is not possible for real property transactions, and it is uncertain for other transactions to what extent foreign notarial deeds could be acknowledged in Germany.

On the other hand, a German notary may record documents in any language in which he or she is conversant. However, any document which must be filed with any of the public registers must be translated into German.

LEGAL ADVICE

Legal advice and assistance in disputes are provided in Germany by attorneys at law (*Rechtsanwälte*). There is no distinction as between barristers and solicitors. Each *Rechtsanwalt* is a member of a local bar and is permitted to plead before the Civil Courts in his or her precinct. However, he or she may act in other places for any matter other than civil litigation.

Generally, German law prohibits any person other than a *Rechtsanwalt* from giving legal advice with certain exceptions as to tax matters etc.

German attorneys are bound to a fee structure set out by federal legislation which provides for a percentage fee based on the value of the matter. However, it has become customary to agree on a different fee scheme agreement which will require formal drafting. As the statutory fees can be substantial, particularly in transactions with a high value but involving a limited amount of work, it is highly advisable to agree on a specific fee structure when retaining a German attorney.

REUNIFICATION

During the political reunification of Germany the five states in the former German Democratic Republic have acceded to the Federal Republic of Germany. With effect from 3 October 1990 the legal system of the Federal Republic of Germany has been introduced in the five new – formerly East German – states.

The details of the transition have been laid down in the Treaty of Unification and its annexes. Under these rules certain parts of the law of the German Democratic Republic, e.g. the bankruptcy law, have remained in force, and other specific legislation has been enacted which mainly relates to the transfer of real property or the protection of residential tenants etc. In general, however, the differences between the legal systems in the two parts of Germany have almost totally disappeared.

33

Employment Law

Clifford Chance

In Germany no uniform statute exists on employment law. There are a large variety of different statutes applicable in this field. The statutory rules leave numerous gaps which have been filled by jurisprudence of the labour courts.

The legal framework of labour relations comprises the following main elements:

- individual employment contracts;
- legal rules relating to individual employment agreements and protective rules for relating to, for example, termination or holidays;
- collective bargaining rules applying to collective bargaining agreements, strikes etc;
- co-determination rules: workers' participation in the business and in corporate governance is statutorily protected under the *Shop Constitution Act* and the *Co-Determination Act.*

INDIVIDUAL EMPLOYMENT AGREEMENTS

Term

In employment law freedom of contract is restricted. Employment contracts generally must be made for an indefinite period of time. Unless justified by specific circumstances no fixed-term contracts can be made. This would exceptionally be permissible in the event that temporary staff were needed, or a specific job limited in time has to be fulfilled etc. A statutory exemption exists under the *Employment Promotion Act* which allows conclusion of fixed-term contracts for a period not exceeding two years.

It is generally not possible to enter into a sequence of fixed-term contracts. Those agreements will be considered as indefinite in time.

It is possible in an employment contract to agree on a trial period, the term of which must be reasonable in view of the work to be performed and may not exceed six months.

Remuneration

Generally the salary can be individually agreed in the employment contract. However, where the parties are bound by a collective bargaining agreement, certain minimum wages and other conditions, such as holidays, overtime payment etc, must be observed.

In case of illness the employee is entitled to salary for a period of up to six weeks. Recent legislation has limited the employer's obligation to make full salary payments during an illness, but as many collective bargaining agreements contain clauses on salary payments during illness, the practical implementation of the new legislation is proving difficult.

Social security and taxes

Employees must contribute to a regulated pension scheme, health and nursing insurance and unemployment insurance (social security).

One half of the social security contributions will be deducted from the employee's salary and the other half must be borne by the employer.

For pension insurance there is a government-controlled insurance to which all employees must pay contributions. For certain professional groups, such as miners or farmers, specialised insurance organisations exist.

Mandatory health insurance is provided by various organisations which are subject to statutory rules. Membership of the health insurance scheme is mandatory for those employees whose salary does not exceed a certain limit. However, this threshold is raised from time to time.

The social security rules apply to all employees, including persons in managerial functions, except owner-managers, ie persons who are appointed managing directors in a company which they control by shareholding.

The employer is responsible for the payment of the social security contributions and is obligated to deduct the proportion payable by the employees from their salaries.

Also, the employer must withhold income tax from the salaries paid and forward the amounts withheld on a monthly basis to the revenue authorities.

Termination

As employment agreements are generally made for an indefinite period of time, they can only be terminated by notice or by termination agreement. The notice may be either an ordinary or an extraordinary notice.

The notice period for an ordinary notice is normally stipulated in the employment agreement. However, the law provides for certain minimum notice periods. If the employee wishes to terminate the employment, notice may be given with effect from the 15th day or the end of a calendar month, observing a notice period of four weeks. If the employer wishes to terminate the agreement notice can be given only to the end of a calendar month, the notice period depending on the duration of employment. The minimum notice periods for the employers are as follows. If the employment has existed:

- for two years   : one month;
- for five years   : two months;
- for eight years   : three months;
- for ten years   : four months;
- for twelve years   : five months;
- for fifteen years   : six months;
- for twenty years or more   : seven months.

Only where employment has existed for less than two years is the notice period four weeks to the 15th day or the end of a calendar month.

During a trial period of employment, either party may terminate the agreement at any date with a notice period of two weeks.

Statutory employee protection

On request of the employee the termination may be declared ineffective by the labour court if it is considered to be unfair. In this case the employer must establish that the termination was justified for:

- reasons resulting from the personal circumstances or behaviour of the employee;
- urgent business requirements.

The reasons based on the employee's circumstances or behaviour may include such events as disobedience, rudeness, constant quarrels with other employees, and, subject to a heavy burden of proof long-term sickness etc. For minor offences one or two written warnings must be given before the notice for termination.

Business requirements which could justify a termination can be occurrences such as the closing of a department, substantial changes in the business organisation or structure, lack of orders or financial difficulties. However, in these cases the employer must give consideration to the social aspects of the termination. In the first instance it would be required to offer an employee becoming redundant under the given circumstances another workplace. Where this is not possible, the persons to be terminated must be selected considering the social aspects. This means that the employer has to take into account the employee's age, qualification, number of dependents and the duration of the employment and difficulties in finding new employment. Therefore, in practice, younger employees with no dependents are less protected than those having responsibility for families and who have been with the employer for many years.

An extraordinary notice for cause can be given at any time without observing a notice period. In this event the employer must establish that a cause exists which clearly requires an immediate termination of the employment. In practice only serious offences can be regarded as cause for termination, such as accepting bribes, theft, violence. Also, a sequence of minor offences may give reason for an extraordinary termination if incorrect behaviour continues in spite of several written warnings having been given.

An extraordinary notice for cause must be given within two weeks after the employer became aware of the relevant facts.

As it is sometimes not certain whether an extraordinary termination can be upheld in court, it can be combined with an ordinary termination. In this case the ordinary termination continues to exist if the extraordinary termination is voided by the labour court.

Notices do not require a specific form. However, most collective or individual agreements provide for a written form. Before notice can be given, the works council (*Betriebsrat*), if any must be informed and asked for comment.

In addition, there are some special protections. The employment of pregnant women cannot be terminated except in very exceptional cases. A member of the works council can only be terminated with the express consent of the council. For the termination of handicapped persons the approval of the welfare authority is needed.

Specific rules apply for mass layoffs. In such cases the labour authorities must be notified. Also, if a works council exists the employer will have to provide a social plan which often grants certain severance payments to the persons dismissed.

An employee requesting protection against the termination must seek recourse from the labour court by filing a complaint within three weeks of the date of receipt of the notice.

In a court procedure it is normal that the rights of the employee will be interpreted in a quite extensive manner. On the other hand, the dispute will frequently end with a compromise. In many cases the court will offer a settlement to the parties under which the termination is considered effective if the employer agrees to a severance payment. For the sum of the severance payment no rule exists, but in practice the rates offered are approximately one half to one month's salary payment for each year of employment.

If no compromise is found and if the claim is not dismissed, the employer can be ordered to reemploy the employee.

The employment can also be terminated by an agreement out of court.

The statutory rules for employee protection do not apply to company directors. Also, employees who have not been employed for more than six months are not protected. Following a recent change in the law the protective statute now only applies to a business which employs more than 10 people (previously the number was 5). It should be noted that those employees protected by this statute as at 30 September 1996 will continue to be protected until 30 September 1999.

COLLECTIVE AGREEMENTS

In many areas of business collective bargaining agreements exist which in most cases have been negotiated between the trade unions and the employers' associations. German trade unions and employers' associations are usually responsible for very large sectors of the economy. Consequently the collective agreements normally cover wide business areas. Trade unions have so far been very reluctant to enter into collective agreements for a single company only.

As a general rule collective agreements are binding only for members of the respective trade union and the respective employers' association. However, the government may declare certain collective agreements to be generally binding. In this event the collective agreement obtains, in practice, the quality of statutory law. It is also customary in individual agreements to make reference to certain collective agreements, which then become binding for the parties of the respective employment agreement even if there are no trade union members.

IMMIGRATION

German law requires every person wishing to reside in Germany to obtain a residence permit. The rules applicable differ considerably for nationals of EU member states and other nationals.

EU nationals

Nationals of the EU member states are entitled to residence permits in Germany without restrictions. Also, if they wish to take up employment they need no work permit. Restrictions may apply if an immigrant EU member state national desires to exercise a profession or to work on a self-employed basis where the desired activity requires certain qualifications.

Other nationals

Nationals of states other than member states of the EU wishing to reside in Germany must obtain a residence permit.

Generally the residence permit is granted in the form of a visa which the immigrant must apply for in the country of permanent residence before entering Germany. If a person desires to work in Germany the availability of a work permit must be cleared in advance. It is normally not possible for persons having entered Germany as a tourist or a student to have their visa status changed after their entrance. It is mandatory for them to return to their home country and apply for their visa from there.

Certain nationals are exempted from these visa procedures and may apply for their residence permits at their final destination in Germany. This applies, for example, to United States, Canadian or Australian citizens.

In addition to the residence permit nationals from non-EU member states require a work permit before beginning an employed working position. The work permit is granted by the local labour authority, in most cases only for a limited time and for a specific employment. However, nationals of countries which are party to a respective bilateral treaty are exempt from the work permit requirement; this is the case for Swiss nationals, for example.

Compliance with the rules on work and residence permits is strictly controlled on the level of the employer. On-site check by the government authorities can be expected, specifically in areas such as the building industry or in restaurants. It is a criminal offence to employ a person without a valid work permit.

EMPLOYEE CO-DETERMINATION

German law provides for employee co-determination on the levels of operational business and of corporate governance.

Works councils

The creation of a works council can be requested by the employees in businesses employing more than five persons. The members of the works council are elected by the employees; the number of council members depends on the number of employees in the business. It is possible to create specific group works councils for groups of companies in addition to the works councils in the separate units of the group.

The works council is in charge of the working conditions in the operation of the business; wherever a business decision influences working conditions the employer must consult with the works council and, in some cases, seek its approval.

In particular, the employer shall consult with the works council on dismissals. For the employment of new staff the approval of the council may be needed. Also the council has rights of co-operation in social matters such as working conditions, working hours, safety regulations etc.

The works council can enter into collective agreements with the employer which bind all employees of the business. Such internal agreements may, however, cover matters of internal significance only, such as working conditions, meal breaks, working hours, special premiums etc, but cannot regulate matters which are normally dealt with in collective bargaining agreements between the trade unions and the employers' associations, such as salaries.

Co-determination in corporate governance

German law provides for co-determination in larger companies. The level of co-determination depends on the number of employees in the company.

For companies with more than 500 employees a supervisory board must be formed, even where this would not be mandatory under corporate law. In such a supervisory board one-third of its members must be elected by the employees.

In companies employing more than 2000 persons one half of the supervisory board members are elected by the employees. The chairperson of the supervisory board will be one of the members elected by the shareholders; in the event of a tied vote the chairperson has a double voting right.

Specific rules apply to the mining and steel industries; here companies with more than 1000 employees must have a 50 per cent participation of employee representatives on the supervisory board. In addition to the equal number of shareholder and employee representatives, a further 'neutral' member will be appointed.

34

Corporate Governance – Managers' Rights and Duties

Clifford Chance

In German corporate entities, managing directors are responsible for the conduct of business and administrative matters. Their authority to manage and represent the corporation is generally speaking unlimited under the law, and cannot be restricted in third-party dealings. It is therefore unnecessary, in specific transactions, for managing directors to have express authorisation from the shareholders, or from the supervising body. Even acts which run contrary to shareholder instructions, or which exceed statutory business limits, will be binding on the corporation and might only result in a claim for damages from the corporation.

Certain specific factors apply to the managing directors of limited companies and stock corporations.

LIMITED COMPANY (GmbH)

A limited company will be managed and represented by one or more managing directors (*Geschäftsführer*). They represent, jointly or separately, the GmbH in third-party dealings. Only actual individuals (with unrestricted business capacity) can serve as managing directors. Shareholders or other persons, regardless of nationality or residence, can be appointed managing directors. There is no rule prohibiting foreign nationals not actually resident in Germany from becoming managing directors of a German limited company. A foreign resident may also be appointed as the sole managing director of a German company. However, this may result in practical problems, as there are some duties which must be performed at short notice by the managing director in a notarial form.

Any change in managing director, or to their signing authority, must be filed in the commercial register. The managing directors of a limited company may be subject to specific shareholder approvals or instructions. These may flow from the articles of association, standing orders for the management, employment agreements, or case-by-case resolutions, and would be binding on the managing directors for internal corporate purposes. They have no bearing on third-party dealings.

In a limited company, the shareholders exercise ultimate control. Acting in the shareholders' meeting, they may have the power of veto over the activities of the managing directors, but they may not actually manage the corporation.

Sometimes a limited company's articles of association may provide for a supervisory board or committee, in which some or all of the shareholders' rights of control over the management may be vested. A supervisory board may be mandatory where the company falls under the co-determination rules.

STOCK CORPORATION

There are three principal representative bodies in a stock corporation (*Aktiengesellschaft*):

- the shareholders' general meeting (*Hauptversammlung*);
- the supervisory board (*Aufsichtsrat*);
- the management board (*Vorstand*).

The shareholders have a limited role to play in corporate governance, which they exercise at properly convened meetings. They only pass resolutions on fundamental corporate matters, such as amendments to the articles of association or mergers with other corporations. The shareholders' meeting also has the power to appoint supervisory board members. Shareholders may vote on the distribution of dividends (but generally not approval of the annual accounts) and on the nomination of auditors. They may not interfere in corporate management and they may only approve corporate transactions at the specific request of the management.

The supervisory board is appointed at the shareholders' general meeting and is elected for a period not exceeding four years. A stock corporation must, generally speaking, have three supervisory board members, but the articles of association may provide for more up to a maximum limit, (depending on the amount of stated capital). The number of board members must always be divisible by three.

Where the co-determination rules apply, a proportion of board members is appointed by the employees, in a statutorily defined procedure.

There is no restriction on the nationality or residence of supervisory board members, but corporate entities are not eligible. Restrictions apply to those persons holding numerous mandates as supervisory board members in various corporations. The mandate is strictly personal, and no representation by proxy is permitted.

The supervisory board controls management and can request regular reports on corporate developments. It has access to all corporate books and records. But, although the articles of association may provide for board approval to certain corporate transactions, the supervisory board may not otherwise interfere in the management of the actual business.

The supervisory board appoints the members of the management board and represents the company's interests in any dealings with the managing directors (eg their employment contracts).

By contrast to the shareholders' limited role is the management board's dominant role. It is the management board which manages and represents the corporation in all third-party dealings and members of the management board have sole responsibility for exercising their duties.

Depending on the articles of association, the management board may comprise one or more individuals. If there is more than one person on the management board, a chairman will usually be appointed (*Vorstandsvorsitzender*).

Anyone may serve as managing director, irrespective of nationality or country of residence, provided that there are no restrictions on their capacity to transact business. A member of the management board may be appointed for a maximum period of five years. A renewal of the appointment is possible, but this may not take place more than one year before the expiry of the current term.

LIABILITIES

The managing directors of a limited company, or of a stock corporation, will not generally be personally liable for their dealings with third parties. Third parties may only raise personal claims against managing directors in exceptional cases (eg if a managing director has been involved in fraud in a personal capacity).

However, managing directors may be held liable for all criminal acts occurring in the conduct of business (eg violations of environmental protection rules).

Managing directors must exercise their duties with the due diligence and care of any prudent business person. They are responsible to the corporation for their actions. This also applies to members of the supervisory board.

The managing directors must ensure that the corporation meets its tax and social security obligations. Should they fail to do so, they must assume personal responsibility for all outstanding sums owed by the corporation to the revenue authorities.

These liabilities apply to all managing directors. It makes no difference if standing orders, corporate agreements or resolutions stipulate specific allocations of duties between managers. Each managing director is held legally responsible for the business as a whole, and must ensure both that he or she is aware of all ongoing matters and that the other managing directors comply with their duties. Where a managing director is unable to fulfil these obligations (eg due to the non-performance of other managing directors, or to instructions from the shareholders or the supervisory board which he or she considers illegal or detrimental), he or she is expected to resign.

35

Disputes and Arbitration

Clifford Chance

Germany has an elaborate judicial system for the resolution of disputes. Five different types of courts exist, each having jurisdiction over specific areas of law.

CIVIL COURTS

Civil courts handle disputes in civil matters. They would normally also deal with most cases under commercial law.

There is a wide network of local courts (*Amtsgericht*) which have jurisdiction over smaller matters not exceeding a value of DM10,000.

Civil law matters with a value exceeding this amount will be tried before the district courts (*Landgericht*). Any party engaged in litigation before the district court or higher civil courts must be represented by an attorney. Only attorneys admitted to the bar of the respective district are allowed to plead. The district courts have specific chambers for commercial matters which generally work faster and more efficiently than normal chambers.

Parties may appeal against the decisions of the local or the district courts. An appeal against a judgment of the local court is tried by the district court, and no further appeal is generally possible. An appeal against a decision of a district court is tried by the court of appeals (*Oberlandesgericht*).

A further appeal against a judgement of the court of appeals is possible and may be brought to the Federal Court (*Bundesgerichtshof*) if the value of the litigation is more than DM60,000 or the dispute concerns matters of fundamental importance. Where all other courts will consider matters of fact and of law, the Federal Court will deal with points of law only.

LABOUR LAW

For matters of labour law, specific labour courts exist. There are local labour courts (*Arbeitsgerichte*), state labour courts (*Landesarbeitsgerichte*) and a Federal Labour Court. The state labour courts have jurisdiction over appeals against judgments of the local labour courts, and the judgments of the state labour courts can be appealed to the Federal Labour Court which will consider only points of law.

ADMINISTRATIVE LAW

In a similar manner, administrative courts (*Verwaltungsgerichte*) exist with a three-tier appeal system and have jurisdiction in matters of administrative law, with local administrative courts, administrative courts of appeal and a Federal Administrative Court.

SOCIAL SECURITY

For matters concerning social security, social courts exist which are organised in a similar manner to the administrative courts.

TAX DISPUTES

Tax disputes must be brought before tax courts. This is the only specialist court which will consider facts. In addition, Germany has a Federal Tax Court which considers questions of law only, but appeals to the Federal Tax Court are limited to cases where the lower tax court has permitted the appeal or which the Federal Tax Court itself accepts on request as having fundamental importance or deviating from a Federal Tax Court precedent.

CONSTITUTIONAL MATTERS

Above the judicial system described, Germany has a Federal Constitutional Court (*Bundesverfassungsgericht*). The constitutional court shall decide on a possible infringement of a party's constitutional rights through acts of public authorities. The constitutional court may declare any court judgment or law null and void. It has also been increasingly used by parliamentary parties to reconsider acts of legislation. German states also have their own constitutional courts.

JUDGES

German courts are mainly composed of legally trained judges who are appointed by the government and exercise this profession as a career. They are normally appointed for a period until the age of retirement and are not subject to any election.

In some cases, such as labour, social, administrative and tax courts, associate judges can be appointed for a limited period of time who do not have legal training, but these associate judges serve periodically in all pending matters and are not appointed to judge on a specific matter. A similar system applies to the chambers for commercial cases organised with the district courts in civil matters, where persons with business experience may be appointed associate judges.

CIVIL CASES

In civil matters the procedure is mainly conducted by presenting writs. It is even possible with the consent of the parties to render a judgment without a formal hearing.

The main principle governing German procedural law in civil cases is party autonomy. Each party has to present all facts of its case and all evidence supporting such facts. Then the other party must present and show evidence of its own opposing presentation of facts if it does not wish to be construed to have accepted the facts presented. The court considers only those facts presented by the parties, and evidence is heard only where a party expressly opposes the facts presented by the other.

If the court feels that a claim is not sufficiently supported by facts, the claim can be dismissed immediately. If a defendant in a civil case does not appear in court or is not represented by an attorney admitted to the respective regional bar, a judgment in default can be issued on the basis of the facts presented by the claimant.

German procedural law rules that all legal fees and expenses, including court fees and lawyers' fees as calculated according to the statutory tariffs, must be borne by the unsuccessful party in a litigation.

ARBITRATION

Arbitration is possible under German law. However, as German courts act normally in a relatively cost-effective and speedy manner, arbitration has much less importance than in other countries.

Except between merchants, an arbitration procedure requires a written agreement separate from any other agreements among the parties concerned. In a normal arbitration agreement it is customary for either party to nominate one arbitrator; the two arbitrators then in turn nominate the chairperson of the arbitration court. It is customary to provide that in the event that the arbitrators nominated by the parties can not agree within a given period of time on a chairperson, the latter is nominated by a neutral party, such as the chamber of commerce or the president of the court of appeal.

Except in cases where a civil procedure undergoes one or two appeals, the arbitration procedure is not much more advantageous as regards time. On the other hand, as the arbitrators normally charge fees on the basis of the statutory attorneys' fee tariff, the arbitration procedure can be substantially more expensive than an ordinary court procedure. For this reason, arbitration agreements are generally made in Germany only in cases where either a specific expertise is needed (eg in highly complicated technical matters) or where the parties wish to avoid a public hearing in the ordinary court.

Alternative dispute regulation procedures exist in Germany but must be agreed between the parties on a case-by-case basis. No procedural rules exist for this.

36

Intellectual Property Protection

Clifford Chance

The protection of intellectual property in Germany is governed by various statutes, many of which have been amended recently (eg the Copyright Act):

- *Patent law:* German patent law protects major technical inventions and is codified in three (concurrently applicable) versions of the German Patent Act. The Patent Act 1981 protects all patent applications brought after 1 January 1981; the Patent Act 1978 applies to patents granted and applications made between 1 January 1978 and December 1980; and the Patent Act 1968 applies before 1978. The amendments in 1978 and 1981 were aimed at harmonising the German patent law with European regulations.
- *Utility patent law:* The Utility Patent Act, the 'little sister' of the Patent Act, protects less creatively inventive technical inventions, such as improved designs of corkscrews.
- *Trademark law:* To harmonise with European law, Germany passed a new Trademark Act in 1994. Its principal aim is to protect trademarks and trade names.
- *Copyright law:* The German Copyright Act, last amended in 1993, protects the results of creative inspiration, such as literature, speeches, computer programs and music. Copyright protection dates from the act of creation.
- *Designs and models:* Registered and protected under the Design Act of 1994; creators of newly cultivated plants can obtain protection under the Cultivation Act (*Sortenschutzgesetz*) and semiconductors are protected under the Semiconductor Protection

Act. Business secrets are protected by S17 UWG (Unfair Competition Act); anybody abusing business secrets gained illegally, or through employment, faces criminal (and civil) prosecution.

Except for copyright protection (and, to some extent, trademark and designs), other statutory protection usually requires registration at the German Patent Office in Munich. Germany has fought hard against product piracy, providing for border seizure applications (see s111e Copyright Act and the Patent and Trademark Acts) allowing the rightholder to seize counterfeit products.

PATENTS

A patent can only be granted for a (technical) *invention* which is *new*, results from *inventive creativity* and is *commercially applicable* (s1 German Patent Act 1981).

Technical invention

Only inventions of a technical nature are patentable. A technical invention is defined as 'a repeatable instruction to harness natural forces in order to directly reach a determinable success'. This does not include computer programs, plans, algorithms or genetic inventions.

Novelty

Only technical developments which are objectively new and are not part of public knowledge are considered patentable (as defined by s3 German Patent Act). This encompasses all oral or written descriptions of, uses of, or other forms of opening public access to, the invention, made anywhere in the world before the relevant priority date.

Inventive creativity

'Inventive creativity' has been one of the characteristics essential to qualification for patent protection since 1978. The invention requires an inventive step which the 'average' technician would not consider. This is, of course, difficult to define and has led to a range of precedents – these indicate that 'inventive creativity' is present whenever a technical problem has been resolved for the first time, a new technical area has been opened, a substantial influence on technical development has been made, or a generally acknowledged technical 'difficulty' has been overcome.

Commercial applicability

An invention is 'commercially applicable' if its subject may be of use in any commercial area (including agriculture); some procedures for medical treatment and diagnosis may not be commercially applicable, but the resulting products may be considered as such.

PROCEDURAL REQUIREMENTS

Some procedural requirements must be met to obtain patent protection for the normal period of 20 years. In Germany, specialist patent lawyers with additional technical training can apply for patent protection at the German Patent Office in Munich and it is advisable to consult these specialists.

An application for the registration of the invention is necessary (ss35–37 Patent Act). This must include the patent claims and a clear description and drawing of the invention. The application costs DM100; registration will cost an additional DM400. Failure to pay these fees will result in a withdrawal of the patent application or protection.

The Patent Office will check the application for 'obvious' flaws (such as insufficient description); if acceptable, it will be publicised 18 months after the application date (or priority date). A thorough examination is only carried out if requested by the applicant within seven years, giving him or her time to see whether the invention is actually worth patenting. If the deadline is missed, the application is deemed withdrawn.

The first person entitled to claim patent protection is the inventor. Subject to licensing agreements, he or she can transfer the right to apply for protection and ownership to a third party (often a legal entity, marketing or using the invention). However, the Patent Office will not check the actual right to apply; if no objections are raised within three months of publication, the patent is issued to whomever applied first (principle of priority). The inventor may raise a set of claims after the patent has been issued to a non-entitled person, but will then have full burden of proof as regards inventorship, ownership and patentability.

Following registration, only the patent owner may use, reproduce and market the invention; he or she can raise, cease and desist claims, information and indemnifications and also apply for public prosecution against anybody violating his or her exclusive rights without permission.

UTILITY PATENTS

A utility patent also requires an invention, but one with less technical merit than a full patent. The Utility Patent Act only asks for an inventive step concerning a tool or other utility step. Protection will only be granted for a period of three years, although three extensions can be applied for, providing for a maximum of protection of 10 years. Double protection of an invention – patent and utility patent protection – can be applied for. This will be of interest if patentability is doubtful but the applicant wishes to keep the priority date.

A more attractive design for a known object will not qualify for utility patent protection, but may be protectable under the Design Protection Act.

The procedural requirements are very similar to those under patent law. An application for registration must be made to the Patent Office containing a brief technical description of the invention, drawings and the name of the applicant. The fee is DM50. Examination procedures do not exist; neither novelty nor inventive merit are reviewed, but may later be the subject of objections by third parties. However, the applicant can ask for novelty examination.

TRADEMARK LAW

The principal statute is the new German Trademarks Act (*Marken-gesetz*), in force since 1 January 1995, which, aside from protecting registered trademarks, also covers business names, geographical indications of origin, get-ups and titles of printed matter. Various relevant provisions are also scattered across other statutes.

Trademarks identify and distinguish the origin of the owner's goods or services, and are considered as a form of guarantee as to the quality of those goods and services.

Protection of trademarks

Registered and unregistered trademarks

The Act protects both registered and unregistered trademarks (if well known within their sector). Protection of the former begins on the date of registration, while protection of the latter begins when the trademark owner can establish the trademark as well known under the Act, which means that it must be recognised by a minimum of 30–50 per cent of the relevant public.

Protection of registered trademarks

A registered trademark can be owned by a natural person, as well as a legal entity capable of acquiring rights in its own name.

The new Act has enlarged the registrability of trademarks. It permits registration of any visible marks, namely names, words (whether coined or existing), devices, three-dimensional marks, acoustic marks, even individual letters or numerals, colours and the packaging or shape of the goods. The mark must be capable of distinguishing the goods or services (s3 of the Act), so most marks are registrable. Technical necessities, or features which give the goods their specific value, are not registrable, neither are marks devoid of any distinctiveness, composed exclusively of descriptive signs or terms or in violation of general laws.

A registered trademark must be used within five years of registration, or protection will be lost and it may be deleted from the Register.

The registration procedure is set out in ss32 *et seq* of the Act. Applications must be filed with the German Patent Office in Munich. Official forms are available on request. The date of receipt of the application is the date which determines the priority (s6 of the Act). If priority under the Paris Convention is claimed, this must be notified with the application. There is a flat fee of DM500 which covers registration in up to three classes of goods or services, and a further fee of DM150 for each additional class. The registration procedure takes between six months and one year but, for an additional fee of DM420, a preferred procedure is available, usually completed within two to four months.

The Act also provides an opposition procedure for trademark owners claiming prior rights.

Rights afforded by trademarks and protection against infringements

Under s14 of the Act, the trademark owner has the exclusive right to use the trademark for goods or services which it protects. The trademark owner can oppose any use made of the mark by unauthorised third parties. There is a two fold test to establish a trademark infringement. It must first be determined that the protected trademark and the other mark are identical or confusingly similar (relevant criteria are basically the visual or acoustic similarity, or a similar meaning) and secondly that the goods or services for which the respective trademarks are used are identical or similar. An identical trademark for identical or similar goods or services constitutes a trademark infringement. The goods to be compared are not the individual goods as such, but the categories of goods which are usually distributed in the same market. This is not limited to goods or services of the same type. With well-known trademarks, if someone uses an identical or similar mark for goods or services different to the trademark-protected goods or services, the right-holder may still prohibit this, if such use unfairly affects the well-known trademark's reputation. The remedies offered include actions for an injunction and for damages if the infringer acted negligently, which will nearly always be the case as prudent business people are expected to check the Register. The right-holder may also demand information about the origin and distribution channel of the infringing goods, and goods bearing infringing trademarks may be subject to destruction. A wilful infringement is a criminal offence.

If a trademark is famous (known by at least 85–90 per cent of the German population), the trademark owner may oppose any use of identical or similar marks likely to dilute its 'unique advertising capacity', so long as the public would make a connection between the famous trademark and the other mark. The famous marks doctrine stems from the Civil Code (s823 BGB) and is designed to protect the exceptional goodwill connected with a famous mark; consequently, protection there under is seldom granted.

The right-holder may also file an application with customs authorities for the seizure of infringing goods when they cross into Germany (ss 146 *et seq* of the Act, adding protection under European law). Trademarks can be transferred and licensed.

Limitations

Rights under s14 of the Act may not be invoked if the trademark has been unused for five consecutive years, neither can they be invoked against fair use of the trademark in a descriptive manner (describing characteristics of goods or services, or their origin – s23 of the Act).

Geographical designations of origin

Sections 126 *et seq* of the Act protect geographical designations of origin – eg a sausage named 'Saucisson Lyonnais', which has not been produced in the appropriate French region, would violate a respective geographical designation.

Protection of business names and special commercial designations

This runs along the same lines as the protection of trademarks. However, there is no Register for business names or commercial designations and therefore the risk for a trader to infringe third parties' trademark rights. Section 5 of the Act affords an exclusive right to the owner of a business name or special commercial designation (ie a logo or abbreviation) denoting a particular undertaking. The rights arise when the name or designation is first put into use, assuming the name or designation is capable of distinguishing the business. If not distinctive, it is protected once it acquires a secondary meaning within the relevant trade circles (eg 'Car Centre' will not be a distinctive name for a car dealer, but may acquire a secondary meaning if connected with a particular car dealer). Secondary meaning requires public awareness of at least 30–50 per cent.

Under s15 of the Act, use of a business name (or similar) in the course of business constitutes an infringement if there is a possibility that use may confuse the relevant public as to the bearer of the respective names or designations. Well-known business names or designations, similarly to trademarks, are protected against unfair use by third parties.

Right of name, s12 German Civil Code, BGB

Section 12 of the German Civil Code affords more general protection, conferring an exclusive right of use on the bearer of a name and empowering them to oppose the unlawful use of their name by third parties. Nobody who lawfully bears an identical or confusingly similar name will, under this section, be hindered from using their own name, but in a commercial environment they may be required to add distinguishing parts to the name. The negligent infringer is liable for damages.

Unfair competition law

The protection of trademarks, trade names and business designations is supplemented by the Act Against Unfair Competition; s1 of the Act prohibits unfair competition in general. The courts have established a number of precedents in which certain business practices have been characterised as unfair competition, eg, impeding a competitor's business and misleading or disparaging advertising. Certain ways of using trademarks, trade names or competitors' business designations have also been held to constitute unfair competition. This will be if usage unfairly damages the reputation of the competitor's trademark, or tries to take a 'free ride' on the competitor's reputation.

COPYRIGHT LAW

German copyright law follows the European approach. The copyright owner will always be the actual creator of the work, and is afforded various unassignable 'personality' rights, including the publication right. The standard right of economic exploitation is transferable to licensees (replication, distribution and performance of a work needs the creator's prior consent, which is generally granted in license agreements – s15 Copyright Act). Unlawful exploitation of the creator's rights is subject to prosecution (ss 97 *et seq* German Copyright Act).

The law is designed to give the greatest possible protection to the creator, which explains why provisions in licence agreements granting exploitation rights for future usage unknown at the time of closing the agreement are deemed void (authors can claim additional royalties for CD-ROM versions of their works written when the distribution of works on CD-ROMs was unknown, as may movie producers of old films now sold on video). Because of this 'creator-friendly' approach, a 'work-for-hire' concept does not exist, so employers should define the scope of rights they intend to receive from employed software developers.

Copyrightable works

The law (s2) defines copyrightable works and includes:

- Works of language (literature, speeches and – since 1993 – computer programs, resulting from the 1991 European Directive on Computer Software Protection).
- Works of music.
- Pantomimic and dance works.
- Graphic art (paintings and sculptures).
- Photography.
- Movies.
- Drawings of a scientific and technical nature.

Any such works must be unique creations with intellectual content and not simply workmanlike products. However, the level of required creative merit varies under German case law. For works of literature, a *kleine Münze* ('little gem') is protectable, which may apply to marketing slogans and simple texts showing limited individual inspiration. In other areas (eg graphic works and fashion drawings) a greater degree of individual creativity (*Schöpfungshöhe*) is required.

Rights granted by copyright law

Copyright protection extends for 70 years after the author's death. As rights also apply to those who publicise and market the work (eg recording artists – *Leistungsschutzberechtigte*), the protection period relating to the performance must be taken into account, generally a term of 50 years following performance or publication of the work.

Rights granted under copyright mainly comprise 'personality rights', including:

- right of publication (the right to release a work for publication);
- right of creative integrity (preventing amendments or disfiguration);
- right of acknowledgement (the – renounceable – right to be named as creator).

There is also a second group of 'exploitation rights' covering the work's commercial value. German law recognises the following types of (transferable) exploitation rights:

- physical forms of exploitation (reproduction, distribution or presentation to the public);
- non-physical forms of exploitation (recital, radio or television transmission).

The creator is also granted various supplementary rights based on the right of access to his or her own work – including the right to inspect, copy or reproduce the work and the right to participate in sales revenues (enabling painters to share in the profits of reselling their work).

Protection granted under copyright law

Intentional violation constitutes a criminal offence and is punishable by a jail sentence of up to three years or – for commercial activity – up to five years, or by significant fines.

Civil remedies are more commonly applied, including claims for injunctive relief and indemnification against illegal (intentional or negligent) violation. In calculating damages, the copyright holder can choose whether to claim the actual financial damage suffered, the lost profit, or a reasonable average licence fee. The main thing, however, is to establish the actual copyright violation – this is easy with straightforward copying of entire works, but copies of parts of works pose difficulties. Partial copies must be established as characteristic original parts of the work; the Copyright Court exercises its discretion on this.

Claims for information on the extent of illegal activity may also be made; the right-holder may also apply for border seizure of counterfeit product (s111 Copyright Act).

Licence contracts and collection societies

With the exception of publishing contracts, there is no specific statutory regulation of licensing contracts – creator and licensee are largely free to define their own terms. However, licence contracts are governed by the Standard Contract Terms Act (which provides for protection against unduly disadvantageous provisions), binding provisions of the Copyright Act (including the provision prohibiting transfer of as yet unknown forms of usage) and, of course, the provisions of EU cartel law (particularly important for exclusive licence contracts).

The collecting societies play an important part in helping creators derive profit from their work. GEMA, the best known collection society, covers works of music; all composers, lyricists and phonographic societies can become members. Literary authors are generally members of the VG Wort and other collection societies exist for cinematic works. The Collecting Societies Act governs the division of profits between members and societies' constitutional requirements.

OTHER PROTECTION

Designs and models

The Design and Model Protection Act 1876 is among the oldest German statutes governing intellectual property, and is closer to copyright than to patent law. It protects both two- and three-dimensional models and so applies to the outer appearance of a given product. Protection is available for designs and models which result from above-average individual creative merit with aesthetic appeal. However, the design or model need not attain artistic status to be protectable. It is often hard to draw the legal line between average creation and aesthetically valuable work, and the courts decide this on a case-by-case basis.

The design or model must be 'new', but this does not mean objective novelty (as in patent law) or subjective novelty (as in copyright law). A model is deemed new if, when registered, the characteristics forming its originality are unknown to domestic experts.

Protection against copying is secured on registration. The Registry is also kept by the German Patent Office. The application must include a (photo)graphic description clearly demonstrating characteristic features, and registration is published with a photograph of the design or model. Protection is granted for an initial period of five years, but three extensions can be applied for, meaning that the ultimate expiry date can actually be 20 years from registration.

Protection of business names and secrets

Business names are protected under various laws; however, s37 Commercial Code is the most important. This makes it unlawful to use a business name which has not been properly obtained or which is owned by another person. The Registration Court may impose a fine, and the lawful owner of the name may seek an injunction or damages.

Business secrets are protected by s17 Unfair Competition Act – one of the few provisions in the Act which also provides for criminal sanctions. Section 17 covers both abuse of business secrets by former employees or service providers (para 1) and criminal industrial espionage. Para I provides for a jail sentence of up to three years for former employees who abuse for private purposes a business secret entrusted to or made accessible to them in the course of an employment contract; the same sanction may be imposed on any third person obtaining access by technical means (computer hacking), by taking copies or by removing the actual 'secret'. In severe cases (particularly industrial espionage), the jail sentence may be up to five years (s2); a 'severe' case will be held to exist if it is known that the secret is intended for use abroad. Of course, a violation of s17 may also have civil consequences, including claims for indemnification and injunctive relief.

DATA PRIVACY PROTECTION

Germany is acknowledged to have a high standard of privacy protection – the world's first Data Protection Act was enacted there by the *Land Hessen* in 1970. Eight years later, the Federal Government passed a Data Protection Act imposing restrictions on the processing of personal data by public authorities and private businesses. The Act was amended in 1990. It mainly affects commercial activity in two ways. First, the collection, processing and use of personal data is only allowed if expressly permitted by the Data Protection Act (the Act), by another legal provision or by the data subject. Secondly, the Act requires the appointment, under certain conditions, of a Company Data Protection Commissioner and the registration of data processing with the Data Protection Authorities.

Legal requirements
Application of the Data Protection Act

The Act covers personal data stored either electronically or in structured manual files. This will probably apply to most of the personal data processed by a company. At present, the only exemptions relate to structured manual files used for the company's internal purposes and to electronic files temporarily set up exclusively for processing purposes.

The Act covers the collection of personal data. The data must be obtained fairly and lawfully. Companies should not attempt to conceal the reasons for data collection and should not use any illegal methods during collection.

The Act distinguishes between the storage, communication and use of personal data for the company's own ends and for communication purposes. If the business does not have as its purpose the communication of data to third parties, then personal data may only be stored, modified or communicated in four instances:

- where the processing is in line with the contractual, or quasi-contractual, relationship with the data subject;
- where the processing is necessary for scientific research;
- where the processing is required by law;
- where the processing is necessary to safeguard the justified interests of the controller of the data file, if there is no reason to assume that the data subject has an overriding legitimate interest in the data being excluded.

In most cases, the processing of personal data will be covered by a contractual relationship with the customer. However, it should be remembered that this will not cover the processing of all customer data and that the Act also includes an obligation to delete or block data after the contract has been carried out. Consequently, storage and use of personal data – for marketing purposes, for example – may be restricted.

In practice, the most important justification for the processing of personal data is to be found in the 'balance of interest' clauses. Storage, modification or communication of personal data will be admitted if this is necessary to safeguard the justified interests of the data file controller. Such a justified interest could include carrying out business activities.

While businesses will attempt to extend the 'balance of interest' clauses in their own favour, the data subject should be assumed to have an overriding legitimate interest in his or her data being excluded from processing or use in certain circumstances – for instance, where he or she objects to the data being used, or where the data cover very sensitive personal information. The law courts and the public Data Protection Authorities tend to use the balance of interest clauses to restrict data processing. Therefore, to avoid legal uncertainties, it is often better for businesses to ask the data subject to consent to the processing of his or her personal data (see below).

The Data Protection Act also provides several other legal grounds for processing in specific cases. One example is the use of personal data for scientific projects. Some companies have tried, unsuccessfully, to use this provision to justify their marketing activities.

There are other specifically listed circumstances where it is unlikely, based on the concept of the balance of interest clauses, that the data subject has an overriding legitimate interest in the data – for example, the use of generally accessible personal data, or the processing and use of non-sensitive data such as name, title, academic degree or address:

The Data Protection Act is currently under revision by the German government. This is due to the European Directive on Data Protection, passed in October 1995, requiring member states to implement several provisions before October 1998. The directive may lead to changes to the law covering data processing, including the interpretation of the 'balance of interest' clauses, so businesses should not rely on them unduly.

Besides the Act, data processing is also registered by other statutory provisions. For example, there are certain data storage requirements under tax and company law.

The Act sets out provisions for companies storing data in the normal course of business for communication. These cover companies selling data (credit ratings, business registrations or marketing data) to third parties, and strike a balance between the commercial necessity for professional data collection and the right to privacy. The law grants Data Protection Authorities extended rights to control such companies.

Consent

If data processing cannot be justified under any of the above circumstances, the data subject's consent should be sought. The Act sets out some requirements as to how this consent should be obtained – the subject must be informed of the reasons for storage and any envisaged communication of his or her data and, at the subject's request, about the consequences of withholding consent. Consent must, in most cases, be given in writing. If the consent is given along with other documentation, the declaration of consent must be distinguishable.

Aside from any requirements under the Act, the German Standard Contract Terms Act might apply. Because the courts have sometimes ruled that consents supplied in standard form contracts were too broad to be valid, businesses should pay particular attention to the drafting of any such standard forms.

Practical considerations

Organisational requirements

The Act also sets out certain requirements for the organisation of companies. Employers must undertake to maintain the confidentiality of all personal data, most usually in the employment contract. They must also appoint a Company Data Protection Commissioner. This applies to any companies with five or more permanent employees handling electronic data processing, or at least 20 employees employed to process structured manual files. The Data Protection Commissioner, who is directly answerable to the management, has various statutory rights enabling him or her to control data processing and usage.

The Data Protection Commissioner must file a list of all personal data processing carried out by the company. This list can be inspected by the public Data Protection Authority. In some cases, the company must also register with the Data Protection Authority.

The Act also sets out data subject rights which must be safeguarded by the company (and effected, in most cases, by the company data protection commissioner). In some cases, the data subject must be notified by any company which processes or uses his or her data. The subject also has the right to obtain information about any such personal data.

Transfer of personal data abroad

Under German privacy law, a problem for foreign businesses arises if they want to transfer personal data outside Germany to countries without, or with only limited, statutory data protection. Currently the Act offers only vague solutions, since the overseas transfer of personal data is not regulated – the only provisions dealing with this concern data bureaux which service German companies from outside Germany.

At present, overseas data transfer requirements are the same as for transfer from one company to another within the jurisdiction. With cross-border data flows, the legitimate interests of the data subject may be compromised by low standards of data protection in the recipient's jurisdiction. This makes it difficult to use the 'balance of interests' clauses to justify cross-border data transfer. To solve this problem, the sender and the recipient of the data agree in a contract to ensure that the data will not be used in a manner which does not comply with the Act and provides certain rights for the data subject.

The European Data Protection Directive will change this situation. Once implemented, intra-European transfers will be differentiated from transfers outside the European Union. The directive does not allow member states to restrict the transfer of personal data between themselves, but it restricts the transfer of personal data to countries outside the European Union. Consequently, businesses needing to transfer data outside the European Union must justify such transfers on legal grounds. One solution may be for companies to implement contractual relationships between the sender and recipient, to guarantee the data protection rights of the data subject as against the recipient.

The directive expressly states that such contractual relationships can be used where other countries do not provide adequate levels of protection, and no other justification for the transfer is given by the law. Such contractual relations have to ensure that, even though the data are transferred to a country outside the European Union, the data subject is still protected. Therefore such contracts must include the main data-protection rights and the main organisational requirements, in order to ensure adequate levels of protection.

Sanctions

The Act provides for fines and imprisonment as sanctions for businesses operating in breach of it. In addition, competitors may be able to stop the business activity, based on the fact that it is in breach of the law. The data subject also has certain rights, including a claim for damages for the breach of privacy rights. In addition to these sanctions, all German *Länder* have installed Data Protection Authorities to control businesses. The size of these authorities does not allow them to carry out regular checks of companies, nor are they permitted to do so without some hint that a business is operating in breach of the law. However, where a breach is alleged, the authorities do take action and they have the right to inspect the company concerned.

Appendix 1: Contacts for Investors Seeking Financial Support in Germany

FEDERAL (*BUND*) AND EU LEVELS:

General information and orientation

Business Location Germany
(BMWi office in the USA)
401 N. Michigan Ave., Suite 2525
Chicago, IL 60611–4212
USA
Tel: +1 312 494 2167
Fax: +1 312 644 3988
e-mail: 106007.502@
        compuserve.com

**Foreign Investor Information
  Center**
(Federal Ministry of Economics)
Bundesministerium für Wirtschaft
  (BMWi)
Scharnhorststr. 36
D-10115 **Berlin**
Tel: +49 30 2014 7750
Fax: +49 30 2014 7036
e-mail: 101350.3305@
        compuserve.com
Website: http://www.bmwi.de

Favourable credit and bank guarantee programmes

Bank for Equalisation
(Deutsche Ausgleichbank (DtA))
Ludwig-Erhard-Platz 3
D-53170 **Bonn**
Tel: +49 228 831 2400
Fax: +49 228 831 2255
Sarrazinstr. 11–15
D-12159 **Berlin**
Tel: +49 30 85085 0
Fax: +49 30 85085 299
Website: http://www.dta.de
e-mail: 106007.502@
        compuserve.com

Bank for Reconstruction
(Kreditanstalt für Wiederaufbau
  (KfW))
Palmengartenstr. 5–9
D-60325 **Frankfurt/Main**
Tel: +49 69 7431 0
Fax: +49 69 7431 2944
Charlottenstr. 33/33a
D-10117 **Berlin**
Tel: +49 30 20264 0
Fax: +49 30 20264 188

European Investment Bank (EIB)
100 Boulevard K Adenaur
L-2950 **Luxembourg**
Tel: +352 437 91
Fax: +352 437 704

Federal Bank Guarantee Program
(C & L Treuarbeit)
Auf'm Hennekamp 47
D-40225 **Düsseldorf**
Tel: +49 211 3394 0
Fax: +49 211 3394 260

R&D / innovation support programmes

Research Center Jülich
(Forschungszentrum Jülich GmbH)
(for biotech, energy & environment)
Breiterstr. 3
D-10178 **Berlin**
Tel: +49 30 23199 3
Fax: +49 30 23199 479

VDI/VDE- Technologiezentrum Informationstechnik GmbH
Rheinstr. 10B
D-14513 **Teltow**
Tel: +49 3328 435 0
Fax: +49 3328 435 141
Website: http://www.vdivde-it.de

Working Group of Industrial Research Associations
(Arbeitsgemeinschaft Industrieller Forschungsvereinigungen e.V. (AIF))
Tschaikowskistr. 49
D-13156 **Berlin**
Tel: +49 30 48334 3
Fax: +49 30 48334 401

Grant programmes that support trade fair participation

Confederation of German Trade Fair and Exhibition Industries
(Ausstellungs- und Messe-Ausschuß der Deutschen Wirtschaft e.V. (AUMA))
Lindenstr. 8
D-50674 **Köln**
Tel: +49 221 20907 0
Fax: +49 221 20907 12

Grants that support certification of quality management systems

German Management and Productivity Centre
(Rationalisierungs-Kuratorium der Deutschen Wirtschaft e.V. (RKW))
Düsseldorferstr. 40
D-65760 **Eschborn**
Tel: +49 6196 495 1
Fax: +49 6196 495 303
Website: http://www.rkw.de

Employment support programmes

Federal Institute for Employment
(Bundesanstalt für Arbeit)
Regensburgerstr. 104
D-90327 **Nürnberg**
Tel: +49 911 179 0
Fax: +49 911 179 2123

STATE (*LAND*) LEVEL

Initial contacts for grant, credit, bank guarantee and other programmes administered by state governments (Länder):

NEW FEDERAL STATES & BERLIN

Berlin Economic Development Corporation
(Wirtschaftsförderung Berlin GmbH)
Hallerstr. 6
D-10587 **Berlin**
Tel: +49 30 39980 213
Fax: +49 30 39980 239

Brandenburg Economic Development Corporation
(Wirtschaftsförderung Brandenburg GmbH)
Am Lehnitzsee 7
D-14476 **Neu Fahrland**
Tel: +49 33208 55 220
Fax: +49 33208 55 100
e-mail: 101450.2652@compuserve.com

Business Promotion and Development Company Saxony-Anhalt
(Wirtschaftsförderungsgesellschaft für das Land Sachsen-Anhalt)
Schleinufer 16
D-39104 **Magdeburg**
Tel: +49 391 56899 30
Fax: +49 391 56899 99
Website: http://www.wisa.sachsen-anhalt.de

Economic Development Corporation Mecklenburg-Vorpommern
(Gesellschaft für Wirtschaftsförderung Mecklenburg-Vorpommern
mbH)
Schlossgartenallee 15
D-19061 **Schwerin**
Tel: +49 385 59225 0
Fax: +49 385 59225 22

Saxony Economic Development Corporation
(Wirtschaftsförderung Sachsen GmbH)
Bertolt-Brecht-Allee 22
D-01309 **Dresden**
Tel: +49 351 3199 1128
Fax: +49 351 3199 1099
Website: http://www.sachsen.de

State Development Agency Thuringia
(Landesentwicklungsgesellschaft (LEG) Thüringen mbH)
Mainzerhofstr. 12
D-99084 **Erfurt**
Tel: +49 361 5603 443
Fax: +49 361 5603 327
e-mail: legusa@aol.com
Website: http://www.legusa.com

OLD FEDERAL STATES

**Baden-Württemberg Agency for International Economic
Cooperation**
(Gesellschaft für internationale wirtschaftliche Zusammenarbeit (GWZ)
Baden-Württemberg mbH)
Willi-Bleicher-Str. 19
D-70174 **Stuttgart**
Tel: +49 711 22787 0
Fax: +49 711 22787 22
Website: http://www.gwz.de

**Bavarian Ministry for Economic Affairs, Transport and
Technology**
(Bayerisches Staatsministerium für Wirtschaft, Verkehr und Technologie)
Prinzregentenstr. 28
D-80538 **München**
Tel: +49 89 2162 2642
Fax: +49 89 2162 2803

Business Development Corporation of Schleswig-Holstein
(Wirtschaftsförderung Schleswig-Holstein GmbH)
Lorentzendamm 43
D-24103 **Kiel**
Tel: +49 431 59339 0
Fax: +49 431 59339 30

Economic Development Agency and Investment Bank of Hesse
HLT Wirtschaftsförderung Hessen Investitionsbank AG
Abraham-Lincoln-Str. 38-42
D-65189 **Wiesbaden**
Tel: +49 611 774 357
Fax: +49 611 774 265

Economic Development Corporation Bremen
(Wirtschaftsförderungsgesellschaft der Freien Hansestadt Bremen GmbH)
Hanseatenhof 8
D-28195 **Bremen**
Tel: +49 421 30885 0
Fax: +49 421 30885 44

Economic Development Corporation North Rhine-Westphalia
(Gesellschaft für Wirtschaftsförderung Nordrhein-Westfalen mbH)
Kavalleriestr. 8-10
D-40213 **Düsseldorf**
Tel: +49 211 13000 0
Fax: +49 211 13000 64

Economic Development Corporation Saarland
(Gesellschaft für Wirtschaftsförderung Saarland mbH)
Trierer Str. 8
D-66111 **Saarbrücken**
Tel: +49 681 94855 0
Fax: +49 681 94855 11

Hamburg Business Development Corporation
(Hamburgische Gesellschaft für Wirtschaftsförderung (HWZ) mbH)
Hamburger Str. 11
D-22083 **Hamburg**
Tel: +49 40 227019 0
Fax: +49 40 227019 29
e-mail: hwz@t-online.de

Investment and Economic Structure Bank of Rhineland-Palatinate
(Investitions- und Strukturbank (ISB) Rheinland-Pfalz GmbH)
Wilhelm-Theodor-Römheld-Str. 22
D-55130 **Mainz**
Tel: +49 6131 9852 00
Fax: +49 6131 9852 99

Investment Promotion Agency (IPA) Niedersachsen
(Lower Saxony)
Hamburger Allee 4
D-30161 **Hannover**
Tel: +49 511 343466
Fax: +49 511 3615909

Bremen Business International GmbH
World Trade Centre Bremen
Birkenstr. 15
D-28195 **Bremen**
Tel: +49 421 17466 13
Fax: +49 421 17466 22

Technology transfer

Principal Agents and Intermediaries

ZENIT,
Dohne 54
D-4330 Mülheim/Ruhr 1
Germany
Tel: +49 208 3000 421
Fax: +49 208 3000 429

TVA - Berlin (Technologie Vermittlungs Agientur)
Kleiststrasse 23-26
D-1000 Berlin 30
Germany
Tel: +49 3021 2957
Fax: +49 3313 0807

Erfinderzentrum Norddeutschland GmbH
Hindenburgstrasse 27
D-30175 Hanover
Germany
Tel: +49 511 813051
Fax: +49 511 283 4075

For a further list see *TII Membership Directory*, published by TII, 3 Rue des Capucins, L-1313 Luxembourg.

UK Partner

The Technology Exchange Ltd
Wrest Park
Silsoe
Bedford MK45 4HS
UK
Tel: +44 1525 860333
Fax: +44 1525 860664

Research Organisations

Max Planck Gesellschaft fur Forderung der Wissenschaften eV
(Max Planck Society for the Advancement of Science)
Hofgartenstrasse 2
80539 München
Germany
Tel: +49 89 21080
Fax: +49 89 2108 1111

Fraunhöfer Gesellschaft zur Forderung der Angewandten
 Forschung eV
(Fraunhöfer Society for the Promotion of Applied Research)
Leonrodstrasse 54
80636 München
Germany
Tel: +49 89 1205 01
Fax: +49 89 1205 307

Steinbeis Foundation
Steinbeis Stiftung Für Wirtschaftsforderung
Willi-Bleicher-strasse 19
D-70174 Stuttgart
Germany
Tel: +49 711 18395
Fax: +49 711 226 1076

For a full list see *European Research Centres* published by Longman.

Patent Agents

Address list of over 900 patent agents from: Patentanwaltskammer
Molassistrasse 2
8000 München 5
Germany
Tel: +49 89 226141
Fax: +49 89 2998

Official German institutions providing information on business with Eastern Europe

Bureau for East West Cooperation
Kooperationsbüro der Deutschen Wirtschaft
Uhlandstraße 28
D-10719 Berlin
Tel: +49 0 30 8826596
Fax: +49 0 30 8825193

Eastern committee of the German economy
Ost-Ausschuß der Deutschen Wirtschaft
Gustav-Heinemann-Ufer 84-88
D-50968 Köln
Tel: +49 0 221 3708452
Fax: +49 0 221 3708540

Federal office for foreign trade information
Bundesstelle für Außenhandelsinformation (BfAi)
Scharnhorststraße 36
D-10115 Berlin
Tel: +49 0 30 20145263
Fax: +49 0 30 20145204

Appendix 2: German Chambers of Industry & Commerce

ARGENTINA

**Cámara de Industria y Comercio
Argentino-Alemana**
Florida 547, Piso 19°
1005 Buenos Aires
Tel: +54 1 3220173, 393 9006/7, 3940098/9
Fax: +54 1 394 0979, 3935151
e-mail: ahk@isol.net.ar
Contact: Dr Gert Schiefelbein

AUSTRALIA

**German-Austrian Chamber of
Industry**
St Andrew's House, Level 2
Sydney Square, Sydney NSW 2000
Tel: +61 2 9261 4475, 9261 4478
Fax: +61 2 9267 3807
e-mail: ahkaust@magna.comau
Contact: Heinrich E Zimmermann

Melbourne

**German-Australian Chamber of
Industry and Commerce**
Hoechst House, 5th Floor, 606 St Kilda
Road
Melbourne, Vic 3004
Tel: +61 3 9510 5826
Fax: +61 3 9510 1835

AUSTRIA

**Deutsche Handelskammer in
Österreich**
Wiedner Hauptstr 142, 1050 Wien
Tel: +43 1 545 1417
Fax: +43 1 545 2259
e-mail: ahkwien@mail.ahk-germany.de
home page: http:www.ahk-germany.de/
ahkwien/ahkwien.htm
Contact: Dr Rolf Schäfer

Salzburg

Getreidegasse 13, A-5020 Salzburg
Tel: +43662 847952 0
Fax: +43662 840589
e-mail: ahksalz@mail.ahk-germany.de
Contact: Paula Koppensteiner

BELARUS

Repräsentanz der IHK Bonn in Minsk
Prospet Gasety Prawda 11, 220116 Minsk
/ Rep Belarus
Tel:/Fax: +375172 703893
Contact: Herr Ulrich / IHK Bonn

BELGIUM/ LUXEMBOURG

Brussels

debelux Handelskammer
Bolwerklaan 21
B-1210 Brüssel
Tel: +32 2 2035040
Fax: +32 2 2034758
e-mail: debelux@arcadis.be
Contact: Dr Peter Toebelmann

Cologne

debelux Handelskammer
Cäcilienstraße 46
50667 Köln
Tel: +221 2575477, 2575485
Fax: +221 2575466
Contact: Gerd Marmann

Luxemburg

Chambre de Commerce DEBELUX
7, Rue Alcide de Gasperi
L-1615 Luxemburg-Kirchberg
Tel: +35 2 435853, 436451
Fax: +35 2 438326

BOLIVIA

Cámara Boliviano-Alemana
Casilla 2722
La Paz
Av Mcal Santa Cruz, Edif Hansa, piso 7°
Tel: +5912 327596, 370166
Fax: +5912 391736
Contact: Olaf Kleinstück

BRAZIL

São Paulo

Câmara de Comércio e Indústria
Brasil-Alemanha
Rua Verbo Divino 1488
BR-04719-904 São Paulo-SP
Tel: +5511 247 0677
Fax: +5511 524 7013
e-mail: ahk-brasil@originet.com.br
Contact: Dr Klaus-Wilhelm Lege

Rio de Janeiro

Câmara de Comércio e Indústria
Brasil-Alemanha do Rio de Janeiro
Av Rio Branco 123, s/708/711
Rio de Janeiro-BR-20040 005 RS
Tel: +5521 224 2123
Fax: +5521 252 7758
e-mail: ahk-rio@-rio.com.br
Contact: Peter Klam

Rio Grande do Sul

Câmara de Comércio e Indústria
Brasil-Alemanha do Rio Grande do Sul
Rua Dr Florêncio Ygartua 70
BR-90430-010 Porto Alegre-RS
Tel: +5551 222 5766
Fax: +5551 222 5556
Contact: N N

BULGARIA

Repräsentanz der Deutschen Wirtschaft
F J Curie Str 25 A
BG-1113 Sofia
Tel: +359 2 659 472, 669 491
Fax: +359 2650 561
e-mail: int0052@ibm.act
Contact: Dr Mitko Wassilev

CANADA

Canadian German Chamber of Industry and Commerce Inc
480 University Ave, Suite 1410
Toronto, Ont M5G 1V2
Tel: +1 416 598 3355
Fax: +1 416 598 1840
e-mail: 106170.2643@compus*
Contact: Uwe Harnack

Montreal

Canadian German Chamber of Industry and Commerce Inc
1010 Sherbrooke Street West, Suite 1604
Montréal, Que H3A 2R7
Tel: +1 514 8443051
Fax: +1 514 8441473
e-mail: 76443.2106@compuserve
Contact: Bernd G Höhne

Vancouver

Canadian German Chamber of Industry and Commerce Inc
1030 West Georgia Street, Suite 617,
Vancouver BC V6E 2Y3
Tel: +1 604 6814469
Fax: +1 604 6814489
e-mail: 102717.2241@compuserve.com
Contact: Thomas W Felber

CENTRAL AMERICA

Cámara de Comercio e Industria Alemana Regional para Centroamerica y el Caribe
5 a Avenida 15–45 Zona 10, Edificio
Centro Empresarial, Torre I, Of 505
Guatemala/Guatemala, CA
Tel: +502 363 9562, 363 9572
Fax: +502 333 7044
e-mail: ahkzakk@netxpress.com.gt

Guatemala

e-mail: camalegu@tikal.net.gt

El Salvador

e-mail: camalem@es.com.sv

Nicaragua

e-mail: cicna@ns.tmx.com.ni

Panama

e-mail: ihkpanam@ns.sinfo.net
Contact: Wolfgang Schilling

CHILE

Cámara Chileno-Alemana de Comercio e Industria
Av El Bosque Norte 0440 of 601, Santiago
Tel: +56 2 203 53 20
Fax: +562 203 53 25
Contact: José-Volker Rehnelt

CHINA

Delegation of German Industry and Commerce Shanghai
Shanghai Bund Center
555 Zhongshan Dong Er Road
200010 Shanghai
Tel: +86 21 63269791/2
Fax: +86 21 63269794, 63269205
e-mail: ahksha@stn.sh.cn
Contact: Dr Klaus Grimm

Delegate of German Industry and Commerce in Guangzhou
Representative Office
2915 Metro Plaza
Tian He North Road
Guangzhou 510620
China
Contact: Mrs Kate Gong

COLUMBIA

Cámara de Industria y Comercio Colombo-Alemana
Carrera 13 No 93–40 Piso 4
Santafé de Bogotá
Tel: +571 6233330, 6233097, 6233186,
      6233330
Fax: +571 6233308
e-mail: 102213.2244@compuserve.com
Contact: Norbert Pudzich

CZECH REPUBLIC

Cesko-Nemecká Obchodní a Prumyslová Komora
Masarykovo-Nábrezí No 30
CZ-11000 Praha 1
Tel: +422 24915216/7, 24916154, 24916206
Fax: +422 24913827
e-mail: 106025.371@compus*
Contact: Dieter Mankowski

DENMARK

Det Tysk-Danske Handelskammer
Bórsen
DK-1217 København K
Tel: +4533 913335
Fax: +4533 913116
Contact: Gerhard Glaser

ECUADOR

Cámara de Industrias y Comercio
Av Atahualpa 1116 y Amazonas
Ed Pérez Pallares, Piso 7°
Tel: +5932 435506 7
Fax: +5932 436057
e-mail: ahkecua1@ahkecuador.org.ec
    ahkecuall@ecnet.ec
Contact: NN

EGYPT

German-Arab Chamber of Commerce
3 Abu El Feda Street, Abu El Feda Bldg
14th Floor, Zamalek-Cairo
Tel: +202 3413662, 3413663, 3413664
Fax: +202 3413663
e-mail: gacc.gacc.awadalla@gacccomm.
    attmail.com
    106025.336@compus*
Contact: Dr Peter Göpfrich

ESTONIA

**Repräsentanz der Deutschen
Wirtschaft**
EE-0001 Tallinn
Tel: +372 2 446726
Fax: +372 6 460248
e-mail: rdwe@ktk.uninet.ee
Contact: Dr Ralph-Georg Tischer

FINLAND

**Saksalais-Suomalainen
Kauppakamari**
Annankatu 25, FIN-00100 Helsinki
Tel: +358 9 642855
Fax: +358 9 642859
e-mail: info@dfhk.fim,aurerQdfhk.fi
Contact: Hans-Joachim Maurer

FRANCE

**La Chambre Franco-Allemande de
Commerce et d'Industrie**
18, rue Balard
F-75015 Paris
Tel: +331 40583535, 40583585
Fax: +331 45754739
e-mail: ahk@isp.fr
    ccfia@isp.fr
Contact: Dr Cornel Renfert

GREECE

**Deutsch-Griechische Industrie- und
Handelskammer**
Dorilaiou Str 10–12/IV
GR-11521 Athen
Tel: +30 1 6444524/5, 6444502/3,
    6444546/7
Fax: +30 1 6445175
e-mail: ahkathen@mail.ahk-germany.de
home page: http://www.ahk.germany.de/
    ahkgrie.htm
Contact: Götz Funck

HONG KONG

**Delegate of German Industry and
Commerce**
Der Delegierte der Deutschen Wirtschaft
Hong Kong,Vietnam/
German Business Association of Hong
Kong
36/F,Lippo Tower , Lippo Centre
89 Queensway
Hongkong
Tel: +852 2526 5481
Fax: +852 2810 6093
e-mail: ahkhkg@hk.net
Contact: Ekkehard Goetting

HUNGARY

**Német-Magyar Ipari és Kereskedelmi
Kamara**
Stefánia út 99
H-1143 Budapest XIV
Tel: +361 2522478, 2522000, 4672140
Fax: +361 1632427, 2520869

INDIA

Bangalore

Indo-German Chamber of Commerce
403 Shah Sultan, 4ᵗʰ Fl
Cunningham Road
Bangalore-560 052
Tel: +91 80 2265650
Fax: +91 80 2203797
Contact: Audrey D'souza

Bombay

Indo-German Chamber of Commerce
Maker Tower E, 1st Floor
Cuffe Parade
Bombay (Mumbai) 400 005
Tel: +91 22 2186131 (9 lines)
Fax: +91 22 2180523
e-mail: igcc.igccb@axcess.net.in
Contact: Dr Günter Krüger

Calcutta

Indo-German Chamber of Commerce
3, West Range
Calcutta-700 017
Tel: +91 33 2474147, 2405645
Fax: +91 33 2476165
Contact: C Dasgupta

Madras

Indo-German Chamber of Commerce
Temple Tower, 4ᵗʰ Floor, "B" Block
476 Anna Salai, Nandanam
MADRAS 600 035
Indien
Tel: +91 44 4348161, 4348027
Fax: +91 44 4344816
Contact: T R Gopalan

New Delhi

Indo-German Chamber of Commerce
German House
2, Nyaya Marg,
Chanakyapuri
New Delhi 110 021
Tel: +91 11 3018721, 3018730
Fax: +91 11 3018664
Contact: Ajay Singha

INDONESIA

**Gedung Perkumpulan Ekonomi
Indonesia-Jerman**
Jl Haji Agus Salim no 115, Jakarta 10310
Tel: +62 21 3154685
Fax: +62 21 3155276
e-mail: sys-dept.@rad.net.id
        trade-de@rad.net.id
Contact: Dr Fritz Kleinsteuber

IRAN

**Official Irano-German Chamber of
Industry and Commerce**
Ave Khaled Eslambouli ,
19th Street No 21,
1st floor
Tel: +9821 8712230, 8715210, 8719250
Fax: +9821 8711123
e-mail: 106025.453@compus*
Contact: Matthias Boddenberg

IRELAND

**German-Irish Chamber of Industry
and Commerce**
46, Fitzwilliam Square/Dublin 2
Tel: +353 1 6762934
Fax: +353 1 6762595
e-mail: gerircha@indigo.ie
Contact: Dr Dieter Tscherning

ISRAEL

**Israeli-German Chamber of Industry
& Commerce**
Migdal Te'umim II, 35, Jabotinsky Rd, 3ʳᵈ
Floor
JL-52511 Ramat Gan (Tel Aviv)
Tel: +9723 6133515
Fax: +9723 6133528
e-mail: ahkisgerQinter.net.il
Contact: Jack A Rosenthal

ITALY

**Camera di Commercio Italo-
Germanica**
Via Napo Torriani 29,
I-20124 Milano
Tel: +39 2 679131
Fax: +39 2 66980964
e-mail: 106030.3323@compus*
Contact: Heinz Friese

JAPAN

Zainichi Doitsu Shoko Kaigisho
Sanbancho KS Bldg, 5F
Sanbancho, 2 Banchi
Chiyoda-ku, Tokyo 102,
Japan
Tel: +81 3 5276 9811
Fax: +81 3 5276 8733
e-mail: 106025.351@compus*
Contact: Manfred Dransfeld

Osaka

Umeda Sky Building, Tower East 35F
1-88-3502-Oyodo-naka 1-Chome
Kita-ku, Osaka 531
Japan
Tel: +81 6 440 5991
Fax: +81 6 440 5992
Contact: Dr Hans Georg Mammitzsch

KAZAKSTAN

KVES International Ltd, Company for Foreign Economic Cooperation
Dostyk Prospekt 38 (Zi 525–532)
480100 Almaty
Tel: +7 3272 617233, 613738, 651669
Fax: +7 3272 542555, 651669
Contact: Dr Galia S Shunusalijewa

KOREA

Korean-German Chamber of Commerce and Industry
45, Namdaemunro 4-Ka, Chung-Ku
KCCI Bldg 10th floor
Seoul 100-094
Tel: +82 2 776 1546, 2837
Fax: +82 2 756 7828
e-mail: kgcci@bora.dacom.co.kr
100053.1642
Contact: Florian Schuffner

LATVIA

Repräsentanz der Deutschen Wirtschaft
World Trade Centre Riga
Elizabetes iela 2a,
offis 421–422
LV 1340 Riga
Tel: +371 7 320718
00371-9-346528 (Mobiltelefon)
Fax: +371 7 830478
Contact: Dr Guntis Strazds

LEBANON

The Delegate of German Industry and Trade
Caracas, Venus St 31
Hatoum Bldg Beirut
Tel: +961 1 742612
Fax: +961 1 742612
e-mail: dihtddwb@inco.com.lb
Contact: Herr Alexis Nassan

LITHUANIA

Repräsentanz der Deutschen Wirtschaft in Litauen
c/o Industrie- und Handelskammer Vilnius
Algirdo Str 31, LT-2600 Vilnius
Tel: +370 2 23 31 83
Fax: +370 2 23 66 53
Contact: Aldas Kikutis

MALAYSIA

Malaysian-German Chamber of Commerce and Industry
UBN Tower, 27th Floor
10 Jalan P Ramlee
50250 Kuala Lumpur
Tel: +60 3 238 35 61/2
Fax: +60 3 232 11 98
Contact: Hans-Joachim Böhmer

MEXICO

Cámara Mexicano-Alemana de Comercio e Industria AC
Bosque de Ciruelos No 130–1202
Col Bosques de las Lomas,11700 Mexiko DF
Tel: +525 2514022
Fax: +525 5967695
Contact: Manfred Hoffmann

MOROCCO

Fédération d'Industrie et de Commerce Allemande au Maroc
Zweigstelle Tanger
2, Rue Ibn AL Banna
90000 Tanger, Maroc
Tel: +212 9 94 14 79
Fax: +212 9 94 61 57

NETHERLANDS

Nederlands-Duitse Kamer van Koophandel
Nassauplein 30,
NL-2585 EC Den Haag
Tel: +31 70 311 4114
Fax: +31 70 363 2218
e-mail: ndkvk@bart.nl
Contact: Michael Krieg

Düsseldorf

Deutsch-Niederländische Handelskammer
Freiligrathstr 25, 40479 Düsseldorf
Tel: +211 4987201
Fax: +211 4920415
e-mail: ndkvk@bart.nl
Contact: K van der Beek

NEW ZEALAND

New Zealand-German Business Association Inc
Chamber of Commerce Building, 3rd Fl
100 Mayoral Drive
Auckland 1
Tel: +64 9 307 1066
Fax: +64 9 309 0209
Contact: Karen Sherry

NIGERIA

Delegate of German Industry and Commerce
Plot PC 10, Engineering Close,
Off Idowu Taylor Street, Victoria Island,
Lagos
Tel: +2341 2619751
Fax: +2341 2619752
e-mail: ngbcahk.nig@lagosmail.sprint.com
Contact: Ute Schröder

NORWAY

Norsk-Tysk Handelskammer
Drammensveien 111B
0273 Oslo
Tel: +47 22 12 82 10
Fax: +47 22 12 82 22
e-mail: 106025.355@compuserve.com
Contact: Ernst-Otto Gelfert

PALESTINIAN TERRITORIES

The Delegate of German Industry and Trade
Dahiet El Barid – Ramallah
Building of Ministry of Industry and Trade
Ramallah 3 Etage
Tel: +972 2 5740533
    +972 50 383308
    +972 50362223
Fax: +972 2 5740533
e-mail: dgit@palnet.com
Contact: Dr Peter Göpfrich

PARAGUAY

Cámara de Comercio e Industria
J E O'Leary 409 esq Estrella
Edif Parapiti – 2 Piso – Of 201, Asunción
Tel: +59521 446594, 490919
Fax: +59521 449735
e-mail: ahkasu@mail.pla.net.py
Contact: Henning B Höltei

PERU

Cámara de Comercio e Industria
Peruano-Alemana
Camino Real 348, Torre el Pilar, Piso 15
Lima 27 – San Isidro
Tel: +511 441 8616/7/8/9, 440 6896,
    421 0355
Fax: +511 442 6014
Contact: Daniel M Scheidel

PHILIPPINES

European Chamber of Commerce of
the Philippines
19th Floor, PS BANK Tower
Sen Gil J Puyat Avenue cor Tindalo Street
Makati City, Metro Manila
Tel: +63 2 759 6680, 845 1324
Fax: +63 2 759 6690, 845 1395
e-mail: eccpcom@globe.com.ph
home page: http://www.eccp.com
Contact: Henry J Schumacher

Cebu

Cebu Desk
Suite 104 Centro Maximo Bldg
D Jakosalem Street, Cebu City
Tel: +63 32 213389; 223765
Fax: +63 32 213387

POLAND

Polsko-Niemiecka Izba Przemyslowo-
Handlowa
ul Miodowa 14
PL-00-246 Warszawa
Tel: +48 22 635 33 53, 635 80 34
    +4839 120219 (via Satellit)
Fax: +48 22 635 81 06, 635 99 09
Contact: Dr Thomas Hardieck

PORTUGAL

Cámara de Comércio e Indústria
Luso-Alema
Av da Liberdade, 38–2°
P-1250 Lisboa
Tel: +3511 3211200
Fax: +3511 3467150
e-mail: ahklisboa@mail.telepac.pt
home page: http://www.ahk-germany.de/
ahklis/ahklis.htm
Contact: Dr Günter Metzger

Porto

Cámara de Comércio e Indústria
Luso-Alema
Av da Boavista 3525, Sala 308, P-4100
Porto
Tel: +3512 6101080
Fax: +3512 6172014
e-mail: ahkporto@mail.telepac.pt
Contact: Christine Malpricht

REPUBLIC SLOVENIA

Repräsentanz der Deutschen
Wirtschaft
Trg republike 3 (TR 3)
61000 Ljubljana
Republika Slovenija
Tel: +386 61 1262567, 1763026, 1763027,
    /8
Fax: +386 611264780
Contact: Frau Senka Andrijanic

ROMANIA

Repräsentanz der Deutschen
Wirtschaft
Jean Louis Calderon Str 6, 1 Stock, App 1
RU-70202 Bucarest
Tel: +401 61463 03, 6130897
Fax: +401 3123841
e-mail: 106004.2601@compus*
Contact: Christina Nitescu

RUSSIA

Moscow

Delegierte der Deutschen Wirtschaft in der Russischen Föderation
Predstawistelstwo nemezkoi ekonomiki w Rossiskoi Federazii
ul Dubininskaja, 98
RF-113 093 Moskau
Tel: +7095 2367288, 9548573, 9585152
   +7502 2221072 (via Satellit)
Fax: +7095 9585163, 9585146
Contact: Dr Andrea von Knoop

Staliningrad

Delegation der Deutschen Wirtschaft in der Russischen Föderation Außenstelle Kaliningrad
Predstawitelstwo nemezkoi ekonomik w Rossiskoi
Federazii, Otdelenije Kaliningrad
RF 236000 Kaliningrad
Tel: +70112 211538, 279855
Fax: +70112 279827
Contact: Stephan Stein

St Petersburg

Delegation der Deutschen Wirtschaft in der Russischen Föderation Außenstelle St Petersburg
Predstawitelstwo nemezkoj ekonomiki St Petersburg
WO, Bolschoj Prospekt 10
RF-199034 St Petersburg
Tel: +7 812 2137991 93,
Fax: +7 812 3505622
Contact: Dr Dieter Schubert

SAUDI ARABIA

German-Saudi Arabian Liaison Office
Dhabab Street, 5th Floor, Suite 1
Chamber of Commerce Building
Tel: +966 1 403 1500
Fax: +966 1 403 5121
e-mail: 106005.3622@compuserve.com
Contact: Dr Rainer Herret

SWEDEN

Tysk-Svenska Handelskammaren
Verdandigatan 2, S-114 24 Stockholm
Tel: +468 7914060
Fax: +468 7903098
e-mail: info@handelskammer.cci.se
Contact: Dr Jörn Gallwitz

SWITZERLAND

Handelskammer Deutschland-Schweiz
Tödistrasse 60
CH-8002 Zürich
Tel: +41 1 2836161
Fax: +41 1 2836100
Contact: Martin Theurer

SINGAPORE

The Delegate of German Industry and Commerce in Singapore
Asia Pacific Support Office
25 International Business Park
#04-65/77 German Centre
Singapore 609916
Tel: +65 5629000
Fax: +65 5630907
e-mail: ahksing@diht.com.sg
home page: www.diht.com.sg
Contact: Jürgen Franzen

SLOVAK REPUBLIC

Delegát nemeckého hospodárstva na Slovensku
Palisády 36
SK-816 45 Bratislava
Tel: +427 531 1464, 531 8889
Fax: +427 53158 86
e-mail: 106025.371@compus*
Contact: Dieter Mankowski

SPAIN

Cámara de Comercio Alemana para España
Avda Pio XII, 26–28, E-28016 Madrid
Tel: +34 1 3597010
Fax: +34 1 3591213
e-mail: 100726.164@compuserve.com
Contact: Dr Helmuth Treiber

Barcelona

Cámara de Comercio Alemana para
España
Calle Córcega 301–303/E–08008
Barcelona
Tel: +343 4155444
Fax: +343 4152717
Contact: Peter Moser

SOUTH AFRICA

**SA-German Chamber of Commerce
and Industry Ltd**
47 Oxford Road (Entrance Waltham Rd)
Forest Town, Johannesburg
Tel: +2711 486 2775
Fax: +2711 486 3625, 486 3675
e-mail: gchamber@lia.co.za
Contact: Klaus Volker Schuurman

TAIWAN

German Trade Office Taipei
4 Fl 4, Min-Sheng E Road, Sec3
Taipei 10444/Taiwan ROC
Tel: +8862 5069028
Fax: +8862 5068182
e-mail: ahktpe@ms7.hinet.net
Contact: Gunther Tetzner

THAILAND

German-Thai Chamber of Commerce
699 Silom Road, 4th Floor, Kongboonma
Bldg,Bangkok 10500
Tel: +662 236 2396, 23535103, 2664924
Fax: +662 2364711
Contact: Dr Paul R Strunk

TUNISIA

**Chambre Tuniso-Allemande de
l'Industrie et du Commerce**
6, rue Didon
1002 Tunis-Notre Dame
Tel: +216 1 785 910, 785 238
Fax: +216 1 782 551
Contact: Karlgerd Quink

TURKEY

Alman-Türk Ticaret ve Sanayi Odasi
PK 22, TR-80840 Ortaköy-Istanbul
Muallim Naci Cad 118/4
TR-80840 Ortaköy – Istanbul
Tel: +90 212 2591195 96, 2590840
Fax: +90 212 2591939
Contact: Marc Landau

UKRAINE

Delegierter der Deutschen Wirtschaft
wul Puschkinska, 34
UA-252004 Kiew/Ukraine
Tel: +38 044 2245998; 2245595
Fax: +38 044 2254234
e-mail: diht@gu.kiev.ua
        106025.374@compus*
Contact: Karin Rau

UNITED KINGDOM

**German-British Chamber of Industry
& Commerce**
Mecklenburg House, 16 Buckingham Gate
London SW1E 6LB
Tel: +44 171 2335656
Fax: +44 171 2337835
e-mail: 100634.3032@compus*
Contact: Klaus Balzer

URUGUAY

**Cámara de Comercio Uruguayo-
Alemana**
Calle Zabala 1379, IV
Tel: +5982 970307,8
Fax: +5982 963281
e-mail: ahkrug@adinet.com.uy
Contact: Dr Klaus Rössler

UZBEKISTAN

**Repräsentanz der Deutschen
Wirtschaft**
ul Murtazaeva 6, kv 82/83
700 000 Taschkent
Tel: +73712 346127
Tel:/Fax: +7 3712 406424 (Kombifax)
e-mail: diht@infotel.tashkent.su
Contact: Peter Hoehne

USA

Atlanta

German American Chamber of Commerce of the Southern United States, Inc
3340 Peachtree Road, NE Suite 500
Atlanta, GA 30326
Tel: +1 404 239 9494
Fax: +1 404 2641761
e-mail: 74672.3117@compuserve.com
Contact: Thomas Beck

Chicago

German American Chamber of Commerce of the Midwest
401 North Michigan Ave, Suite 2525
Chicago IL 60611-4212
Tel: +1 312 644 2662
Fax: +1 312 644 0738
e-mail: 106025.402@compus*
Contact: Christian Röhr

Houston

German American Chamber of Commerce, Inc
5599 San Felipe, Suite 510
Houston, TX 77056
Tel: +1 713 8771114
Fax: +1 713 8771602
e-mail: 74672.3117@compus*
Contact: Wolfgang Schönborn

Los Angeles

German American Chamber of Commerce of the Western United States, Inc
5220 Pacific Concourse Drive, Suite 280
Los Angeles, CA 90045
Tel: +1 310 2977979
Fax: +1 310 2977966
e-mail: 104165.3056@compus*
Contact: NN

New York

German American Chamber of Commerce, Inc
40 West 57th Street, 31st Floor
New York, NY 10019-4092
Tel: +1 212 974 8830
Fax: +1 212 974 8867
e-mail: 72700.3042@compus*
Contact: Werner Walbröl

Philadelphia

German American Chamber of Commerce, Inc
1515 Market Street, Suite 505
Philadelphia, PA 19102
Tel: +1 215 6651585
Fax: +1 215 6650375
e-mail: 104753.426@compus*
Contact: Barbara Afanassiev

San Francisco

German American Chamber of Commerce of the Western United States, Inc
465 California Street, Suite 910
San Francisco, CA 94104
Tel: +1 415 3922262
Fax: +1 415 3921314
e-mail: 76375.1513@compus*
Contact: Lawrence A Walker

Washington

Representative of German Industry and Trade
1627 I Street, NW, Suite 550
Washington, DC 20006
Tel: +1 02 6594777
Fax: +1 02 6594779
e-mail: 104075.1540@compuserve.com
Contact: Jacob Esser

VENEZUELA

Cámara de Comercio e Industria
Edificio Coinasa, Piso 4,
Av San Felipe, La Castellana/Caracas
Tel: +582 2671411, 2670852, 2671630,
    2671945
Fax: +582 2666373
e-mail: 102213.22@compuserve.com
        106001.1111@cpmpus*
home page: www:http://www.ahk-
germany.de//ahk.htm
Contact: Sven Heldt

VIETNAM

**Delegate of German Industry and
Commerce Hanoi**
41, Ly Thai To
Hanoi/SR Vietnam
Tel: +84 4825 1420
Fax: +84 4825 1422
Contact: Ekkehard Goetting

Appendix 3: Major Investment Incentives

NEW FEDERAL STATES AND EASTERN BERLIN

Tax Incentives

Since 1 January 1996 western Berlin is eligible for some of these incentives.

Investment Allowance (Investitionszulage)

- Investment deadline extended from 31 December 1996 to 31 December 1998.
- 10 per cent of investment deducted from tax debt (loss-making firms receive refunds) for manufacturing or commercial craft firms with up to 250 employees and for wholesale and retail trade firms with up to 50 employees and not located in business, industrial, or special parks/zones (maximum yearly investment allowable for the latter is DM 250,000).
- 5 per cent of investment with more than 250 employees. Effective 1 January 1997 only manufacturing firms are eligible (until then all firms except banks, utilities, insurance and trade remain eligible).

Special Accelerated Depreciation Allowance (Sonderabschreibung)

- Investment deadline extended from 31 December 1996 to 31 December 1998.
- The special allowance is in addition to the straight-line method and can be used over a 1–5 year period.
- Effective 1 January 1997 the conditions change from a special 50 per cent allowance for the purchase or production of depreciable movable and immovable assets to:

- 40 per cent for commercial construction by manufacturing firms (cannot be rented or sold); for the modernization/ renovation of buildings; and for the purchase of plant and equipment.
- 25 per cent for new housing construction.
- 20 per cent for non-manufacturing, non-housing construction as well as construction by manufacturing firms which is rented or otherwise not used directly.

Capital Asset Tax Exemptions

- Exemption from net worth taxes (*Vermögensteuer*) on assets was extended from 31 December 1995 to 31 December 1998.
- Exemption from municipal trade capital taxes (*Gewerbekapital-steuer*) until 31 December 1996. This tax may be eliminated for all of Germany.

Capital Gains Tax Exemption

- Exemption effective 1 January 1996 to 31 December 1998 on any equity invested in, or money loaned to, firms in the new states with up to 250 employees.

The Eastern Germany Equity Fund

- Effective 1 January 1996 to 31 December 1998, 12 per cent of long-term equity invested in this new fund (take-in ceiling: DM 500 million per year) can be deducted from tax debts.
- These funds are in turn loaned through programmes of the *KfW* and *DtA* (see below).

Investment Grants

The Improvement of Regional Economic Structures Programme (Gemeinschaftsaufgabe *or* GA *funds; from federal, state and EU budgets)*

- The following programme conditions are good until 31 December 1999:
  - Most firms can receive up to 35 per cent of an investment. This is the ceiling for the percentage of all incentive programmes taken together. *GA* funds can account for the full amount.
  - Small- and medium-sized manufacturing firms with up to 250 employees and a maximum turnover of ECU 40 million or balance sheet sum of ECU 20 million can receive up to 50 per cent of an investment.

- Beginning on 1 January 1997 maximum grants as a percentage of new investments in the cities of Berlin, Dresden, Erfurt, Halle, Jena, Leipzig, Schwerin, and Weimar will be limited to 28 per cent for large firms and 43 per cent for small- and medium-sized firms. In rare cases these cities (except for western Berlin) may be able to award the higher amounts of 35 per cent or 50 per cent.
- Note: Through 31 December 1996 investors in western Berlin are eligible for 35 per cent/45 per cent maximum grants. From 1 January 1997 rates are the same as in eastern Berlin (28 per cent/ 43 per cent).

Grants for Research and Development and Consulting and Training Costs

- 6 major programmes with grants ranging from DM 4,000 to DM 1 million.
- Up to DM 100,000 per firm for consulting and training costs.
- Up to DM 60,000 per firm over two years for 'human capital development.'

Credit Programmes

The loans described below chart below-market rates of interest.

Consolidation Funds (money provided by the former Treuhandanstalt)

- Established in December 1994 and administered by the states, these monies are considered emergency funds for small- and medium-sized firms (same definition as applied in GA funds above) with liquidity difficulties.
- Up to DM 2 million can be lent at especially favorable terms, or up to DM 2 million in silent shares can be invested in the firm.

Deutsche Ausgleichsbank (DtA) (equalization funds bank)

- 4 major programmes of up to and between DM 700,000 and DM 10 million.
- The DtA's most popular programme, Equity Capital Assistance (EKA) has been extended to year-end 1998.

Kreditanstalt für Wiederaufbau (KfW) (reconstruction funds bank)

- 4 major programmes of up to DM 10 million.
- Programmes with negotiable amounts and with a 50 per cent of investment ceiling.

European Recovery Programmes (ERP) **(Marshall Plan funds)**

- 4 major programmes of up to and between DM 2 and 5 million (*DtA* or *KfW* administered).

European Union (EU) Programmes

- 2 major programmes offering up to DM 50 million or 50 per cent of investment.

Loan Guarantee Programmes

- 3 major programmes for up to DM 1 million and DM 20 million.

OLD FEDERAL STATES AND WESTERN BERLIN

Tax Incentives

Special Accelerated Depreciation Allowance **(Sonderabschretbung)**

- For the purchase or production of new, movable capital goods.
- Up to 20 per cent in the first year or over a five year period.
- This is in addition to the regular straight-line or declining balance methods.
- Eligible firms cannot have more than DM 240,000 of income-producing assets or more than DM 500,000 in employed trading capital at the time of purchase or production.

Capital Reserves Allowance **(Ansparabschreibung)**

- For the planned purchase or production of depreciable, movable goods over the two following tax years.
- Taxable profits can be reduced (capital reserves increased) by 50 per cent of the value of the planned purchase or production.
- Same eligibility requirements as in special accelerated depreciation allowance above.

Effective 1 January 1996 to 31 December 1998 western Berlin is also eligible for some of the more generous tax incentives available for the New Federal States.

Investment Grants

The Improvement of Regional Economic Structures Programme (Gemeinschaftsaufgabe or GA funds)

- For investment in specially-designated areas that are under-developed or depressed. Such areas currently cover about 22 per cent of the population of the old Federal States.
- Maximum grant is 28 per cent (small firms) or 18 per cent (large firms) of investment for the start-up, expansion or modernization of most businesses. Acquisitions are eligible if a business is closed or about to be closed.
- Through year-end 1996 maximum grant rates in western Berlin are 35 per cent/45 per cent and from 1 January 1997 the same as eastern Berlin, 28 per cent/43 per cent.
- Grant amounts are decided at the state (Land) level and vary considerably. Investments in manufacturing facilities and start-ups usually receive the highest grants.
- The purchase of real estate and transportation vehicles are not covered by the plan.
- The programme also offers loan guarantees of up to DM 20 million per year.

Grants for Research and Development, Consulting Fees and Training Costs

- Up to DM 500,000 per firm for cooperative R & D arrangements.
- Up to DM 200,000 per firm to support the exchange of R & D personnel.
- Up to DM 8,000 over a 5 year period for management consulting costs.
- Up to DM 8,000 over a 5 year period for energy efficiency consulting.
- Up to DM 8,000 over a 5 year period for environmental protection consulting.
- Up to DM 8,000 over a 5 year period for consulting support for a business start-up.
- Up to DM 2,800 for training programmes that last 1–4 days.

Credit Programmes

The loans described below offer below-market rates of interest.

Deutsche Ausgleichsbank (DtA) (bank for equalization)

- For the support of start-ups or firms less than 8 years old: usually up to DM 2 million with a term of up to 10 years and 2 year grace period.
- For a start-up or an investment within 2 years afterwards: up to DM 700,000.
- For the implementation of environmental improvement projects: usually up to DM 10 million with up to a 20 year term and 3 year grace period.

Kreditanstalt für Wiederaufbau (KfW) (bank for reconstruction)

- For small- and medium-sized companies to purchase real estate, machinery, equipment and vehicles; support R & D; help finance an acquisition or MBO/MBI: up DM 10 million with a 20 year term and up to a 3 year grace period.
- For R & D programmes: up to DM 10 million with a 10 year term and up to a 2 year grace period.
- For the implementation of environmental improvement programmes: up to DM 10 million with a 10 year term and up to a 2 year grace period.

European Recovery Programme (ERP) (Marshall Plan)

- For the start-up, expansion or modernization in GA designated regions: up to DM 1 million with a 10 or 15 year term and up to a 2 year grace period (KfW administered).
- For the implementation or expansion of programmes which save energy, improve disposal of waste and sewage or cut down on noise and air pollution: up to DM 1 million with a 10 or 15 year term and up to a 2 year grace period (DtA administered).
- For business start-ups: up to DM 1 million with a 10 or 15 year term and up to a 3 year grace period (DtA administered).
- For the support of equity investments in firms which need capital to finance cooperation and innovation projects, start-ups, expansions or modernizations: usually up to DM 1 million for up to 10 years (KfW administered).

European Union (EU) Programmes

- 2 major programmes which offer loans through the European Investment Bank (EIB) and venture capital financing through the European Venture Capital Association (EVCA).

Loan Guarantee Programmes

- Guaranty banks in each state (*Land*) offer coverage of usually up to DM 1 million over a 15 or 23 year period.
- A special guarantee programme is available for independent professionals.
- For the production of innovative, environmentally friendly products or construction of environmentally sound manufacturing facilities: up DM 1 million (*DtA* administered).
- The *GA* investment grant programme offers loan guarantees of up to DM 20 million.

Other Major Programmes

- For small technology firms: the refinancing of up to DM 4 million in equity shares through the *KfW*; and a co-equity investment of up to DM 3 million through the *DtA* with private lead investors.
- For large-scale demonstration projects which provide models for environmentally sound production processes and products: up to 70 per cent of the costs with up to a 30 year term and 5 year grace period (*DtA* or *KfW* administered).

There are over 100 federal incentive and support programmes as well as dozens of others at state and local levels. For further information on any programme contact the Foreign Investor Information Center at the Federal Ministry of Economics, Scharnhorststr. 36, D-10115 Berlin; Tel: (+49 30) 2014 7751; Fax: (+49 30) 2014 7036; e-mail: 101350_3305@compuserve.com

Appendix 4: Contributor Addresses

Bayerische Vereinsbank
Kardinal
Faulhaber Str. 1
80311 Munich
Tel: +49 (0) 378 26859
Fax: +49 (0) 378 25699
Contact: Kaevan Gazdar

British Chamber of Commerce in Germany
Sevorinstreße 60
50678 Köln
Tel: +49 221 31 44 89
Contact: Bernhard Wingenbach

Boss Group Limited
Grovebury Road
Leighton Buzzard
Bedfordshire
England LU7 8SR
Tel: +44 1525 215000
Fax: +44 1525 215105
Chairman's Office fax: 01525 215009
Contact: Teresa Tiller
　　　　Secretary to **R.A. Bichof**

Bundesinstitut für Berufsbildung (BIBB)
Dienststelle Berlin
Hausanschrift
Fehrbelliner Platz 3
01707 Berlin
Tel: +49 (0)　30 8643 2212
Fax: +49 (0)　30 8643 2600
Contact: Dr. Hermann Schmidt

Bundesverband der Deutschen Industrie (BDI)
Department for General Economic Policy
Gustav-Heinemann-Uter 84 88
50968 Köln (Bayenthal)
Tel: +49 (0) 3708 545
Fax: +49 (0) 3708 690
Contact: Gabriele Hintzen

Bureau for East-West Co-operation
Uhlandstrasse 28
10719 Berlin
Germany
Tel: +49 (0)　30 8826 596
Fax: +49 (0)　30 882 5193
Contact: Michael Harms

CDH Haus
Geleniusstrasse 1
50931 Köln
Tel: +49 (0) 221 51 40 43
Fax: +49 (0) 221 52 57 67
Contact: Ute Sellhorst

Clifford Chance
200 Aldersgate Street
London
EC1A 4JJ
Tel: +44 (0) 600 1000
Fax: +44 (0) 600 5555
Contact: Joan Fulton

Commerzbank
ZGB Marketing & Research
Neue Mainzer Str. 32–36
D-60261 Frankfurt
Tel: +49 691362 3215
Fax: +49 691362 9096
Contact: Klaus Holschuh

Coopers & Lybrand
1 Embankment Place
London
WC2N 6NN
Tel: +44 (0) 171 583 5000
Fax: +44 (0) 171 822 4652
Contact: Peter Drummond

Dipi-Kfm
Management Consultant and former
President of
"Berufsverband deutscher Markt-und
Sozialforscher e. V. (BVM)
Sindmuhlenweg 20
33605 Bielefeld
Tel: +49 521 25779
Fax: +49 521 25779
Contact: Walter Tacke

**Foreign Investor Information
Center**
Federal Ministry of Economics
Scharnhorststr. 36
D-10115 Berlin
Tel: +49 30 2014 7755
Fax: +49 30 2014 703
Contact: John M Zindar

**German-British Chamber of
Industry & Commerce**
16 Buckingham Gate
London SW1E 6LB
Tel: +44 171 233 5656
Fax: +44 171 233 7835
Contact: Klaus Balzer

Hans Bockler Stiftung
Bertha-V-Suttner
Platz 3
40227 Düsseldorf
Telefax direct: 77 78 210
Contact: Wolfgang Lecher

**Landesbank Hessen-Thuringen
Girozentraie (Helaba)**
Finanzgruppc
Junghofstraße 18–26
60297 Frankfurt am Main
Tel: +49 (0) 69 132 01
Fax: +49 (0) 60 29 15 17
Contact: Jutta Sundermann

Laura Covill
Financial Journalist
Dachbergstraße 48
65812 Bad Soden
Tel: +49 (0) 6196 641253
Fax: +49 (0) 6196 641290

LCT Consultants
Adam-Kraft-Strasse 45
D-90419 Nuremberg
Tel: +49 (0) 911 39 7702
Fax: +49 (0) 911 33 1477
Contact: Eric Lynn

**Lehrstuhl für
Volkswirtschaftsiehre**
Wirtschaftsthcorie
Universitat Bayreuth
95440 Bayreuth
Tel: +49 921 55 2880/1
Fax: +49 921 55 2886
Contact: Prof. Peter Oberender

Technology Exchange Ltd
Wrest Park
Silsoe
Bedford MK45 4HS
Tel: +44 1525 860333
Fax: +44 1525 860664
Contact: Brian Padgett

Index

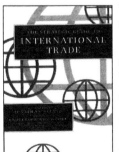

CBI European Business Handbook 1997

Fourth Edition
Consultant Editor:
Adam Jolly

£35.00 Paperback
January 1997
ISBN 0 7494 2088 X
Order ref: KT088

"...this handbook should be on your desk, not on your shopping list. This has to be the best value for money for a handbook of this type for a long while."

SALES AND MARKETING MANAGEMENT JOURNAL

With an expert analysis of the business, economic and political prospects in 26 European countries, the CBI European Business Handbook is the ideal source book for trading and investment in the new Europe.

The Export Handbook 1997

Fourth Edition
Consultant Editor:
Harry Twells

£30.00 Paperback
May 1997
ISBN 0 7494 2157 6
Order ref: KT157

Completely revised and updated the handbook contains practical advice on how to export successfully to the world's major trade areas including principles of exporting; export opportunities and difficulties in the European Single Market; contacts and advice for export trading; and a unique directory of export services.

A detailed directory and a new section indicating the best places to go for further information and advice make, The Export Handbook 1997 an invaluable reference source for anyone wishing to carve a niche in international markets, and vital reading for all students of international trade.

International Executive Development Programmes

Second Edition
Consultant Editor:
Philip Sadler

£75.00 Paperback
January 1997
ISBN 0 7494 1625 4
Order ref: KS625

The guide is the only truly international guide and directory of international development programmes - invaluable to those businesses that view human development as an ongoing part of essential business practice.

With editorial overviews from some of the world's leading companies and bodies, a comprehensive reference section and an extensive profile of business schools and management centres worldwide, the guide provides you with all the information you need to transform your managment and hence your business capabilities.

Germany's Top 500

In association with
Frankfurter Allgemeine
Zeitung

£90.00 Paperback
December 1996
ISBN 3 929368 38 2

A unique single information source to evaluate and compare the performance and structure of germany's major companies banks and insurers. Updated annually the guide profiles the companies' addresses, full names, business activities, shareholders, share earnings, dividends and equity and fully comprehensive financial reports over four consecutive years.

Germany's Top 500 is the most complete, authoritative, English-language reference book on German companies, giving you all the information you require to evaluate the performance of a single company or an entire industry.

More information on these and other titles can be found in Kogan Page's comprehensive *International Business Catalogue*. To request a copy please phone or fax the marketing department on:
Tel. 0171 278 0433 Fax. 0171 837 6348.
Kogan Page's international business books can be brought from good booksellers or direct from Kogan Page's customer services department on 0171 278 0433, quoting the reference number for the title and your credit card details.
Payment can also be made by pro-forma, or by cheque made out to Kogan Page Ltd and sent to:
Kogan Page, 120 Pentonville Road, London N1 9JN, England

Index of Advertisers